EFFECTIVE STUDY SKILLS

Maximizing Your Academic Potential

JUDY M. ROBERTS
Jefferson Community College,
Louisville, Kentucky

Prentice Hall
Upper Saddle River, New Jersey 07458

39627492

Library of Congress Cataloging-in-Publication Data

Roberts, Judith M.
    Effective study skills : maximizing your academic potential / Judy
M. Roberts.
       p.   cm.
    Includes bibliographical references and index.
    ISBN 0-13-095061-0
    1. Study skills. I. Title.
LB2395.R63   1999
378.1'7'0281—dc21   98-33861
                                                      CIP

Publisher: Carol Carter
Acquisitions Editor: Sue Bierman
Managing Editor: Mary Carnis
Production: Holcomb Hathaway, Inc.
Director of Manufacturing and Production: Bruce Johnson
Manufacturing Buyer: Marc Bove
Cover Design: Marianne Frasco
Editorial Assistant: Michelle M. Williams
Marketing Manager: Jeff McIlroy
Marketing Assistant: Barbara Rosenberg

 © 1999 by Prentice-Hall, Inc.
A Simon & Schuster Company
Upper Saddle River, New Jersey 07458

Printed in the United States of America

10 9 8 7 6 5 4 3 2 1

ISBN 0-13-095061-0

Prentice-Hall International (UK) Limited, London
Prentice-Hall of Australia Pty. Limited, Sydney
Prentice-Hall Canada Inc., Toronto
Prentice-Hall Hispanoamericana, S.A., Mexico
Prentice-Hall of India Private Limited, New Delhi
Prentice-Hall of Japan, Inc., Tokyo
Simon & Schuster Asia Pte. Ltd., Singapore
Editors Prentice-Hall do Brazil, Ltda., Rio de Janeiro

Contents

To all of my students—past, present, and future,
and
To Steve

Preface

To the Instructor

Research has revealed that a major difference between the successful and the unsuccessful student is the use of metacognitive strategies. The good student knows what to do when confronting problems with comprehension, memory, concentration, test preparation, or any other type of information processing. Strategies used will differ according to learning styles and training, but there *will* be strategies. Any successful instructor of study skills methods believes that study strategies can be taught, enabling all students to learn to their maximum potential. First-year college students enrolled in reading and study skills classes have frequently remarked that study skills should have been taught to them in high school, or earlier.

Although the various study skills books have been very helpful to the majority of students, several features would improve and update these books. The purpose of the added or improved features in this book is to create a textbook that will be more inclusive of the diverse college population and will address students of all learning styles, ages, and backgrounds. The text also offers to instructors presentations and activities in different modalities so that instruction can be relevant to all students. In addition, this textbook addresses the needs of both the traditional and the nontraditional student.

SIGNIFICANT FEATURES

- Cooperative learning activities for each chapter designed to offer consolidated practice of skills described in that chapter.
- Reading selections from a wide variety of college textbooks, complete with higher level thinking questions.
- Increased opportunities for students to link reading and study material with prior knowledge and interest.
- Reading selections pertaining not only to multicultural groups but also written by members of diverse populations.
- Newspaper and newsmagazine editorials on timely, significant issues of interest to college students.
- More complete coverage of critical reading and analytical thinking strategies.
- Opportunities for greater use of academic patterns of organization through training in everyday reading and culminating in academic reading and writing.

- Special emphasis on college writing through academic patterns of organization.
- A comprehensive learning styles inventory covering the various modalities and also including such learning preferences as study environment, organizational preferences, and peak periods of concentration.
- A wide array of graphic illustrations extended to note taking and test preparation.
- Note taking and test preparation by lecture styles of instructors.

To the Student

Effective Study Skills: Maximizing Your Academic Potential is designed to help you learn and practice skills that will enable you to be successful in your academic courses. In addition to practice provided in the book, you should consistently practice the reading and study skills while you are attending classes and while studying your textbooks. Mastering and practicing the strategies in this book can lead to your becoming the best student you can be.

Several features of the book will help you comprehend and apply the information.

- The objectives tell you what you should learn in each chapter. If, at the completion of the chapter, you feel you have not mastered one of the objectives, you should study that part of the material again or in a different way.
- The headings and subheadings within each chapter tell you the topic of that section. Practice turning headings into questions. Then read to find the answers.
- Key terms, some of which may be new to you, appear in bold print. All of the terms are explained, so you should try to learn the new vocabulary.
- Many examples are provided to clarify new ideas and concepts.
- Chapter summaries reinforce the major topics of a chapter.
- A glossary of all of the key terms in the book will act as a quick reference tool for you.
- Opportunities for both individual and group work will reinforce skills learned in the chapters.
- Reading selections are placed at the ends of all chapters to help you with both comprehension and reinforcement of skills.

In order to maximize your academic potential, or become the best student you can be, you must be willing to work hard. Nothing worth having comes without effort.

Acknowledgments

I would like to thank two people who helped with the development of this book: Cathy Leist, Coordinator for Reading and Study Strategies at the University of Louisville, initially suggested that I consider writing a study skills book, and Todd Rossell of Prentice Hall was instrumental in guiding me during the early stages of the book.

I wish to thank all of those who took time to review this manuscript and offer their valuable suggestions: Mary Bixby, University of Missouri, Columbia; George Ann Drennan, University of New Mexico; Jacqueline Heisler, Hope College; Cheryl K. Miller, Wichita State University; Jo-Ann Mullen, University of North Colorado; Rebecca Pollard Cole, Northern Arizona University; Nancy Roberts, Grant McEwan Community College; Elaine Wright, Quinnipiac College.

A special thank you goes to Steve Roberts and Damon Roberts for their technical expertise, assistance, and encouragement.

ABOUT THE AUTHOR

Judy Roberts received her A. B. degree in English from West Georgia College, her M. Ed. degree in education from Georgia State University, and her Ed. D. in reading from the University of Miami. She has taught developmental reading and study skills courses at five colleges and universities in Florida and Kentucky. Prior to beginning a career in college teaching, she taught for sixteen years in the public school systems of Georgia, Florida, and Kentucky. She is a member of Phi Delta Kappa and the Kentucky Association of Developmental Education.

She maintains the belief that all students can become more successful after being taught some basic metacognitive strategies, which can be applied to all of their college courses.

STUDY SKILLS

This section presents life skills that will enable you to perform more efficiently in all settings, from the classroom to the workplace. It covers the skills of time management, concentration and memory, learning styles, and critical thinking. These skills are interrelated; each plays a crucial role in our being able to move beyond functioning to achieving and succeeding. For example, in our hectic and busy lives, time management has become increasingly imperative. To achieve goals and, just as important, to have sufficient time left for leisure activities and relaxation, efficient time management skills are a must. Any task also requires the ability to concentrate and to remember what is learned. Concentration and recall are enhanced if the learning styles most appropriate to us and the situation are used. Finally, critical thinking is one of the most valuable of skills in a world where people are bombarded with information that must be processed to determine what is accurate and what is important.

In Section I:

Time Management

CHAPTER OBJECTIVES

- To learn the principles of good time management
- To learn how to get organized and use time effectively
- To recognize and monitor stress
- To learn how to control stress through effective use of time

Time management is an important part of the life of every person of every age and occupation. How many times have you heard someone say, "I didn't have time"? Unfortunately, no one ever seems to have enough time to do everything that needs to be done. This chapter concentrates on the time management problems of college students and offers solutions to those problems.

College students should understand that their primary activity is learning. Those who do not realize this may soon find themselves on academic probation. Much time is spent in classes or labs as well as in study outside of class. It is usually the unsupervised study outside of class that poses the greatest problem for many freshmen and, sometimes, upper-level students. Freshmen have often recently come from a very structured academic setting in high school where they had to be in class most of the day, and where teachers monitored their work and behavior. Older, returning students may have been out of school for many years and feel that handling classes, work, and family responsibilities will be challenging. This chapter presents suggestions for dealing with college schedules through effective time management.

A TALE OF THREE STUDENTS

Today's college students are very different from those of a generation ago when students who attended college usually did so immediately after high school. Those students rarely were married or had children, and fewer of them worked full-time. Today students of all ages are considered a welcome addition to college campuses. The older students who have many responsibilities are often called "nontraditional students" or "returning students." They have time management problems that are different from those of most younger students. Among the younger students, there is also great variability in terms of work, family responsibilities, and extracurricular activities. Three very different students will be profiled to lead into the discussion of analyzing commitments and getting organized according to those commitments.

Glenn

Glenn has only been out of high school for two years. He would have liked to attend college immediately after high school, but finances dictated that he work and save money. Glenn did earn money but not as much as he needs, so now that he is a college freshman, he still must work 25 hours a week. He takes a full load at college, belongs to an archery club, and attends church every week. He also volunteers to drive the church bus every Thursday night to take a senior citizens' group to and from their weekly social activities. Glenn works out at the college gym one hour every day if he can.

In order for any student to organize time, it is first necessary to analyze commitments, preferably by the week. Glenn's weekly commitments are listed on the following page.

Glenn has accounted for 117 out of the week's 168 hours. Later in the chapter, schedules will be assessed to show how to determine both how much time is available to study and how to discover *where* that time is.

ACTIVITY	HOURS PER WEEK
Work	25
Class attendance	12
Transportation to work and classes	5
Archery club	3
Church and volunteer work	5
Exercise	7
Sleep	49
Eating	7
Grooming	4
Total	117 hours

Sharon

Sharon is a nontraditional student, having graduated from high school fifteen years ago. She is now attending college for the first time because all three of her children are in school, giving Sharon a little more free time. She is still very busy with the children after school and on weekends and holidays. She works thirty hours a week to help augment her husband's income, although she would prefer to concentrate only on her college courses. In addition to work and child care, Sharon is very busy doing the cooking and housework for the family and driving the children to school and after-school activities. Sharon has tried to estimate her weekly commitments, without any overlapping, in the following chart:

ACTIVITY	HOURS PER WEEK
Work	30
Child care	45
Class attendance	12
Transportation	8
Cooking and housework	15
Sleep	45
Eating (not counted since with children)	
Grooming	4
Total	159 hours

Sharon's problem appears to be a real time management dilemma because she has accounted for 159 out of 168 hours in the week. As you will read in a later section, it is going to be necessary for Sharon to combine some activities. If she is successful in this, she can still manage to attend college. She may also consider getting help from other family members for some of her duties, such as transporting children, cooking, and doing housework.

Time may seem like a particularly difficult problem for the older, nontraditional student. The solution for people like Sharon is to be even more organized. If you are a busy, nontraditional student, you should make the phone and the mail work for you, even before classes begin. Most colleges now allow some type of mail or phone registration. This is preferable to standing in long lines all day and is a good time management tip for students of any age.

Nontraditional students may have the added stress of family members and friends making too many demands on their time or failing to understand the need or desire of an older person to return to college. Communication with those who are closest is needed before returning to classes so that everyone's needs and goals are expressed and the necessary compromises are made.

Brad

Brad is a full-time student on a football scholarship. He does not have to work, but he must maintain good grades in order to remain in college. He has many daily and weekly activities that are required by the coach. He must attend all practices, weight training sessions, and games. The athletic department requires attendance at its own daily study hall as well. Brad's football-related activities take as much time as a job, so he is also very busy, as you can see from his weekly hours:

ACTIVITY	HOURS PER WEEK
Class attendance	12
Football practice, training, and games	35
Study hall	7
Transportation	10
Sleep	56
Eating	7
Grooming	6
Total	133 hours

Since Brad's football activities take as many hours as a job, he also must manage his time well if he is to be a successful student. Fortunately, the team offers a study hall, which is accounted for in Glenn's schedule, but seven hours a week are insufficient for college study. He has enough time left for additional study if he finds out where the time is and then uses it.

 **GETTING ORGANIZED**

The three students profiled, and all other college students, can manage time more effectively, but first they must get organized. This can be accomplished by first analyzing commitments, then learning and using timesaving tips.

Analyzing Commitments

You will need to take the time to record how you spend your time for one week. You should use Figure 1.1 for this project; make more than one copy of the table so that you can work on using your time more effectively in the future. (Figure 1.2 is an example of a person's record of how the time was spent.) It is important not to estimate but instead to record exactly what you did in the hourly block of time, even if you have to record "goofing off" or "sitting and thinking." After you have done the time chart for one week, you can write down your weekly hours per activity as was done in the three examples of Glenn, Sharon, and Brad.

When analyzing your commitments in order to find time to study, remember the following six important points.

1. To ensure an accurate number of hours, do not count any activity more than once. There should not be any overlapping. For example, the nontraditional student, Sharon, was always with her children during meals, and that time had already been allotted in the category of "child care."

2. Use a typical week when estimating your hours. Obviously, there are weeks when the activities vary, such as during vacations or family emergencies. You need to use the times of a normal week for school and work.

3. Realize that some study time may be found during another listed activity. To use Sharon as an example again, the time allotted for child care consists of caring for her school-aged children from the time they get out of school at 3:00 P.M. until they go to bed at 8:00 P.M. on school nights as well as caring for them ten hours a day on weekends. She did not count the time when the children were

Figure 1.1 Blank weekly schedule form.

WEEKLY SCHEDULE

	Sunday	Monday	Tuesday	Wednesday	Thursday	Friday	Saturday
6:00 A.M.							
7:00 A.M.							
8:00 A.M.							
9:00 A.M.							
10:00 A.M.							
11:00 A.M.							
12:00 P.M.							
1:00 P.M.							
2:00 P.M.							
3:00 P.M.							
4:00 P.M.							
5:00 P.M.							
6:00 P.M.							
7:00 P.M.							
8:00 P.M.							
9:00 P.M.							
10:00 P.M.							
11:00 P.M.							
12:00 A.M.							

Figure 1.2   *Sample weekly schedule form.*

WEEKLY SCHEDULE

	Sunday	Monday	Tuesday	Wednesday	Thursday	Friday	Saturday
6:00 A.M.	Slept	Slept	Slept	Slept	Slept	Slept	Slept
7:00 A.M.		Got ready Rode bus	↓	Got ready Rode bus	↓	Got ready Rode bus	
8:00 A.M.		Biology class	Got ready	Biology	Talked with friends	Biology	
9:00 A.M.	↓	Studied	Went to mall	Studied		Rested	
10:00 A.M.	Got dressed	English class		English		English	↓
11:00 A.M.	Church	Art class		Art		Art	Got dressed
12:00 P.M.	Went to lunch	Lunch	↓	Tutor	↓	Lunch	Talked on phone
1:00 P.M.	↓	Work	Math class	Work	Math class	Work	Work
2:00 P.M.	TV		↓		↓		
3:00 P.M.			Work		Work		
4:00 P.M.							
5:00 P.M.	↓	↓		↓		↓	↓
6:00 P.M.	Boyfriend came over	Dinner with parents	↓	Dinner	↓	Dinner with friends	TV
7:00 P.M.			Dinner	TV	Dinner	and movie	
8:00 P.M.		↓	Studied		Studied		
9:00 P.M.	↓	TV			↓		
10:00 P.M.	Studied math		↓	↓	Slept	↓	↓
11:00 P.M.	Slept	↓	Slept	Slept		Slept	Read
12:00 A.M.	↓	Slept	↓	↓	↓	↓	Slept

sleeping. During the 45 hours of child care, Sharon can also study while the children do their homework, thereby setting an excellent example for them. She can also find study time when the children are busy with their own activities in the homes of friends or in their own rooms.

4. Be prepared to assign priorities to your activities if you really cannot find adequate amounts of time to study. If college is truly important to you, you may have to give up or cut back on time spent in some of the other activities. Remember that college requires a certain amount of sacrifice, and some activities may have to be relinquished, at least temporarily. Obviously, some activities cannot be given up, such as caring for one's own children or participating in football when on a football scholarship. However, there are many areas to explore in anyone's schedule.

5. Keep a calendar on which you place important events and appointments. Figure 1.3 is an example of a college student's calendar. Notice that he or she has filled in important academic due dates and tests as well as personal appointments and important events. A quick glance at the calendar will reveal the time slots when the student may study.

6. Ask yourself honestly if you must work as many hours as you do. Are you working to support a family or pay tuition, or are you simply trying to purchase extras? Remember again that college requires both commitment and a certain degree of sacrifice.

Working Around Work

A real problem for many modern college students is the job. Many must work full-time in order to attend college. If this is your situation, consider the following suggestions to make your job more beneficial.

Find a job with an employer who understands the demands placed on a student. You can have serious problems with an employer who is so inflexible that he or she will not change your hours with each new, and different, semester. If your employer is a college graduate, you will probably receive more understanding in this area. You may also need additional time off to study for tests, especially for final exams. If needed, request a meeting with your boss to discuss how conflicts can be resolved.

Don't work any more hours than necessary. Many colleges have work-study programs where students work in exchange for money toward tuition. Most of these programs limit the weekly work hours to twenty. If you can manage, keep your work hours to a minimum.

Figure 1.3   *Sample college student calendar.*

SEPTEMBER 1999

Sunday	Monday	Tuesday	Wednesday	Thursday	Friday	Saturday
			1 1:00— Go to Financial Aid office	2 2:00— Dental appt.	3	4
5	6 Labor Day	7	8 Visit Frank	9 Math test	10	11 8:00— Date for dance
12	13 3:00— Meet w/ tutor	14 History test	15	16	17 3:00— Pick up Mom Flight 84	18 6:00— Meet Cindy at Red Lob
19	20 3:00— Tutor	21	22 Biology test	23 Art test	24	25 8:00— Dance
26	27 3:00— Tutor	28	29	30		

Whenever possible, get a job in the area in which you have the greatest academic interest, maybe even a future major course of study. If you are planning to become a veterinarian and you can work part-time in a pet-related occupation, it would look good on your resume. You also would not be totally inexperienced.

Don't be afraid to change jobs if your present job is causing too much conflict with college. This is a responsible reason for leaving a job, so take advantage of any opportunity to have a more manageable schedule.

Ten Guidelines for Successful Time Management

There are many **time traps,** those things that take your time away from studying. Some of these time traps are socializing with friends, worrying, and procrastinating. Most people have some problems managing their time and avoiding traps, but anyone can apply these ten important principles and begin to manage time better.

1. Set goals for yourself. You need both short-term and long-term goals. If you are in college, your long-term goal is probably to graduate with your preferred major and then to enter a certain career field. To reach your long-term goal, you need to set immediate and daily goals for yourself. For example, if you have trouble concentrating on your assigned reading, set a goal such as, "In one hour, I will have read and annotated Chapter 6 of my biology text." When you set a study goal, include both a time period and a specific task.

2. Make a habit of recording all of your assignments. Do this routinely in an organized way. You may use a form such as the one used in Figure 1.4. If you do not record assignments for every class meeting, you will inevitably forget an important assignment sooner or later. You should write the *exact* assignments, as a student has done in the example in Figure 1.4.

3. Make lists daily and/or weekly. People who make and use daily "to-do" lists report that they accomplish more and forget less. You can make both a personal and an academic list, or you can combine them, as in the example on page 14.

If you prefer, you can prioritize your list. Do not hesitate to list chores you perform every day or classes you must attend. When you look back at the list at the end of the day, having checked off the completed tasks, you will have a sense of accomplishment. If some tasks do remain uncompleted, put those tasks at the top of the list for the next day.

Figure 1.4   *Sample assignment form.*

Course Name	Monday Date: 9-13	Tuesday Date: 9-14	Wednesday Date: 9-15	Thursday Date: 9-16	Friday Date: 9-17
History		Read Ch. 2 and prepare to discuss.		Decide on a research topic. Answer ques. on pp. 25–27.	
English comp.	Write essay on controversial topic.		Revise notes from 9/14.		Write original poem.
Algebra		Work problems #1–25 on pp.18–21.		Study for test on Ch. 1 & 2.	
French	Define new terms in Ch. 2.		Read and learn conversational phrases pp. 21–28.		Work with group on project.
Music		Check out and listen to tapes 2 & 3. Make notes.		Answer ques. on handout. Read Ch. 3.	

	TO-DO LIST FOR MONDAY
	1. Review history notes.
	2. Attend all classes and take notes.
	3. See financial aid officer.
	4. Clean apartment.
	5. Go to dental appointment.
	6. Decide on topic for English term paper.
	7. Study for biology test for one hour.
	8. Read assigned chapter in art.

4. Don't procrastinate. Putting off until later what you should be doing now will have certain negative effects. Your stress level will probably increase because of your having to rush at the last minute. Also, your academic grades will probably suffer because work done in a frantic rush is rarely as good as that which is well planned. Procrastination is a habit with many people, but try to determine the cause of your procrastination. Do you dislike the courses you are taking? Do you really want to be in college? You probably will not like every course you have to take in your college career, but if graduation is your goal, you must stop putting things off.

5. Use your peak periods of concentration for difficult assignments or subjects. Find out when you perform better—when you are at your "peak." Study your most difficult subjects then, or try to schedule the most difficult classes at that time. You can perform more routine tasks, such as organizing note cards or reviewing notes, when you are getting tired.

6. Use review to your advantage. Students who review on a regular basis will not feel the need to stay up all night the night before a big test. Such a marathon study session may not be possible anyway, due to other responsibilities. Many experts recommend review at a time that is close to the time the class meets. For example, you might read the notes made on an assigned chapter before the class meets, or review your lecture notes right after the class.

7. Plan for two to three hours of study for each hour spent in class. This rule of thumb is an estimate of the time required to be a successful college student. Although you may actually be in a class for three hours a week, you must realize that most of the work takes place outside of the classroom. You should expect to spend six to nine hours of outside study for every three hours in class. Plan for this as you make your schedule.

8. Use distributed, not mass, practice. **Distributed practice** or study means a smaller amount spread over several days instead of several hours in one day. **Mass practice** or study means a large amount of time studying in one session. If two students both decided to spend five hours on an assignment, the one using distributed practice could work for one hour on five consecutive days. This would be less arduous and each session would serve as a review, aiding recall and effectiveness. The student using mass practice would work for five hours in one session. You can use the principle of distributed practice even when reading assignments in a textbook. If you must have one hundred pages read and underlined in five days, you could process twenty pages of the material a day:

Distributed Practice	Mass Practice
M (1 hour), T (1 hour), W (1 hour), Th (1 hour), F (1 hour)	Saturday (5 hours)

9. Use small amounts of time if large blocks are not available. Many students who have analyzed their time for one week report that they have no time to study. Some very busy students actually may not have an hour or more at a time, but they must learn to use small periods of time to study. Much time is wasted while waiting. Consider the following situations in which conscientious students used time that would otherwise have been wasted:

Janice receives allergy injections every week. She must wait for about fifteen minutes before and another fifteen minutes after getting the injections. She uses this half-hour to study her biology notes.

Bob rides to class with another student who always arrives at the college about a half-hour early. Bob uses this time to read part of the assigned material before history class.

Ming must work full-time as a ticket agent for an airline. Between customers, she has another ticket agent quiz her on the terms she has written on index cards. These five- or ten-minute segments add up to about three hours a week.

Mary Ann drives her children to and from school and other activities. The children enjoy taking turns asking Mom questions they compose from her geology notes.

Matteo is in the Army Reserves. Once a month he has to drive 130 miles to spend a weekend in the military. He realized years ago that he is an auditory learner, so he tapes the material he is trying to learn for a test and plays the tape during his drive.

Steve has to ride the city bus to and from classes as well as to and from work at an automobile plant. He always takes a textbook or some important notes and studies on the bus.

10. *If you discover that you have too many activities, don't be afraid to withdraw from some of them.* If you have analyzed your time and your commitments, you may find that you really don't have enough time to do everything. You will have to assign priorities to the activities in your life. The less important activities will have to be eliminated so that you can attain your goals. It is not a sign of weakness to rearrange your schedule.

Preparation for Handling Emergencies

Emergencies often prevent students from being able to attend classes. However, some emergencies do not have to interfere with your daily routine if adequate preparation is made in advance:

1. *Have a responsible "partner" in the class who can inform you of information and announcements missed when you are ill or injured.* Always choose a student who is responsible and who has regular attendance. You will need to reciprocate, so you also must be responsible.

2. *Arrange for an alternate ride to class in the event that you miss the bus or your own car is malfunctioning.* Prepare to leave home early enough to take advantage of your other arrangements if they become necessary.

3. *If you have children, make alternate arrangements for babysitting services.* Even if you have very responsible and reliable babysitters, they will also have illnesses or emergencies that prevent them from working for you. Arrange for backup babysitters in case you need them; do not merely assume that someone will be available. Most people have busy lives, so ask them in advance if you can call on them in case of emergencies. If your children are in school, make arrangements for their care when they are too ill to attend school.

4. *A death in the family can take you out of town for a few days, so notify the instructor of your reason for being absent.* If possible, notify the instructor in advance. The courtesy will be greatly appreciated, and the instructor will know you care about your class performance and your grade.

5. *Keep an old-fashioned windup clock in case your electricity fails at home.* This backup clock will also help you get a better night's sleep because you will not be worrying about sleeping too late.

MANAGING STRESS

Stress is certainly a part of life, especially for busy people. Some stress is good for people. For example, feeling some stress before a job interview or an important test causes people to prepare and do their best. However, prolonged severe stress can cause physical problems and illnesses, so it should be controlled. Stress is considered an important part of a time management chapter because poor time management can increase stress. Some of the physical manifestations of stress are listed below:

Headaches	Fatigue
Problems with digestion	Weight loss/gain
Difficulty concentrating	Depression
Sleep problems	Psychosomatic illnesses

Ten Guidelines for Reducing Stress

1. *Manage your time well through the tips given earlier in the chapter.* Poor time management can lead to more stress. People who find themselves getting more and more behind schedule suffer more of the symptoms of stress.

2. *Avoid simultaneous life changes.* Figure 1.5 lists some of the life events that may cause stress in our lives. Many of the changes on the list are unavoidable, and some are even welcome and pleasant. However, too many changes *at once* can cause severe stress. Give thought to which of these you may be experiencing. If you are under great stress because of certain life events, you may want to seek counseling. College students have counselors available at no cost, so take advantage of this valuable service.

3. *Eliminate the stressors you can do without.* You may be feeling stress because you are in danger of failing math. Do something about this as soon as

Figure 1.5   *Examples of life events that can cause us to experience stress.*

1. Death of a spouse or loved one
2. Divorce or separation
3. Personal injury or illness
4. Marriage
5. Being fired or laid off at work
6. Retirement
7. Pregnancy
8. Birth of a child
9. Change in financial state
10. Change to different line of work, or in responsibilities at work
11. Death of close friend
12. Foreclosure of mortgage or loan
13. Son or daughter leaving home
14. Trouble with in-laws
15. Outstanding personal achievement
16. Begin or end school
17. Change in residence, school, recreation, church or social activities
18. Change in sleeping or eating habits
19. Vacation
20. Christmas

the stress begins: Seek a study group or a tutor; schedule a conference with the instructor or a counselor; consider withdrawing from the course and taking it at a later date (especially if you are already too far behind). If you are feeling stress because of your job, consider changing jobs or discussing the problem with your boss. In short, if you can do something about a stressful situation, take action.

4. Make careful plans in the future to prevent more stress.   Schedule your classes at the most convenient time. Ask a lot of questions before accepting a job because you need to know if the employer will be supportive of your college plans. Don't accept too many responsibilities; you may have to learn to say "no" to all requests except those that are most important to you at this time.

5. Make time for fun and physical activity.   Some people report that a walk every day is very relaxing for them. You may prefer swimming, working out in a gym, or playing some team sport. Decide what you like to do and give yourself a break. Make time for your friends or family, and do something you enjoy. If you see a good movie, you may then be ready to get back to your studies.

6. Employ good health habits.   Get enough rest and nutritious food. Many college freshmen are exhausted mentally and physically. Concentration will be optimum if you are in good physical condition.

7. Use your daily to-do lists and weekly schedule to avoid added stress and to realize that you are accomplishing something.   It is a good feeling to check off each finished item. You will get more done and feel better about yourself.

8. Set realistic goals. Consider your available time, energy, and commitments. Be willing to modify your goals if necessary. A few suggestions will help you set realistic goals:

- Consider your background, training, and financial resources.
- Make sure the goals represent what you really want to do in life.
- Use your short-term goals to achieve a feeling of making progress.
- Don't overreact when you must modify or change a goal.

9. Assume responsibility for your own life events. Resist tendencies to become passive, and do not become a victim. No one can make you lead your life a certain way. You should try to surround yourself with positive, upbeat people as much as possible; avoid the negative and the pessimistic ones because they can have a detrimental effect on your attitude.

10. Don't be afraid to ask for help when you need it. College students have access to many professional resources that would be very costly in the private sector. You can get help with academics from professors, advisors, and the college catalog. In addition, there are study skills centers, learning labs, study groups, and tutors. If you have special physical or learning problems, you can get help from the disability resource centers. Personal problems can be addressed by counselors. It is reassuring to know that, whatever the source of stress, there are many campus resources to which you can turn for assistance.

SUMMARY

Successful college students must master the skills of concentration and memory. Since today's college population is so diverse, three very different students were profiled. The three had various time constraints and responsibilities, and they were discussed separately.

A section on getting organized stressed the importance of analyzing commitments and setting goals and priorities. Because of the large number of students who work, suggestions were presented for dealing with work and employers, and for deciding on the ideal number of hours for college students to work.

The chapter contributed guidelines for successful time management, which would enable all students to effectively deal with commitments and find time to study. Included were suggestions both for advance preparation for handling inevitable emergencies and for managing stress.

Cooperative Learning Activities

GROUP 1. Phil has a problem with finances. Like many other students, he must work in order to attend college. If he takes fewer courses, he will lose his financial aid. But if he works less, he cannot afford to attend college. He knows that he has too much to do, but he cannot see any way out of his present situation. What are some alternatives for Phil so that he can use his time as efficiently as possible? What special guidelines for time management would you recommend for Phil?

GROUP 2. Dolores is a single mother of a three-year-old son. She works twenty-five hours a week and takes four college courses. In addition to her regular job, she teaches aerobic dancing two nights a week. On the weekends, she drives two hours one way to visit her parents. She drives home late Sunday night because she has to be at work Monday morning. She feels tired all the time and always feels rushed; she is afraid that she does not spend enough time with her son. She hardly has any time to study and feels tired and sleepy when she does study. Analyze Dolores's use of her time; tell how you would solve her problems and work out a more feasible semester plan for her.

GROUP 3. Fred is a full-time college student. His parents support him completely and do not feel that he should work while he is in college. Fred does not play any sports or have any other commitments. Although he is free to pursue his education, he finds at midterm that he is failing all his courses. Since he only parties on the weekend and usually attends classes, what could be his problem? Explore all the possibilities, and offer solutions that would enable Fred to be more successful in the future.

GROUP 4. Let each member of the group describe a situation in which he or she mismanaged time, and give the results of the poor time management. Then tell how each situation could have been avoided. After this personal accounting, make your own list of time management guidelines that have worked best for you.

GROUP 5. Compile a list of as many time traps as you can. After listing the time traps, list two solutions or alternatives for each so that work and study can be more productive. Circle all the time traps that any member of the group still feels is a problem.

Reading Selection: *Health and Behavior*

Title: *Getting a Handle on Impossible People**
Author: Karen S. Peterson

Activation of Prior Knowledge and Interest

1. What different behaviors could be described as "impossible"?

    _____

    _____

    _____

    _____

2. Describe a person with whom you are not on good terms. What be-
    havior changes could you or the other person make to improve the re-
    lationship?

    _____

    _____

    _____

    _____

3. Predict ways in which dealing with an impossible person could affect
    you.

    _____

    _____

    _____

    _____

---

*Copyright 1997, USA TODAY. Reprinted by permission.

Think about it for a minute. Is there somebody in your life who is driving you nuts?

"We encounter impossible people in our families, neighborhoods, churches and in our workplace," says Les Parrott in his *High-Maintenance Relationships: How to Handle Impossible People* (Tyndale, $17.99). "Some people are just more difficult, if not impossible, to get along with." Parrott is a professor of psychology and co-director of the Center for Relationship Development at Seattle Pacific University.

You often don't have the luxury of erasing these folks from your life, or you may just choose not to cut them off, Parrott says. But life would be more placid if you could stop them from unraveling your security blanket.

The goal, Parrott says, is not changing the person but changing the way you two interact. "Then he won't wear you down as much."

Parrott surveyed 100 people to find out the types who truly irritate them. Some of the winners, plus how to cope:

Critics. They "find the cloud in the silver lining," Parrott says. They can also be perfectionists, driven, bossy, judgmental, arrogant, exhausting, pedantic and nit-picky.

Critics often think they are just being helpful, Parrott says. They often are natural problem-solvers. And often, they were raised by critics. To cope:

1. *Don't write them off.* They can be "the unpaid watchmen of your soul," he says. See if there is not some core of truth in what is said.

2. *Set limits on the criticism you will accept.* Parrott suggests, for example: "You may critique anything I do, but don't tell me how to correct the relationship with my sister. For right now, that is my business."

3. *Institute a complaint session.* Set aside a specific, limited time to vent complaints. Critics like that; it fits into their problem-solving mode.

4. *Put things into perspective.* Believe, "What you say and what you think about me matters to me. But after I have wrestled with my own conscience—and made my decision—your judgment will not matter much."

5. *Keep your own dreams alive.* Don't allow critics to snuff them out.

6. *Remember the gender difference.* Men and women often regard criticism and requests differently. Women believe fulfilling requests shows love; men equate receiving requests with taking orders.

Control freaks. They're unable to let go and are often obnoxious, tenacious, invasive, obsessive, perfectionistic, critical, irritable, demanding and rigid.

In most cases, Parrott says, control freaks are trying to protect themselves, not trying to hurt you. Accusing them will only make them more fearful. To cope:

1. *Pinpoint their need.* Do they need to be important, recognized, powerful, appreciated? Stroke control freaks' egos.

2. *Drown them in information.* Think of control freaks as overprotective parents, Parrott says. "One of the best ways to help them relax is to keep them informed." Best of all, put your plan in writing, giving them time to think.

3. *Negotiate your role.* Carve out some autonomy. You can assure control freaks you are on their side while at the same time asserting your own style.

4. *Know when it is time to move on.* Control freaks can harm your career. They don't want to share credit or assignments. Consider a change.

Martyrs. They're forever the victim, flattened by the smallest difficulty, and are defeatist, passive, self-blaming, and irrational.

Martyrs are often created in childhood, Parrott says. As adults, they can't understand the gradations from independence to helplessness. They often fear rejection. To cope:

1. *Don't expect too much change.* Martyrs were "raised with self-pity and weaned on guilt." Lower your expectations.

2. *Make martyrs laugh.* They often think they deserve to suffer. Change the pace.

3. *Avoid the guilt trap.* Martyrs seek pity and induce guilt. Avoid the suggestion that you could never do enough to help.

4. *Keep your own tank full.* Monitor your time spent with a martyr and avoid letting your energy be depleted.

Personalities That Can Test Patience

Personalities included in Les Parrott's hall of shame—folks who drive others crazy:

- Wet blankets. Pessimistic.
- Steamrollers. Blindly insensitive.
- Gossips. Spread rumors, leak secrets.
- Back stabbers. Two-faced.
- Cold shoulders. Avoid contact.
- Green-eyed monsters. Seethe with envy.
- Volcanoes. Ready to erupt.
- Sponges. Needy, but give nothing back.
- Competitors. Winning is everything.
- Workhorses. Never satisfied with anything.

- Flirts. Deal in sexual innuendoes.
- Chameleons. Eager to avoid conflict.

Is High Maintenance Part of Your Life?

Want to know if you have an impossible person in your life? Take this quiz, adapted from *High-Maintenance Relationships.* Respond "yes" or "no" to each question. Check scoring below:

_____ 1. Do you feel anxious when this person leaves a message for you to call?

_____ 2. Does dealing with him or her drain your energy?

_____ 3. Do you sometimes dread having to talk to this person?

_____ 4. Do you give more than you get?

_____ 5. Do you second-guess yourself after seeing this person?

_____ 6. Are you more self-critical in his or her presence?

_____ 7. Is your clarity of mind hampered sometimes by having to deal with this person?

_____ 8. Do you calm yourself after being together with some unhealthy habit such as eating more or drinking?

_____ 9. Do you have imaginary conversations, trying to defend yourself?

_____10. Have you become more susceptible to colds, muscle tension, or stomach problems since this person's arrival?

_____11. Are you resentful that he or she seems to treat others better than you?

_____12. Do you wonder why this person rarely acknowledges what you do well but dwells more on himself or herself?

_____13. Do you think of bailing out of a job or marriage because of this person?

_____14. Has he or she made you more irritable or impatient?

_____15. Are you discouraged because your attempts to change the relationship have failed?

SCORING. If you said "yes" to 10 or more, you are in a high-maintenance relationship with a difficult person.

Critical Thinking Questions

1. Of the three personality types discussed in detail (critics, control freaks, and martyrs), which type would be more detrimental to you personally? Explain.

_____

_____

_____

_____

_____

2. Compare and contrast the possible causes of any two of the personality types.

_____

_____

_____

_____

_____

3. What effective parenting methods would you employ to raise a well-adjusted child?

_____

_____

_____

_____

_____

4. Reread the suggestions given for dealing with critics, control freaks, and martyrs. Which suggestions do you feel are most realistic, and why? Are any suggestions unrealistic or unworkable, in your opinion? Explain.

_____

_____

_____

_____

_____

REFERENCES

Bliss, E. C. (1991). *Getting Things Done: The ABCs of Time Management.* New York: Macmillan.

Covey, S. R. (1994). *First Things First.* New York: Simon & Schuster.

Lakein, A. (1989). *How to Get Control of Your Time and Your Life.* New York: Signet Books.

Winston, S. (1978). *Getting Organized.* New York: W.W. Norton & Co.

CREDIT

Peterson, K. S. (1997, April 7). "Getting a handle on impossible people." *USA Today.*

Concentration and Memory

CHAPTER OBJECTIVES

- To learn how to concentrate by controlling distractions
- To learn the types of memory and how memory works
- To develop strategies for improving memory

C oncentration and memory are frequently stated as problem areas for college students. There is often a lack of understanding of the processes of these two closely related skills. If students cannot concentrate, they certainly cannot remember the critical information necessary to perform well in class. What are the reasons for *your* failure to concentrate? When students state their reasons, the answers can usually be classified as (1) external distractions or (2) internal distractions. **External distractions** are interruptions or hindrances that are outside the student—something in the environment. **Internal distractions** are those that are within the person—those not contingent on the surroundings. It is important to identify the type of distraction so that you will be able to control your learning situation better.

CONCENTRATION THROUGH CONTROL OF EXTERNAL DISTRACTIONS

Control the noise around you when you study. Depending on your learning preferences, the noise level in a room may inhibit concentration. Some students report that they can study with noise, such as the television, loud music, other people's conversations, or simply street sounds. There are others who must have absolute quiet in order to concentrate. Be very honest with yourself when you assess your optimum noise level. You may enjoy listening to music, but can you really concentrate as well as when it is quiet? Do your test grades reflect your ability to concentrate in a noisy environment? For some people, the noise really may not be a problem, but you must monitor your studying and then decide for yourself. If you do need quiet, select a quiet study spot every time you study. If your situation prevents you from finding a quiet spot, invest in a set of earplugs that are effective enough to shut out the noise.

If you know you will sometimes be in a position where you must study with constant noise, practice simple tasks under distracting conditions. Many students these days have small children. They often must care for the children and study at the same time, and they cannot use earplugs to eliminate noise completely because the children must be heard if they are in distress. In cases like this, train yourself to concentrate while reading a magazine article, an interesting letter, or a movie review. Practice learning to concentrate for longer and longer periods of time, even with distractions.

Control visual distractions. You may invariably become distracted by looking at things in your surroundings. Do you look up from your book every time someone comes into the library? Do you look at objects such as pictures and memorabilia in your room at home? If so, find a place where you cannot view anything other than your desk and materials. A good place is a study carrel in the library. Unless you get up out of your seat, you should have no visual distractions. If you must study at home, create such an environment for yourself.

Make sure that other people respect your space and your privacy. This can be a problem anywhere, but it can be especially troublesome in a dormitory. If you need to be alone to concentrate on your studying, explain this to your friends and relatives. You may also have to hang a "Do not disturb" sign on your door. Even if you are a member of a study group, the group should remain on the subject being studied and resist socializing. If necessary, change groups.

Study in a place and at a time conducive to concentrating. Study in the same place and at the same time every day. Your study area should be used *only* for study so that you will be in the "mood" or frame of mind to study, associating that time and that place with academics and nothing else.

Organize your materials before you begin to study. When you make a decision concerning your time and place for study, be sure to have all the materials you will need close at hand. Collect these materials before your study session begins. Give yourself no excuse to get up and leave the study area to get pens, paper, books, reference books, or other materials.

CONCENTRATION THROUGH CONTROL OF INTERNAL DISTRACTIONS

Use to-do lists. Make your complete daily to-do list before beginning your study session. During the study session, you will not have to worry about forgetting some important activity or appointment because it will be on your list. Some people may even need to make a "worry list" of all problems that might enter their mind and inhibit study. Tell yourself, "I'll worry about or deal with that at 5:00 P.M." If something new comes to mind while you are studying, add it to the list.

Set study goals for yourself. Instead of studying aimlessly, actually devise a goal that describes exactly what you intend to accomplish. Make sure the goal includes material covered or tasks accomplished, not merely time passed. Some examples of study goals are listed below:

- In one hour, I will have completed reading and taking notes on the first three sections of my art appreciation text.
- I will work until I complete all the algebra problems assigned.
- I will go to the library and locate five sources for my term paper.
- Between 4:00 and 5:00 P.M., I will learn all of my new French vocabulary.

Use the tally method when you begin to lose concentration. The tally method is good for training yourself to concentrate. Every time your mind begins to wander, put a mark on a paper. Do this every time you fail to concentrate, and count how many marks you have in a certain specified period of time. Continue this procedure as you study, using the same amount of time. Your goal is to have fewer and fewer marks on the page. Many students who begin using this procedure report several dozen marks in a thirty-minute period, but the number of marks significantly decreases after a few sessions.

When studying for long sessions, vary your activities. Don't try to continuously read or write research notes or work math problems with no breaks. After reading for some period of time, it would be advantageous to change to a different type of study activity, such as working on math problems or practicing foreign language sentences. It is more difficult to concentrate on one single task for very long periods of time.

Take planned breaks as you study. Since no one can concentrate for very long periods of time, plan to take a break every hour that you are studying. The "50:10" ratio is a good one—after you study for fifty minutes, give yourself a break for ten minutes. During this break, do something you really like that is a change of pace. Some examples of rewards during breaks are listed below:

- A bicycle ride
- A favorite snack
- A quick phone call to a friend
- A ten-minute swim
- A short conversation
- Time with a favorite pet

It is preferable not to use the break to perform an activity that resembles study; do something other than writing or reading to get a change of pace.

Accentuate your successes and strong points. You have probably heard students make negative remarks about themselves, such as, "I'll never learn this." When you begin to engage in self-doubt, think of some of your previous accomplishments. You have achieved your goals in the past; you can do so again.

Study with a supportive partner or study group. Unless you are a completely independent learner, the right study group or partner can be reassuring. If you are anxious about predicting the right test questions, for example, discussing your predictions with those in the group can lead to the sharing of more information. Beware the naysayers and pessimists! They will cause additional anxiety.

If you lose concentration while reading, make notes as you read. You cannot lose with this idea because it also aids memory to employ some muscular activity such as writing. You will concentrate better and remember the material as well.

Try to end your study session on a positive note. Resist the temptation to close a study session when you become confused. For example, if you cannot grasp the concepts involved in solving a math problem, get help then. Most colleges and universities have walk-in math labs where you can get immediate help. If this is not possible for you, call another student or drop by the instructor's office. If you cannot reach anyone to help you at this time, put solving this problem on the next day's to-do list.

 **MEMORY**

Consider the amount of information you have learned in the course of your lifetime. It is a sobering thought to reflect on the minute amount of that information you can recall now. Much research has been conducted on the subject of memory. One very influential study conducted by a German psychologist investigated the rates of forgetting nonmeaningful and meaningful material (Ebbinghaus, 1964). The researcher, Hermann Ebbinghaus, wanted to study nonmeaningful material, such as nonsense syllables, in order to eliminate the effects of prior knowledge. He found that most of the nonmeaningful material was forgotten immediately after learning. After that, the process of forgetting slowed down, and some of the material was remembered. With meaningful material, he found that the rate of forgetting was not quite so fast, but people still forgot about 50 percent of meaningful material in one week. This presents a great problem for college students because they must remember all of the course material for at least one semester; hopefully, they will want to remember the information indefinitely.

Also contemplate the few things you could never forget. Think about possible reasons for your ability to remember some things so well but not other things. People have a great memory capacity, as evidenced by so many experiences that are never forgotten. This chapter offers some insight into learning, remembering, and forgetting.

 **TYPES OF MEMORY**

Psychologists divide memory into three types: sensory memory, short-term (or working) memory, and long-term memory (Wortman, Loftus, & Marshall, 1992). Each of these will be discussed briefly, especially as each type relates to the area of study skills.

Sensory Memory

Sensory memory is a brief lingering of sensory information after the stimulus has been removed. It is like seeing a stranger's face in your mind for a moment after a brief meeting. It could also be like an experiment where the examiner exposes a series of symbols for a second and then removes the symbols. A person can recall some of the symbols for a short period of time. People take in information through the five senses of seeing, hearing, feeling, smelling, and tasting. If something is not done to cause this information to get into the working memory, the information is lost forever. Since the mind is always receiving many sensory messages, it is necessary for a student to screen the messages that come in—in order to pay attention to the important messages. One way this is done is through **selective attention,** which is screening out some information while attending to other information. For example, a student trying to study for midterms may train himself or herself to ignore noises outside or people coming into the library through a creaky door.

When people put information into some form that can be placed into memory, this act is called **encoding.** There are strategies you can use to improve the encoding act:

- *Control distractions by eliminating competing stimuli.* The competing stimuli may be hearing excessive noise, watching television, listening to conversations, or participating in some other activity. Place all your conscious attention on the task at hand to ensure that information is encoded adequately.

- *Use as many sensory modalities as possible.* Listen to a lecture, but also write information in your notes. You should pay close attention to all visual presentations. In some classes, you will also have opportunities to use a hands-on approach or to take a field trip. Use every opportunity to understand the material as it is being presented to you.

- *Perfect your note-taking and text-processing skills.* Remember that, in classes, encoding takes place primarily through lectures and textbook reading. How many times have you heard students complain about not being able to remember? How many times have you complained about this yourself? Before you conclude that your memory has failed, ask yourself two questions:

> Have I attended every class session?
> Have I diligently read my textbook assignments?

If you had to answer "no" to either question, you cannot expect to remember the material because it was never encoded properly.

Short-Term (or Working) Memory

Short-term (or **working**) **memory** has the capacity to hold information for only about twenty seconds unless some active strategies are employed to retain the information. An example is trying to remember a phone number that someone just told you. You may say the number over and over until you can rush to a phone and dial. If something else gets your attention before you dial, you will forget the number. This is comparable to a student's hearing all sorts of history facts but doing nothing to cause the facts to be remembered. After class, all the information will be gone. It is important to realize that information entering short-term memory is rapidly lost without active work or an association with information that is already in long-term memory.

Information can be held in short-term memory longer if the facts are clustered or "chunked." The mental act of **chunking** is putting information in meaningful units. People do this when they read because letters are chunked into words, and words into meaningful phrases. We even divide our Social Security numbers and phone numbers into chunks in order to remember them better. Look at the following series of letters:

O S T T M M Y H R O R E E M R

The series of letters would be difficult to memorize, although it could be done. However, how long would it be recalled since it has no semantic significance? If the letters are arranged in a meaningful way, they would be easy to remember and would have meaning:

SHORT-TERM MEMORY

Long-Term Memory

Long-term memory is the mental receptacle for all of a person's accumulated knowledge. An amazing amount of information is held in long-term memory, and people can retrieve information from there even though they may not have thought of the particular information in years. An example of this is a little girl who, wanting to show off for some friends, memorized the West Point cadets' answer to the question, "What time is it?" The lengthy answer, containing advanced vocabulary, was used a few times and then apparently forgotten. Forty years passed, and the woman discovered, to her amazement, that she could still recite the paragraph word for word although she had not consciously thought of it in decades. Apparently her motive for learning was so strong that the information remained in long-term memory. She also worked very hard, as a child, to learn the information thoroughly.

There are many different learning strategies, but *some* strategies must be used in order for information you are learning in class to get into your long-term memory and remain there for as long as you need it. Some examples of active learning strategies you might use are listed below:

- Paraphrase what the lecturer says and write it down.

- When listening to a lecture, find the corresponding information in the textbook and mark it.
- Think of how you will use information in the future.
- Organize information in some meaningful form, such as an outline or a semantic map (covered later in this chapter).
- Discuss the lecture material with classmates.

All strategies are not for every student. The point is that good students use good learning strategies. Information does not enter the brain through osmosis. (See Figure 2.1 for examples of information that is difficult to remember versus information that is easier to remember.)

 ## GUIDELINES FOR REMEMBERING

The tips for remembering will be divided into three categories: (1) attitude and motivation, (2) organization, and (3) specific study skills.

Attitude and Motivation

Intend to remember. You must make a conscious effort to remember material. In a social situation, if you saw someone new on the street, you probably could not describe him to the police later. However, if that same person forcibly pulled your purse out of your hand, you would concentrate on his looks so that you could give an accurate description to the police. Many students sit in a

Figure 2.1 *Types of information.*

Information Difficult to Recall	Information Easy to Recall
Names of people and places	Material you have a motive to learn
Numbers and dates	Material in manageable parts
Subjects considered uninteresting	Subjects considered interesting
Unpleasant experiences	Pleasant experiences
Information barely learned	Information that is overlearned
Facts that conflict with beliefs	Facts consistent with beliefs
Material learned by cramming	Material reviewed often
Information rarely thought of	Information you talk about often
Material that seems confusing	Material that makes sense
Material you try to learn when tired	Material you learn when rested

class thinking the information will just "sink in." Do not be a passive learner. Instead be active, intend to remember, and take steps to make it happen.

Select what is important. Obviously no one can remember everything, so you must decide what is worth remembering. There are effective ways to do this. If you are trying to decide what parts of a lecture to remember, notice what is stressed by the instructor. Some information may be stressed by repeating it several times. Also pay close attention to information that is written on the board, put on an overhead transparency, or included in a handout. Some instructors will be less subtle and will simply make a statement telling you to remember certain information because it is important or because it will be on a test. There are also clues in textbooks that let the reader know what is most important. Some textbook chapters contain questions on the chapter. Read and learn the answers to these questions because the author has selected that information as important. You should also focus on terms in boldface type or italics, headings, subheadings, pictures, and graphic illustrations.

Make associations. The definition of **comprehension** is to connect new information with known information. With every new bit of knowledge, you should make a connection by thinking of how the new knowledge is similar or dissimilar to another situation. When you learn some seemingly vague concept, try to apply the concept to a real situation. Think of how this concept or idea could possibly affect you or relate to something else you have learned. You must *want* to make these associations.

Be a critical reader and thinker. If you question what you read and hear, it will make an impression on your memory. Some students who are critical thinkers make reflective comments in the margins of their textbooks. Ask yourself how you feel about a situation. For example, if you are reading about the fight for civil rights, question whether your own rights have ever been violated. Have the rights of a friend or family member been violated? How would you feel if such a thing did happen? What could be done to correct an injustice? What problems in society still need to be solved?

Put aside your biases when necessary. Many people have biases and prejudices that exclude conflicting views. While personal beliefs are expected of everyone, sometimes these beliefs interfere with learning new theories and other information. Some examples reported by students are listed below:

- A student who feels very strongly about capital punishment cannot recognize logical arguments for the opposing viewpoint.
- A very conservative and religious student refuses to learn about evolution in science class.

- A student who is so ethnocentric that he cannot understand the viewpoint of the Native Americans in a history class does not remember much of the material in that chapter.
- A student whose religious beliefs are very exclusive has trouble in a class of comparative religion.
- A sexist male student has trouble remembering the historical contributions of women.

All of these students should understand that they are not being asked to change any of their personal beliefs. They are simply broadening their education by learning about other people and ideas.

Organization

Organize your facts to be remembered. There are many ways of organizing material, depending on your personal preference. Some people outline; others make stacks of note cards. Another innovative way of organizing information is by **mapping** (also known as **semantic mapping** or **webbing**), which is a system of placing material in categories. Even a grocery list can be mapped using headings such as *dairy products, meats, fresh vegetables, cleaning supplies,* and so forth. It is easier to remember material that has been categorized because the brain stores information in this way. Mapping is covered in greater detail in another chapter, but the following list (Figure 2.2) and the semantic map of the list (Figure 2.3) will give you a good idea of how the procedure is used.

Figure 2.2   *List of terms to learn.*

Susan B. Anthony	*Plessy v. Ferguson*	poll tax	naturalization
restrictive covenants	expatriation	Jim Crow	Lucretia Mott
political refugees	19th Amendment	literacy test	suffrage

Figure 2.3   *Semantic map of terms.*

Women's Rights	**Racial Civil Rights**	**Citizenship**
Susan B. Anthony	*Plessy v. Ferguson*	naturalization
Lucretia Mott	poll tax	expatriation
19th Amendment	restrictive covenants	political refugees
suffrage	Jim Crow	literacy test

Learn difficult facts and concepts in parts. Difficult tasks can be broken down into a series of easier tasks. This is true of everything from learning to tie shoes to complicated academic tasks. When large tasks are restructured into smaller tasks, you can learn each part really well, and it is also less strenuous. For instance, if you must learn one hundred terms in a physical science class, learn a certain number of them, in an organized way, and let that be your goal for the session. If you take chapters one at a time and master the material, the concepts will come together later to form the whole.

Specific Study Skills

Recite or talk about material you want to remember. You would not think of going to a special ceremony to deliver an unrehearsed speech. Instead, you would practice the speech either before a mirror or before some friends or family members. You would rehearse the speech so that you would remember it on the proper occasion. The same method is often overlooked by students trying to recall course material, but it would be as effective in an academic situation as it is for a speech.

If you make the material a part of your everyday life, you will remember it for a long time, maybe indefinitely. You may be a student who prefers to study alone, so talk to yourself about the material every day; thinking aloud will be as effective as conversing with a partner. The important element of this guideline is to think of the material frequently and make it a part of your knowledge base.

When studying your textbook or lecture notes, paraphrase the main ideas. This guideline is particularly helpful to students who have trouble concentrating. After reading a section of an assignment, look away and attempt to **paraphrase** (tell in your own words) the main ideas. If the assigned reading is exceptionally difficult for you or if you are having a really hard time concentrating, paraphrase after each paragraph.

Stretch yourself to learn and recall material. You may write in a notebook, on note cards, on a typewriter, or on a word processor. Writing helps you to remember the material longer and more effectively than merely underlining it. You should write notes from your underlining after you have read and learned the main ideas of a selection. Also take notes during a lecture instead of simply listening. You may also stretch yourself in other ways, such as recording notes if you are an auditory learner.

Visualize what you are trying to remember. Visualization is easier for some students because they are visual learners. However, it is a skill that can be learned, with ample practice, by any student. When reading literature, picture the characters as television or movie stars you enjoy watching. Even when reading a description of a procedure in mathematics, try to see it as well as read it.

Use textbook aids to help you remember. You should use all of the "extras" offered by the textbook to help you comprehend and remember. Many textbooks provide special features such as graphics, pictures, and even cartoons. These added features may trigger your memory or simply help you form a more profound impression of the material you are trying to learn.

Also use **prediction,** which is trying to anticipate what is coming next in a textbook chapter by looking at the subheadings or at the first sentences of paragraphs. Then read to confirm your predictions. Being really involved in the text is a key to remembering it.

Use distributed, or spaced, practice or study. Both distributed (spaced) and mass practice are defined and explained in Chapter 1. Basically, it is much easier to remember material that you have studied on several occasions than in one long study session. Also, it is much easier to concentrate for shorter periods of time than for several hours in one session. A practice some students consider to be mass practice is cramming. Distinguished from ordinary mass practice, **cramming** is usually done by students who have failed to keep up during the semester and then try to "learn" all of the material in one marathon session. This is not as effective as a mass practice session for a student who has attended class regularly and kept up with assignments. Material learned while cramming, if remembered at all, will not be recalled for very long.

Review directly before sleep. The material you review right before going to sleep will be the last thing on your mind, so there will be no interference. Review is always a key to learning and remembering.

Learn and use specific memory techniques. The specific memory techniques, called **mnemonics** or **mnemonic techniques,** will be discussed individually in the next section. Use the examples given, and proceed to make and use your own mnemonics.

MNEMONIC TECHNIQUES

The section on mnemonics will be a discussion of six techniques: (1) acronyms, (2) acrostics, (3) the keyword method, (4) rhymes, (5) the story method, and (6) the method of loci. These mnemonic techniques will be discussed separately, with examples given for each. Your goal should be to learn to use one or more of these proven memory strategies to help you remember information for tests and other purposes.

Acronyms

An **acronym** is a word formed from initials of other words. An acronym often represents some aspect of the concept being named. Some acronyms are so well known that the words from which the acronym was fashioned are rarely used. Many acronyms appear in the newspapers every day:

NOW—National Organization for Women

MADD—Mothers Against Drunk Driving

AWOL—Absent Without Official Leave

CORE—Congress of Racial Equality

You can observe that in two of the examples, NOW and CORE, you may either include small words like prepositions or omit them. Sometimes the first letters of the small and insignificant words are included in order to form a word, but often the inclusion of such words (such as "for" in National Organization for Women) would destroy the word. As you can see, "NOFW" would not spell a word.

Acronyms such as MADD are especially appropriate because the acronym describes the feelings of the group. The mothers truly are angry or *mad*. You can use acronyms to help you remember things such as items you are learning for a test. You will need practice in creating acronyms in order for them to be easy for you to form and to use. Consider the following acronyms for organizations (you may think of others that are equally appropriate):

An organization that wants to legalize euthanasia:
PAINS—People Against Intolerable Needless Suffering

A group that proposes to ban pornography in town:
COVER UP—Cancel Out Very Explicit Really Uncouth Pornography

An organization that wants to bring back the military draft:
DRAFT—Don't Resist Aid for Tomorrow

EXERCISE 2.1

Practice devising other acronyms for the last organization (an organization that wants to bring back the military draft). The practice will enable you to use this skill effectively. Use the following terms, which are all related to the military.

1. WAR— _____

2. ARMY— _____

3. UNIFORM— _____

4. UNCLE SAM— _____

Acronyms in academic situations. If your geography teacher tells you to remember the five Great Lakes, you could use the acronym **HOMES** to be sure no lake was omitted. If you leave out one lake, you no longer have the word:

HOMES —Huron, Ontario, Michigan, Erie, Superior

Don't limit your use of acronyms to lists. If, for example, you are preparing for an essay test, you should predict questions and practice answering them. On any particular question, you may want to remember to discuss several vital points. If you can devise an acronym for the points you want to recall, it will help you on the essay test.

Acrostics

You may have noticed that sometimes acronyms cannot be used. This is because the list you are attempting to memorize may not have letters that would spell a word, or there may be no vowels at all. An additional problem could be that the instructor said to learn the list *in a particular order.* Take the example of the Great Lakes. You might be told to learn the lakes from largest to smallest, smallest to largest, east to west, or west to east. Suppose that the instructor wanted you to remember the lakes from west to east, which would be Superior, Michigan, Huron, Erie, and Ontario, spelling SMHEO. When you cannot use an acronym, you can still use an acrostic.

An **acrostic** is the use of the first letters of the words (here the lakes) being used as the first letters in other words. The entire acrostic is a sentence that the student can remember to help recall information. It is very suitable for learning all lists that have to be remembered in a specific order.

Here is one sentence that could be used to remember the Great Lakes in order from west to east:

<u>S</u>am	Superior
<u>M</u>ay	Michigan
<u>H</u>ave	Huron
<u>E</u>mergency	Erie
<u>O</u>perations	Ontario

The sentences you form will be easier to remember if they remind you of something or someone in your personal experience. Never worry about how silly or ridiculous your sentences appear because you do not have to share them with anyone. Some students have reported using acrostics they would be embarrassed to share but that are very easy for them to recall.

Another example of how an acrostic can be used to recall a list is a sentence to remember the nine planets of our solar system in the order of their proximity to the sun. The following example might have been devised by a student who enjoys music:

<u>M</u>ay	Mercury
<u>V</u>ery	Venus
<u>E</u>ager	Earth
<u>M</u>usicians	Mars
<u>J</u>ust	Jupiter
<u>S</u>ell	Saturn
<u>U</u>s	Uranus
<u>N</u>ew	Neptune
<u>P</u>ianos	Pluto

Acrostics for spelling. A man who became a very good high school teacher had a difficult elementary school experience because of his spelling disability. His father, trying to solve the problem, taught him to create and use acrostics to learn to spell words. The method may seem like an inordinate amount of work to people who have no spelling problems, but this person felt that it was worth the effort. One of his examples was a sentence to remember the spelling of the word *arithmetic:*

<u>A</u> <u>r</u>at <u>i</u>n <u>t</u>he <u>h</u>ouse <u>m</u>ay <u>e</u>at <u>t</u>he <u>i</u>ce <u>c</u>ream.

Since you will probably be using acrostics more often than acronyms, you will need some practice. For longer lists, you may want to devise acrostics containing more than one sentence. This is perfectly acceptable. Whatever works for you is a method you will recall on a test or in other situations.

EXERCISE 2.2

Devise an acrostic to remember the original thirteen colonies in the order listed below. Remember that you can make more than one sentence if necessary. It would probably help if the two or more sentences were semantically related. You will have to decide what to do about the states containing two words in their names. You are limited only by your imagination. Here are the thirteen colonies.

Delaware	South Carolina
Pennsylvania	New Hampshire
New Jersey	Virginia
Georgia	New York
Connecticut	North Carolina
Massachusetts	Rhode Island
Maryland	

The Keyword Method

The **keyword method** is a multistage process that takes the word to be learned and associates it with both a familiar sound-alike and a visual image. It was originally developed to help students learn foreign language vocabulary (Atkinson, 1975). The keyword method has since been generalized to English words. This is important because vocabulary is such a necessary part of all college courses, and the introductory classes in particular introduce a tremendous number of new vocabulary words.

The initial step in the keyword method involves translating the unknown word to be learned into a familiar, sound-alike counterpart. For example, a word such as *prurient,* meaning "sexually longing," can be phonetically changed into "pure-he-ain't." Then a strong visual image is conceived, linking the keyword ("pure-he-ain't") to the meaning of the word. For the word *prurient,* the student might visualize a high school or college male in a locker room boasting about his experiences with women (Roberts & Kelly, 1985). Observe some other examples of keywords:

- *Taciturn* (disinclined to conversation)—"take-his-turn" (Imagine a man who refuses to take his turn talking.)
- *Ominous* (threatening)—"omen us" (Imagine an evil omen that threatens us.)
- *Naive* (unsophisticated)—"Not-Eve" (Imagine Eve in the Garden of Eden getting into trouble because of a lack of understanding.)

EXERCISE 2.3

Practice using the keyword method by creating keywords for each of the following vocabulary words. Remember that you will have to form a strong visual image for each word. Describe the image briefly in the space provided.

VOCABULARY WORD	KEYWORD	VISUAL IMAGE
1. contraband		
2. prodigious		
3. recalcitrant		
4. fractious		
5. supercilious		
6. ambidextrous		
7. sanctimonious		
8. dermatologist		
9. psychotherapeutics		

Rhymes

Using **rhymes,** which are phrases ending in words that sound alike, to remember information is as familiar as childhood and needs no elaborate explanation. Most children have recited the rhyme, "In fourteen hundred ninety-two,

Columbus sailed the ocean blue," to recall the date for history. The fact that people can remember this rhyme decades after learning it indicates that the method is effective. Realizing this, you can create new and original rhymes to help you remember other information if that is a method you prefer.

EXERCISE 2.4

Look up the following information, and then try to think of rhymes to help you recall the facts.

1. Names of the seven seas

_____

2. Date of the signing of the Declaration of Independence

_____

3. First five U. S. presidents in order

_____

4. The three types of memory

_____

The Story Method

This method will be very effective for some students who excel at writing narratives, but it may have limited use for other students. The **story method** consists of making up a story that connects the items you are trying to remember in some type of narrative. If the items must be remembered in order, they must be in the correct order in the story.

EXERCISE 2.5

Try to create a story to remember some of the following academic lists.

- The Bill of Rights (in order)
- U. S. Supreme Court Justices
- U. S. Cabinet members and their duties

The Method of Loci

The method of loci, which has been used for centuries, is sometimes called the place method. Loci means "place" in Latin. This mnemonic technique is most effective for strong visual learners because the visualization element is extremely important. In the **method of loci,** items that are to be memorized are visualized in a series of familiar places, such as around the living room. The student remembers the items in the list as being in certain places in a room. Then, when trying to recall the items, the student visualizes the room and proceeds by associating each item with a part of the room. It is probably easiest to remember the items in the natural order of the room, beginning at the door. While this method is not for everyone, many students report success with the method of loci.

EXERCISE 2.6

Use the method of loci to remember the following list of objects. If it is helpful, you may want to draw a picture to accompany your list. Here are the objects.

barley	oranges
cotton	tangerines
coal	oats
iron ore	quartz
tomatoes	synthetic carpets

SUMMARY

This chapter dealt with two problems that are experienced by most people from time to time: concentration and memory. For some, the problem may be so severe that academic progress is threatened. Tips were given for controlling external and internal distractions. Background on memory and details on how information is taken into long-term memory led into the types of information that are most often forgotten and the types that are easiest to remember. There were general guidelines for remembering various types of personal and academic information.

Specific memory techniques, called *mnemonics,* were discussed as methods to be used by active learners. The discussion included several mnemonic techniques: acronyms, acrostics, the keyword method, rhymes, the story method, and the method of loci.

Cooperative Learning Activities

GROUP 1. Samantha enjoys going to parties. She has always liked to meet new people and has no trouble remembering their names. When introduced to as many as twenty people, she can usually recall all of their names well enough to introduce them to her old friends. Additionally, she will remember the names long after the party. However, in her college classes, she has great trouble learning new information. She especially dislikes introductory classes like history, which require her to memorize many names and dates. What could be the reasons for Samantha's inability to remember history names even though she has much more time to learn them than the names at a party? How can she solve her problem and become a good student?

GROUP 2. Steve has serious problems with concentration. He realizes that he needs absolute quiet in order to study, so he leaves his dorm room and studies in the library. He becomes distracted at the slightest sound, and sitting in a study carrel has not solved the problem since he often looks out of the carrel to see who is approaching. He cannot seem to get his mind on his studies during his first semester at college. He does not remember having this much trouble in high school even though he lived at home with his parents and two younger brothers. Give possible causes for this seemingly new inability to concentrate. Outline a plan of action for Steve.

GROUP 3. Teresa is capable of remembering large amounts of information in courses in which she is interested. The problem occurs with the classes she dislikes, and she cannot seem to find a way to become interested in them. She knows that she must take all the required courses to remain in college, but she does not think it is possible for her to pass about half of her freshman and sophomore courses. List several ways for Teresa to develop interest in courses she has never liked.

GROUP 4. Refer to the list of "Information Difficult to Recall." Compile a group list of ways in which you have overcome each type of information that is considered difficult to recall. Give specific strategies that were used by members of the group.

GROUP 5. Devise acronyms or acrostics for remembering each of the following (the group may decide whether an acronym or an acrostic would be more appropriate in each case):

- The last ten U. S. presidents in order
- The seven continents from largest to smallest in geographic area
- Any ten of the "Guidelines for Remembering" presented in this chapter

Reading Selection: *Earth Science*

Title: *Hurricane Destruction**
Authors: E.J. Tarbuck & F.K. Lutgens

Activation of Prior Knowledge and Interest

1. How have you learned about destructive weather patterns such as hurricanes, tornadoes, earthquakes, and volcanoes?

   _____

   _____

   _____

   _____

2. In your opinion, do the movies give accurate depictions of these events? Give an example from a movie you have seen.

   _____

   _____

   _____

   _____

3. What did you learn from news coverage of Hurricane Andrew? Did you personally know anyone who was in South Florida at the time of the hurricane?

   _____

   _____

   _____

   _____

A location only a few hundred kilometers from a hurricane—just one day's striking distance away—may experience clear skies and virtually no wind. Prior to the age of weather satellites, such a situation made the job of warning people of impending storms very difficult.

The worst natural disaster in U. S. history resulted from a hurricane that struck an unprepared Galveston, Texas, on September 8, 1900. The strength of the storm, coupled with the lack of adequate warning, caught the population by surprise and cost six thousand people in the city their lives. At least two thousand more were killed elsewhere. Fortunately, hurricanes are no longer the unheralded killers they once were. Once a storm develops cyclonic flow and the spiraling bands of clouds characteristic of a hurricane, it receives continuous monitoring. For example, when hurricanes Hugo (1989) and Andrew (1992) formed, satellites were able to identify and track the storms long before they made landfall. In the United States, early warning systems have greatly reduced the number of deaths caused by hurricanes. At the same time, however, there has been an astronomical rise in the amount of property damage. The primary reason, of course, has been the extensive building of homes and businesses in coastal areas.

Although the amount of damage caused by a hurricane depends on several factors, including the size and population density of the area affected and the shape of the ocean bottom near the shore, certainly the most significant factor is the strength of the storm itself. By studying past storms, a scale has been established to rank the relative intensity of hurricanes. A *category 5* storm is the worst possible, whereas a *category 1* hurricane is least severe. During the hurricane season, it is common to hear scientists and reporters alike use the numbers from the *Saffir-Simpson Hurricane Scale*. The famous Galveston hurricane just mentioned, with winds in excess of 209 kilometers (130 miles) per hour and a pressure of 931 millibars, would be placed in category 4. Storms that fall into category 5 are rare. Hurricane Camille, a 1969 storm that caused catastrophic damage along the coast of Mississippi, is one well-known example.

Damage caused by hurricanes can be divided into three categories: (1) wind damage, (2) storm surge, and (3) inland freshwater flooding.

Wind Damage. For some structures, the force of the wind is sufficient to cause total destruction. This was demonstrated in South Florida in 1992. The billions of dollars in property damages from Hurricane Andrew were largely the result of strong winds. However, wind damage is not necessarily responsible for a hurricane's greatest destructiveness.

Storm Surge. The most devastating damage in the coastal zone is caused by the storm surge. It not only accounts for a large share of coastal property losses but is also responsible for 90 percent of all hurricane-caused deaths. A **storm surge** is a dome of water sixty-five to eighty kilometers (forty to fifty miles) wide that sweeps across the coast near the point where the eye makes landfall. Ignoring wave activity, the storm surge is the height of the water above normal tide level. Thus, a storm surge commonly adds two to three meters (six to ten feet) to normal tide heights—to say nothing of tremendous wave activity superimposed atop the surge.

We can easily imagine the damage this surge of water can inflict on low-lying coastal areas. In the delta region of Bangladesh, for example, the land is mostly less than two meters above sea level. When a storm surge superimposed upon normal high tide inundated that area on November 13, 1970, the official death toll was two-hundred thousand; unofficial estimates ran to five-hundred thousand. This was one of the worst disasters of modern times.

Inland Flooding. The torrential rains that accompany most hurricanes represent a third significant threat—flooding. Whereas the effects of storm surge and strong winds are concentrated in coastal areas, heavy rains may affect places hundreds of kilometers from the coast for several days after the storm has lost its hurricane-force winds.

Hurricanes weaken rapidly as they move inland, yet the remnants of the storm can still yield fifteen to thirty centimeters (six to twelve inches) or more of rain as they move inland. A good example of such destruction was Hurricane Agnes (1972). Although this was just a category 1 storm on the Saffir-Simpson Scale, it was one of the costliest hurricanes of the century, creating more than $2 billion in damage and taking 122 lives. Most destruction was attributed to flooding caused by an inordinate amount of rainfall.

Critical Thinking Questions

1. You have been told by the instructor that you will have an essay test on this material. Select any mnemonic technique discussed in this chapter, and prepare a method for remembering all of the information you want to include in a discussion of the Saffir-Simpson Hurricane Scale.

   _____

   _____

   _____

2. Devise an acrostic for remembering the categories of hurricane damage.

   _____

   _____

   _____

3. Based on this article, make some predictions about future hurricane damage to property in the coastal areas of the United States. What changes, if any, do you think will be made?

_____

_____

_____

REFERENCES

Atkinson, R. C. (1975). Mnemotechnics in second language learning. *American Psychologist, 30,* 821–828.

Ebbinghaus, H. (1964). *Memory: A Contribution to Experimental Psychology.* Mineola, NY: Dover Publishing.

Highbee, K. L. (1988). *Your Memory: How It Works and How to Improve It.* Englewood Cliffs, NJ: Prentice-Hall.

Laird, D. A., & Laird, E. C. (1960). *Techniques for Efficient Remembering.* New York: McGraw-Hill.

O'Neil, H. F., & Spielberger, C. D. (1979). *Cognitive and Affective Learning Strategies.* New York: Academic Press.

Roberts, J., & Kelly, N. (1985). The keyword method: An alternative vocabulary strategy for developmental college readers. *Reading World, 24* (3), 34–39.

Robinson, F. P. (1970). *Effective Study* (4th ed.). New York: Harper & Row.

Wortman, C. B., Loftus, E. F., & Marshall, M. E. (1992). *Psychology* (4th ed.). New York: McGraw-Hill.

CREDIT

Tarbuck, E. J., and Lutgens, F. K. (1997). *Earth Science* (8th ed.). Upper Saddle River, NJ: Prentice-Hall, Inc.

Learning Styles

CHAPTER OBJECTIVES

- To discover personal learning styles that are most effective
- To identify and learn study strategies that are appropriate for each learning style
- To adapt to various teaching styles of professors
- To understand the importance of flexibility and the use of alternate study strategies when needed
- To learn how to recognize and control additional factors that account for ease or difficulty of learning in college

Learning style refers to the way you learn most effectively. There is no "correct" or "better" style; all the learning styles are merely different. Think of your learning experiences in high school and college. Some methods of learning and remembering information probably seemed natural to you, while other methods might not have yielded the same results.

Several formal learning styles inventories are available to take if you would like to know more about your personal learning styles. Examples of these formal measures are the *Hogan/Champagne Personal Style Indicator* and the *Kolb*

Learning Style Inventory. The informal measure included on the following pages is not intended to take the place of the formal inventories. The statements below are intended to make you aware of your preferences and to give you some insight into the study methods you can use for maximum efficiency.

For each pair of statements, circle the letter of the response that best describes you. Answer as honestly as you can. If you think both choices are favorable or unfavorable, choose the one you prefer more. You must make a decision in each case. Each section has nine pairs of statements, eliminating the possibility of a tie. At the end of each section of the informal measure, read the recommended study strategies.

SECTION 1

1. I prefer to
   a. make important decisions by myself.
   b. brainstorm with other people when I have an important decision to make.

2. I prefer to
   a. work alone on a project.
   b. work on a class project with a group.

3. I prefer to take a class in which
   a. my grade is based on how well I perform on tests and assignments.
   b. the professor lectures for part of the period and then allows the class to break into smaller groups to do projects and assignments.

4. If I were having trouble in a class, I would prefer to
   a. work through the difficult subject by spending more time alone in study.
   b. get into a study group or get a tutor.

5. I prefer to
   a. work alone to conduct my science experiments.
   b. work with a partner in a science lab.

6. I prefer to
   a. decide on a topic for a research paper and then get to work on it.
   b. compare my ideas for a research paper with those of others in the class.

7. I prefer to
   a. study alone before final exams.
   b. study with class members or other friends before final exams.

8. I prefer to take a class that
   a. has lecture as its major format.
   b. involves discussion and group work.

9. When working on a class project, I prefer to

   a. do most of the project myself so that it will be done right.

   b. delegate certain tasks to each group member.

Scoring: More *a* responses indicate that you are a **competitive** learner while more *b* responses indicate a **collaborative** learner. Competitive learners probably enjoy working alone for a grade and may prefer the lecture method instead of collaborative or cooperative group work. Both types of learning are in current use on college campuses.

RECOMMENDED STUDY STRATEGIES

COMPETITIVE

1. When outside of class, work alone and try to control interruptions.
2. Use computer-assisted learning whenever possible.
3. Use study guides when you experience difficulty.
4. Try to enroll in classes that use the lecture format instead of groups.

COLLABORATIVE

1. Speak informally or in conferences with the instructor.
2. If you have difficulty in a class, get a tutor early in the semester.
3. Be part of the cooperative learning groups in class or on projects.
4. Join content-related student organizations.
5. Participate in study groups.

SECTION 2

1. I prefer to

   a. have all of my materials on my desk before I begin to work.

   b. gather materials as I need them.

2. I prefer to

   a. keep assignments, books, and papers for each class in a separate place.

   b. keep all of my course materials in one large stack.

3. I prefer to

   a. study at approximately the same time every day.

   b. study whenever I can make time for it.

4. I prefer to take my elective courses
   a. in those subjects that are closely related to my major.
   b. in various areas that I think would be interesting.

5. I like instructors who
   a. follow the curriculum guidelines listed in the syllabus.
   b. allow students to brainstorm about possible alternative class activities.

6. I like instructors who
   a. expect all students to complete the same activities for a grade.
   b. allow students to choose what they want to do for a grade.

7. I prefer to
   a. make to-do lists every day and go by them.
   b. accomplish as much as I can, but without lists.

8. I prefer to
   a. not waste my time learning some new method for reading faster when it may not work.
   b. learn a new method for reading faster.

9. To confirm a prediction, I prefer to
   a. read the research and discover what has been found.
   b. conduct an experiment.

Scoring: More *a* responses indicate that you are a **structured** learner, whereas *b* responses indicate an **unstructured** learning style. Structured learners are fond of organization, routine, and systematic learning. Those who are unstructured tend to plan less and do more on impulse.

RECOMMENDED STUDY STRATEGIES

STRUCTURED

1. Study in the same place and at the same time every day.
2. Use lists, schedules, and organization of your materials to help you accomplish more.
3. When studying for tests, organize your material by outlining or writing summaries.
4. Divide all of your long assignments into manageable smaller units.

UNSTRUCTURED

1. Resist the tendency to procrastinate.
2. Get in a study group with students who are *more* organized than you.

3. Since you like to try new things, learn a new study method. (See Chapter 9.)

4. When bored in a class, associate material with something else that is interesting.

SECTION 3

1. I prefer to play
   a. a guessing game.
   b. a board game.

2. When learning a foreign language, I prefer to
   a. hear taped lessons.
   b. read flash cards and books.

3. I prefer to
   a. listen to a sociology lecture.
   b. read the sociology chapter myself.

4. When I am at a party, I prefer to
   a. be told the names of all the people.
   b. have the people wear name tags.

5. When I am trying to recall information for a test, I prefer to
   a. recite information aloud.
   b. write summaries or make semantic maps.

6. To find an address, I prefer to
   a. receive oral directions.
   b. have a map drawn.

7. I like instructors who
   a. lecture and lead class discussions.
   b. write on the board, use an overhead transparency, or give a handout.

8. I prefer to
   a. have a friend explain how to perform a task.
   b. watch a friend demonstrate a task.

9. I prefer to
   a. listen to a recorded story.
   b. read a story.

Scoring: If you have more *a* responses, you are an **auditory** learner. More *b* responses indicate a **visual** learner. Auditory learners attend more to what they hear, while visual learners prefer to see the information, as in reading or viewing films.

....

RECOMMENDED STUDY STRATEGIES

AUDITORY

1. Take excellent notes during lectures.
2. Tape-record facts you are studying for tests.
3. Recite information aloud, and give "fake speeches" on your material.
4. Study with a group or a partner, and ask each other questions.

VISUAL

1. Read all assigned chapters and outside readings.
2. Read the chapters *before* going to class to help with comprehension of the lecture.
3. If possible, take courses with instructors who use visual aids.
4. Use computer programs and graphic illustrations when applicable.

SECTION 4

1. When studying, I prefer to
   a. make outlines of a psychology chapter.
   b. write summary paragraphs about a psychology chapter.
2. To understand a concept in history, I prefer to
   a. study a map of the ancient world.
   b. read a description of the ancient world.
3. When studying for a test, I prefer to
   a. make graphs or charts of significant ideas.
   b. write summaries of significant ideas.
4. To understand a concept in science, I prefer to
   a. interpret diagrams, charts, or graphs.
   b. read written paragraphs.
5. I prefer to
   a. draw a process I am reading about in my text.
   b. translate drawings into language when reading my text.
6. When reading a textbook chapter, I prefer to
   a. underline important information.
   b. annotate in the margins to mark important information.

7. To find the house of a friend, I prefer to
    a. follow a road map.
    b. follow written directions.

8. To report to my club about money that was donated, I prefer to
    a. create a line graph.
    b. read a written report.

9. When assembling a child's toy, I prefer to
    a. look at a diagram.
    b. have someone explain to me how to do it.

Scoring: If you have more *a* responses, you are a **spatial** learner. You are more comfortable with all types of graphic representations because you can visualize how things are positioned in the space around them. You probably like to draw and may create some type of drawing when trying to remember something you are reading. If you have more *b* responses, you are a **verbal** learner. You would prefer to read descriptions of processes, figures, events, and so forth than to view graphic illustrations.

RECOMMENDED STUDY STRATEGIES

SPATIAL

1. Incorporate drawings, maps, and graphs into your regular notes.
2. Make outlines and semantic maps to study for tests.
3. Draw and fill in number lines for subjects such as history.
4. Make graphic displays before writing.

VERBAL

1. Write verbal translations of the graphics.
2. Write summaries of textbook information.
3. Use your verbal skills to take good notes on both lectures and the text.
4. Paraphrase important ideas instead of using the language of the text or instructor.
5. Keep content area journals in each academic subject.

SECTION 5

1. I prefer to
   a. learn the meaning of Einstein's theory of relativity.
   b. think of possible implications of Einstein's theory of relativity.

2. I like an instructor who
   a. distributes a study guide before a test.
   b. allows the students to contribute questions that will be put on the test.

3. I prefer to
   a. listen to soothing music while I work.
   b. try to compose some music.

4. I prefer to have the instructor
   a. go exactly by the syllabus.
   b. allow the students to help plan ways to earn grades.

5. I prefer to
   a. divide my assignment into an equal amount for each day.
   b. complete my assignment when I feel most inspired.

6. I prefer to know how
   a. calculus will help me in my future job.
   b. an outstanding mathematician arrived at a theory.

7. In a required literature class, I prefer to
   a. read a collection of essays in my field.
   b. write some essays on topics of interest to me.

8. In mathematics, I prefer to
   a. work some problems.
   b. make up some problems for others to work.

9. In class, I prefer to
   a. make good notes as the professor answers the questions asked in the textbook.
   b. predict questions and listen to find out if the professor asks those same questions.

Scoring: More *a* responses indicate a **practical** learning style, while more *b* responses indicate a **creative** style. Practical learners are very methodical and systematic. They are students who like to keep up with assignments, and they prefer assignments of a practical nature, which have great utility, in their opinion. They are willing to amass essential information and acquire skills for the purpose of fulfilling a specific goal. Creative students are more likely to wish to explore and experiment with new things. They enjoy creating something themselves, whether it is a list of predicted questions or a work of art.

....

RECOMMENDED STUDY STRATEGIES

PRACTICAL

1. Organize your study.
2. Make a semester plan for each course.
3. Use to-do lists for both academic and personal tasks.
4. Take courses that are instructor-directed, not courses where students plan assignments.

CREATIVE

1. Take courses that involve experimentation, exploration, or creativity.
2. Write reflective and content journals.
3. Make great use of annotation. (See Chapter 10 on notetaking and annotating.)
4. Use a word processor to keep records.
5. Predict test questions and answer them.

SECTION 6

1. I prefer to learn
   a. how to prevent AIDS.
   b. where AIDS came from.
2. I prefer to learn
   a. which academic major would give me the best chance of finding a job.
   b. why some majors are more popular than others.
3. I prefer to
   a. associate a new theory in psychology with one I learned last semester.
   b. compare and contrast theories in psychology.
4. I prefer to
   a. find out which sociological method gets results with juvenile offenders.
   b. learn the schools of thought in juvenile justice.
5. I prefer to
   a. locate facts that sound like good test questions.
   b. identify organizational patterns used most often in textbooks.

6. I prefer to
    a. take a public opinion poll in my college to see how many people agree with an idea.
    b. study the different philosophies influencing religious thought.

7. I prefer to
    a. replicate an experiment after reading about one.
    b. learn the theories behind the reason for an experiment.

8. I prefer to
    a. go to the biology lab and determine my blood type.
    b. find out how many blood types there are and which is the most prevalent.

9. I prefer to
    a. use the information I learned in finance class to make some money in the stock market.
    b. research the origin of the stock market.

Scoring: More *a* responses indicate an **applied** learner. You would like to understand both how information can be used and how it can be applied to a given situation. You might have been the student in grade school who annoyed the teacher by asking, "How will we ever use this?" You probably like a hands-on approach, such as that in a laboratory or an internship. More *b* responses indicate that you are a **conceptual** learner. The concepts or ideas themselves are interesting to you, whether or not those ideas will be applied to a certain situation in your life. The application of the ideas is not necessary for you to understand the concepts, and you enjoy working with new ideas.

RECOMMENDED STUDY STRATEGIES

APPLIED

1. Think of ways in which ideas can be used.
2. Take courses that offer a lab or an internship of some kind.
3. When studying for tests, think of examples and other applications to help with recall.
4. Connect information with other disciplines in practical ways.

CONCEPTUAL

1. Research interesting ideas in your academic disciplines.
2. Think in terms of organizational patterns when reading texts. (See Chapter 7.)
3. Use your conceptual skills to organize materials from lectures and texts.
4. Read biographies of famous people who had innovative ideas.

SECTION 7

1. I prefer
   a. objective tests.
   b. essay tests.

2. I prefer to
   a. learn what important events led to a war.
   b. consider the results of war on family life.

3. I prefer to
   a. learn the incidence of serial murder now as compared to earlier times.
   b. to discover the reasons why a serial murderer kills.

4. I prefer to
   a. memorize facts and details about the national government.
   b. compare and contrast the various roles of the members of the president's Cabinet.

5. I prefer to
   a. answer questions about the founding of this country.
   b. discuss the high points in the country's history.

6. I prefer to write an article for the college newspaper about the
   a. different student organizations students may join.
   b. types of students who join the various student organizations.

7. I prefer to
   a. learn which poets wrote what poems.
   b. analyze the meanings of poems.

8. I prefer to learn
   a. what different types of family structures exist in the world.
   b. in which family type women are treated more equitably.

9. I prefer to
   a. study facts about family violence.
   b. determine the roles of social service organizations in the prevention of family violence.

Scoring: More *a* responses indicate that you are a **factual** learner, while *b* responses indicate that you are an **analytical** learner. If you are a factual learner, you are good with details and probably enjoy learning interesting and unusual facts. You would have more patience on a long objective test than would a student who is analytical. If you analyze something, you break it down into its parts. You want to understand the whole and also understand each of the parts and how they relate to each other. You are not satisfied to learn just the facts; you want to look for implications. An example of analysis is to examine the roles of different family members, studying the various interactions and the effects of those interactions. You find this far more interesting than the simple facts.

RECOMMENDED STUDY STRATEGIES

FACTUAL

1. Use your preference to excel in introductory and survey courses.
2. Use some effective method to record the facts.
3. Make lists of possible test information.
4. Associate new facts with your prior knowledge.

ANALYTICAL

1. Before tests, compose and answer higher-order questions.
2. As you read textbooks, locate the pattern of organization (see Chapter 7).
3. Use verbal reasoning to comprehend more difficult textbook material.
4. Look for trends and patterns in both textbooks and lectures.
5. Look for comparable situations in all subject areas.

SECTION 8

1. I prefer to
    a. view a movie in history class about survivors of the Holocaust.
    b. have the reasons for the Holocaust listed on an overhead transparency.
2. I prefer to interview
    a. a prisoner in the county jail about events in his early life.
    b. the police about crime statistics.
3. I prefer to know
    a. how a person on death row feels.
    b. whether capital punishment is a deterrent to crime.
4. I prefer to write
    a. an essay about the emotional impact of divorce on children.
    b. a research report on the incidence of divorce in four countries.
5. I prefer to hear a speaker tell how
    a. AIDS affects the family of a victim.
    b. a cure for AIDS might be found.

6. I prefer to view a movie about
   a. a family who became homeless.
   b. how a police force fought crime.
7. I prefer to read
   a. newspaper editorials.
   b. national and local news.
8. I like a professor who assigns outside readings that are
   a. essays on multicultural issues.
   b. research done on multicultural issues.
9. I prefer to have a speaker
   a. tell why she likes a particular method of doing something.
   b. give the steps in a process in an orderly manner.

Scoring: More *a* responses indicate an **emotional** learner, someone who prefers human interest stories and subject areas that include the affective issues, not just facts and logic. If you are an emotional learner, you probably even prefer movies and novels about emotions surrounding events, not just the adventure of the events themselves. Someone with this style might like to help people get in touch with their feelings, such as a psychologist or counselor would do. More *b* responses indicate a **logical** learner, someone who is interested in knowing if an act or an attitude makes sense. A logical person is a good critical thinker and reader, wants arguments to make sense, and would not be easily influenced by advertising gimmicks and emotional appeals.

RECOMMENDED STUDY STRATEGIES

EMOTIONAL

1. When studying a factual subject like history, read biographical sketches.
2. Record your *impressions* of information in the academic disciplines.
3. Take electives that will satisfy your emotional learning style.
4. Apply human interest ideas to factual information.

LOGICAL

1. Apply logic to all of your academic subjects.
2. Develop your natural preference for logic by becoming a very astute critical reader.
3. Consider taking courses in which logic is stressed.

LEARNING STYLES AS RELATED TO PROFESSORS' TEACHING STYLES

Different professors have different teaching styles, just as students have different learning styles. When your style and the professor's style do not match, you are the one who will have to find ways to adapt.

The teaching styles will be discussed in four major categories, and you should contemplate how your personal learning styles relate to the styles of your professors.

1. Major source of information for the class. Some professors use their lectures as the major source of information and material on which you will be tested. This is conducive to the auditory learning style and is usually the format in very large lecture halls. If you are a visual learner, you can still keep pace with the class, especially if audiovisual equipment is also used.

In some classes, the textbook is the major source of information, and this is beneficial to the visual and structured learner. You need to be even more disciplined as a student if the textbook is the major source of information because there will be no set time when you must sit and process the chapters. You will have to structure your learning so that your work gets done.

Some professors are very creative in their choice of materials, and they expect their students to be creative also. They may assign much outside reading and numerous supplementary projects, such as social experiments to be conducted and reported on. If you are a collaborative learner but are not so creative, you may need to work with other class members to complete the project, if this is allowed. If you are a competitive or independent learner, you will probably have the freedom to complete assignments alone. Creative professors are usually also analytical, so you will need to concentrate on higher-order questions instead of on so much fact and detail.

2. Class Organization. If professors are very organized and structured, they will probably dislike disorganization in their students. You should make a special effort not to turn in messy, disorganized, or late work. Tardiness is a sure sign of disorganization. As for your personal attendance in class, do not be absent or tardy. Many instructors report that some students are habitually tardy and often absent. If you are one of these students, ask yourself why this is happening and take steps to correct the problem.

Various learning styles will be compatible with an organized professor, as long as you keep up with assignments and do what is expected of you. You should expect tests to be rather predictable. That means that the tests will probably cover just what the professor has emphasized. You should also read all assignments. Do not think any assignment is unimportant simply because it is not discussed in class. With very structured professors, there are usually no big surprises, at least for those students who have been in regular attendance.

If professors are more unstructured, often called "laid back," they may seem to be preoccupied or less organized; sometimes they may be late to class. However, you should be in class waiting and prepared. The unstructured professors are not as likely as the highly structured to go exactly by the syllabus or by the daily or weekly lesson plans. They will probably be more spontaneous, even occasionally changing the location of the class. They may introduce a completely unexpected topic on certain days. If you are the type of student who is creative, unstructured, and perhaps emotional, you will probably prefer this type of professor.

3. Expectations for Students. If professors are very conceptual and creative, they will expect you to be more creative also. They sometimes seem hard to comprehend or to follow while taking notes. You cannot always know what to expect—in class sessions or on tests. They want you to be able to take a new situation and deal with it, even on tests. Those who are more factual and practical will be much more predictable and, you may feel, easier to understand. If, on the other hand, you like variety, you would prefer the more creative professors.

If you have professors who are more spontaneous, you must study everything that is assigned and also additional material that has not been specifically assigned. You are expected to learn on your own and to seek information. This type of professor often assumes that class members will be self-starters—curious and inquisitive. These professors will often ask questions like the following:

- What if—?
- What might be the result of—?
- What would be the *most* advantageous—?
- Which is the *better* interpretation—?

If you dislike questions like these because no one answer is the only correct one, you must practice these questions. Make them up and answer them. Form a study group to work on this skill; practice asking each other questions, and then discuss the answers. Frequently tests in these classes will be essay tests, with very general questions, such as the following:

- Business—"On paper, start your own business, telling all of the essentials: costs, type of business, overhead, expenses, and so forth."
- Education—"Set up a fourth-grade whole-language classroom, including materials, equipment, and information about methods."

- Art—"Compose an essay about the three Impressionists you consider to be the most influential."
- Music—"Write an essay about early forms of music that influenced *rock and roll*."

4. Class leadership. This refers to the amount of freedom you are given to learn what you want and to help with planning the course assignments and objectives. Some students prefer a professor who tells them exactly what is expected and what they will be doing week by week. These students would be uncomfortable with a professor who did not adhere to a detailed syllabus. If you were doing a research paper, would you prefer to have an assigned topic? A student-directed learning situation would be one in which you would get to choose your own topics for papers as well as choose your own projects and experiments. You would also get to decide how to accomplish the assignments. You might even have some freedom to do additional work aside from the regular topics and activities of the class.

If your professor organizes the class by a student-directed learning approach, he or she probably expects you to organize your own learning, be a disciplined person (not a procrastinator), and prove that you understand how the subject matter relates to your own life and future career goals. You will not be given a firm schedule of due dates for assignments, so you must schedule your activities so that everything is accomplished. Remember that these professors do not simply sit back and let you work or not work; they usually have very high expectations for their students. The learning is more individualized, so everyone in the class may not be learning the same thing.

Professors who take full charge themselves will expect all students to complete a given set of assignments and activities to earn a good grade. The course content is usually not negotiable, an aspect that may offend students who are unstructured and creative. Everyone will be expected to learn the same material, and this is compatible with practical, factual, and structured students who see this as fair to all concerned.

IMPORTANCE OF FLEXIBILITY

Although it is important to know how you learn best, you will have professors who have teaching styles that are incompatible with your learning styles. Therefore, you need to develop the ability to use different methods of study, class participation, and test preparation when it becomes necessary to do so. You may also need to be flexible because of your life situation. A student recently had a family problem that required him to drive home every weekend and return to college by Monday afternoon. The drive was a long one—three to four hours each way. He realized that the only way to keep up was to listen to tape-recorded lessons while driving. This was difficult for him at first because he was a visual learner, but he became proficient as an auditory learner after much practice.

If you would like to develop skill in a different learning style, the following list gives an example of a way to do this in each of the learning styles presented in this chapter.

1. *Competitive*—Start by doing ordinary errands alone, working up to part of a project; then a complete project alone.

2. *Collaborative*—If you are uncomfortable working with a group, start by working with one other person with whom you feel at ease.

3. *Structured*—If you need help disciplining yourself to study, ask a friend to meet you at the library at a certain time every day.

4. *Unstructured*—"Plan" to do something spontaneous one day a week.

5. *Auditory*—When stuck in the car, listen to part of a recorded story, and try to retell it. If necessary, play the tape again.

6. *Visual*—Watch a nature program on television with the "mute" activated.

7. *Spatial*—Learn semantic mapping. It is still mostly verbal, more so than many other types of graphic displays.

8. *Verbal*—When studying a textbook, recite the main ideas in your own words. You can do this after every section or every paragraph, whichever you prefer.

9. *Practical*—Make a to-do list, and reward yourself if you finish the jobs on the list.

10. *Creative*—Practice asking yourself questions like, "What would have happened if the automobile had never been invented?"

11. *Applied*—Learn a new study method, such as SQ3R (see Chapter 9), and use it on your content area textbooks.

12. *Conceptual*—Think of a religious leader or famous citizen whom you admire, and find out what ideas led to the person's enthusiasm and accomplishments.

13. *Factual*—Pretend you have to give the police a detailed description of someone. Look at someone in class and try to memorize enough details to describe the person and his or her clothes.

14. *Analytical*—Ask the reference librarian for a book or a learning kit on analytical thinking skills, and learn how to work some of the problems/activities. An example is the *Whimbey Analytical Skills Inventory,* complete with activities.

15. *Emotional*—Think of how a hunted animal feels. If you cannot, read the short story *The Most Dangerous Game*, by Richard Connell.

16. *Logical*—When you get your daily newspaper, read an editorial every day. Find the evidence used to back up arguments, and determine whether it makes sense.

ADDITIONAL FACTORS RELATED TO LEARNING STYLES

Time of Day

The jokes about not being a morning person are so popular and familiar that many people even wear T-shirts emblazoned with messages such as, "I don't do mornings." This is more than simply a joke or witty saying. People really do have a time of the day when they are more alert and more productive. Some people are morning people, while others perform better in the early or late afternoon or in the evening.

To determine your best time of day, find a time, if possible, when you are free from schedules for a while. In other words, you can go to bed whenever you like and get up when you feel like it. Pay attention to your natural preferences. You may find that, without an alarm clock, you prefer to sleep late and stay up late, even work late into the night. On the other hand, you may find that you can think more clearly and that you feel better early in the day.

When you have determined your "best" time of the day, what does it mean to you as a college student?

- If possible, schedule courses you consider the most difficult at your best time of the day.

- Study for the most difficult courses at your best time.

- Use other times for more routine tasks, those that do not require high levels of concentration.

- If, despite your efforts to schedule courses according to your peak period of concentration, you must take very difficult courses when you are least alert, be aware of your disadvantage. Use all the techniques you have learned about concentration.

- Pay attention to health habits, such as rest and nutritional needs, so that you will feel your best all through the day.

Surroundings

Many students claim that they can study with noise from music, television, or other people. Do their grades support that claim? Many students really do need a quiet study environment in order to concentrate. Some will even close the classroom door to block out noises from the hallway, although the instructor and many of the other students seem oblivious to the noise. Other students actually do seem to be able to concentrate under conditions that would seem like excessive noise to some.

Monitor your study habits, such as degree of quiet needed, and keep a record of your grades to determine whether or not they are adversely affected. If you feel that you can study with external distractions, perhaps you can—when you are very interested in the subject matter. Can you concentrate equally well when you are studying a course in which you have little or no interest? If you decide that you need a quiet environment in which to study, refer to Chapter 2 and use the concentration tips offered.

Task Orientation

When you enroll in college, you should be dedicated to the task of making optimum grades in each course. This will, after all, lead to your career goals. When you have an assignment, do you get right to work, or do you procrastinate? If you have a tendency to put things off, you need to deal with this aspect of your personality. When you habitually procrastinate, the work you eventually complete will not be your best because you will have to resort to a "rush job." When you plan and give yourself ample time to do a task well, it will be your best work. Your grades will reflect your planning and time spent on the task. If you realize you need to work on the problem of procrastination, the following suggestions may help:

- Make a daily or weekly to-do list, and include your assignments on the list. Force yourself to complete the list, marking off the items as they are done.

- Break long or complicated assignments into more manageable tasks. For example, if the assignment is to write a term paper, the first task on the to-do list could be, "Decide on a topic." The next time the task could be, "Go to the library and locate ten sources."

- Reward yourself after you have completed a task or assignment.

After following these guidelines for a while, you will probably notice that you feel better because you will be experiencing less stress, and you will not feel so rushed.

Locus of Control

Locus of control refers to the way in which people evaluate situations. Some people feel that they can control their own fate, while others feel that the control is beyond them (Morris, 1996). Regarding study skills, it means that some students take more responsibility for their own learning and outcomes. Students who have an **internal locus of control** believe that they are responsible for their learning. If they fail a test, they might offer an explanation such as one of the following:

- "I didn't start studying soon enough."
- "I don't have the necessary math background for this course."
- "I should have studied in the library where it was quiet."
- "I should have attended all of the lectures."
- "I should have read all of the material assigned."

People often do not like to blame themselves, but the benefit of having an internal locus of control is the person's ability to change his or her situation, improving on future efforts. If you believe your fate is in your own hands, you know you have the power to accomplish your goals.

On the other hand, a person who possesses an **external locus of control** credits other people and situations, even "luck," with outcomes. Some examples of explanations for failing a test are given below:

- "The professor hates me."
- "My study group is no good."
- "My tutor doesn't know the material."
- "I'm unlucky in school."
- "My high school did not prepare me well enough."
- "The students in the class are too noisy."

These excuses are well known, and the list could go on and on. The point is that you should not give others the power over your learning. You *can* control your own learning.

Influence of Interest and Prior Knowledge

Everyone would prefer to study material that is considered "interesting." People also have more interest in subjects about which they have some prior knowledge. Some students, more than others, are deeply affected by interest and prior knowledge. Reflect on the required courses all college students must take. How will you handle the situation if you are strongly influenced by the factors of interest and prior knowledge? There are several suggestions for this:

- Learn something about the subject, since prior knowledge can build interest.
- Find out why some students and the instructor find the course very interesting. Talking about the course with them may motivate you.
- Associate the course with some other knowledge you already possess. Try to make a connection with something of great interest to you.
- Be a *more* dedicated student in the "uninteresting" class. Take better notes, read every assignment, and attend every class.

Motivation. Motivation refers to a desire to do something. In the study skills context, motivation means that you want to learn and do your best. You may feel more motivated in some classes than in others, and this may relate to interest. However, motivation will be examined as intrinsic motivation and extrinsic motivation. According to the publication, *A Dictionary of Reading and Related Terms* (International Reading Association, 1981), **intrinsic motivation** deals with satisfaction derived from the activity itself—in this case, the love of learning. **Extrinsic motivation** deals with rewards outside the learner, such as grades, money, recognition, and ability to achieve goals in life. Only *you* can determine which type of motivation you possess; either type will encourage you to be a better student. It is a serious problem when a student is not motivated to be in college at all. Ask yourself if you really want to attend college at this time or if you are attending only to satisfy your parents (or friends) or because you have nothing else to do.

SUMMARY

The chapter included an informal method for assessing learning styles in eight categories. After students determined their most effective learning styles, they were given suggestions for study strategies that will benefit their cognitive skills. Since college professors also possess a variety of teaching styles, students were encouraged to be able to adapt to the styles of professors. Suggestions are given for developing strength in study strategies that are not in the preferred learning styles.

In addition to learning styles, some other factors can account for ease or difficulty of learning. Those discussed in this chapter were time of day, surroundings, task orientation, locus of control, influence of interest and prior knowledge, and motivation. Students were encouraged to examine their personal preferences, their goals, and their motivators.

Cooperative Learning Activities

GROUP 1. Dwayne is a visual, collaborative, and structured learner. This semester he is enrolled in a history course that is all lecture. There are only three grades in the entire course, and they are all tests. The professor announced early in the course that attendance was not required. How can Dwayne's learning styles be used or adapted in ways that will enable him to perform well in the history class?

GROUP 2. List characteristics of professors that enable you to take notes effectively and remain focused on the lessons. After each characteristic listed, tell how individual learning styles play a part in your ability to perform well with such professors.

GROUP 3. List characteristics of professors that make learning more difficult for the members of the group. How do your learning styles conflict with these teaching characteristics? What can you do about this conflict?

GROUP 4. Let each member of the group name one course in which he or she needed to adapt a learning style to the professor's teaching style. Tell how the study methods were changed or could have been changed to fit the course.

GROUP 5. Janine is a very unstructured, creative, and verbal learner. She is a college freshman who is finding her courses very difficult. Her advisor has told her that she will have more freedom to express herself according to her own learning styles after the first two years. Janine does not know if she can pass all of the core requirements and is thinking of withdrawing from college. How would you solve her problem?

Reading Selection: *Psychology*

Title: *The Insanity Defense**
Author: Charles G. Morris

Activation of Prior Knowledge and Interest

1. Do you think *insanity* should be a legal defense? Why or why not?

   _____

   _____

   _____

2. What court cases have you been interested in, either in person or on television?

   _____

   _____

   _____

3. What changes in the American judicial system would you advocate?

   _____

   _____

   _____

Particularly horrifying crimes—assassinations of public figures, mass murders, and serial murders, for instance—have often been attributed to mental disturbance because it seems to many people that anyone who could commit such crimes must be crazy. But to the legal system, this presents a problem: If a person is truly "crazy," are we justified in holding him or her responsible for criminal acts? The legal answer to this question is a qualified *yes*. A mentally ill person *is* responsible for his or her crimes unless he or she is determined to be *insane*. What's the difference between being "mentally

*Psychology 9/e. by Morris C. G., © 1996. Reprinted by permission of Prentice-Hall, Inc. Upper Saddle River, NJ.

ill" and being "insane"? Insanity is a legal term, not a psychological one. It is typically applied to defendants who, when they committed the offense with which they are charged, were so mentally disturbed that they either could not distinguish right from wrong or could not control the act—it was an "irresistible impulse."

Actually, when a defendant is suspected of being mentally disturbed, another important question must be answered before that person is brought to trial: Is the person able to understand the charges against him or her and to participate in a defense in court? This issue is known as *competency to stand trial*. The person is examined by a court-appointed expert and, if found to be incompetent, is sent to a mental institution, often for an indefinite period. If judged to be competent, the person is required to stand trial. At this point the defendant may decide to plead not guilty by reason of insanity—which is an assertion that *at the time of the crime* the defendant lacked substantial capacity to appreciate the criminality of his or her action (know right from wrong) or to conform to the requirements of the law (control his or her behavior).

Despite popular belief to the contrary, the insanity plea is rare, arising in less than 1 percent of serious criminal cases. But it became controversial when it was successfully used by John Hinckley, the man who attempted to assassinate President Ronald Reagan in 1981. Many people were very upset that Hinckley, whose action had been clearly captured on videotape, seemed to escape punishment for his crime by pleading insanity in a jurisdiction (Washington, D.C.) that required the prosecution to prove beyond a reasonable doubt that *he was sane.* (In contrast, most states, as well as the federal courts, place the burden on the defense to prove that the *defendant is insane.*) Since his trial, Hinckley has been confined in a mental hospital.

When a defendant enters an insanity plea, the court system relies heavily on the testimony of forensic psychologists and psychiatrists to determine the mental state of the defendant at the time of the crime. Because most such trials feature well-credentialed experts testifying both for the defense and for the prosecution, the jury is often perplexed about which side to believe. Furthermore, there is much cynicism about "hired-gun" professionals who receive large fees to appear in court and argue that a defendant is or is not sane. The public, skeptical about professional jargon, often feels that psychological testimony allows dangerous criminals to "get off." Actually, those who successfully plead insanity—like John Hinckley—often are confined longer in mental hospitals than they would have been in prison if convicted of their crimes. Therefore, the insanity plea is not an easy way out of responsibility for a crime.

Critical Thinking Questions

1. Why were the American people more upset about the Hinckley plea of insanity than they were about other previous cases?

   _____

   _____

   _____

2. Contrast the legal definition of insanity with the medical definition.

   _____

   _____

   _____

3. Which of your learning styles do you use to process this and other text assignments? Give examples from this selection.

   _____

   _____

   _____

REFERENCES

Apps, J. W. (1990). *Study Skills for Today's College Student*. New York: McGraw-Hill.

Harris, T. L., & Hodges, R. E. (1981). *A Dictionary of Reading and Related Terms*. Newark, DE: International Reading Association.

Morris, C. G. (1996). *Psychology: An Introduction* (9th ed.). Upper Saddle River, NJ: Prentice-Hall, Inc.

Sonbuchner, G. M. (1991). *Help Yourself: How to Take Advantage of Your Learning Styles*. Syracuse, NY: New Readers Press.

CREDIT

Morris, C. G. (1996). *Psychology: An Introduction* (9th ed.). Upper Saddle River, NJ: Prentice-Hall, Inc.

Critical Reading and Thinking

CHAPTER OBJECTIVES

- To learn the purposes for writing
- To recognize various factors that help the reader determine the author's purpose
- To evaluate types of evidence
- To understand deterrents to critical thinking
- To recognize errors in logical reasoning

Critical thinking is a purposeful and deliberate evaluation of all the evidence on all sides of an issue in order to form a judgment about the value of information, arguments, or opinions. Critical thinkers temporarily suspend their own opinions in order to look at an issue logically instead of emotionally. They look at all aspects of the issues and hear or read all of the arguments. At the conclusion of this process, they may retain their previous opinions, or they may adopt new ideas.

PURPOSES FOR WRITING

If you were asked to list all of the reasons why you write, your list might include some of the following reasons:

- To fulfill an assignment
- To take notes in class
- To help remember a grocery list
- To inform a friend in another state about a reunion
- To tell people to stay off the newly painted porch
- To develop a speech for French club

Regardless of the length of the list, all of the reasons you might write could be classified into the following three **purposes for writing.**

1. To inform. This includes any information that has as its purpose educating someone, including informing them to "keep off the grass." A few examples of informative writing are *textbooks, the driver's license manual, all how-to books, labels on food and medicine, front-page news articles, regulatory signs,* and even *poison labels.*

Critically reading informative writing includes such mental activities as checking for copyright date, checking the credentials of the writer, and observing the type of publication in which the information appears.

2. To entertain. This writing includes *novels, plays, personal letters, jokes, anecdotes, musical compositions, poetry,* and anything else that is intended to simply be enjoyed by others. This writing may also contain **themes,** important underlying messages with which you may agree or disagree. You also should read the literature written to entertain in order to evaluate its style and worth. Anyone who thinks critical thinking is not necessary for this type of writing needs only to be reminded of ethnic jokes, which are insulting and hurtful to entire populations.

3. To persuade. This is the category that is often mentioned first in association with critical thinking since the writers of persuasive material are usually trying to get you to *buy something, do something,* or *believe something.* Critical thinking is imperative with all types of persuasion. For this reason, most of the examples given throughout this chapter are taken from persuasive writing or speaking. Some forms of persuasion are *political speeches, advertisements* and *commercials, religious brochures, newspaper editorials,* and *letters to the editors of newspapers.*

FACTORS TO HELP DETERMINE AUTHOR'S PURPOSE

Facts and Opinions

In all types of writing, you will encounter both facts and opinions. A **fact** is a statement that is true or, at least, verifiable. The reader or listener is able to verify—prove or disprove—the information by checking a source. Sometimes a statement that is not accurate is mistakenly presented as a fact. Such a statement would be an error, but it would still not be considered an opinion. An **opinion** is someone's judgment or belief.

The following statements are all facts:

- Tallahassee is the capital of Florida.
- The Declaration of Independence was signed in 1776.
- Many people in this country live in mobile homes, or trailers.
- Of the two towns of Clarksville and Simmonsville, Clarksville has more registered voters.
- A spider has eight legs.

All of the above statements can be verified by checking sources such as reference books, town records, and voting records. Therefore, they are facts, not opinions. However, the following statements are all opinions:

- Capital punishment should be outlawed.
- Michael Jordan is the world's greatest athlete.
- Euthanasia is wrong, regardless of the circumstances.
- The TV viewing habits of children should be closely monitored by the parents, not by the government.

Many people have great difficulty separating their own opinions from what they *think* of as facts. A statement such as the second example, "Michael Jordan is the world's greatest athlete," may be confusing since so many sports enthusiasts believe this statement is true. However, since there is no way to verify the statement, such as a worldwide contest for athletes, it must be considered an opinion. All of the opinion statements above could be changed into factual statements by the addition of the words, "many people believe." It *would,* indeed, be a fact that *many people believe* those statements to be true.

People often make predictions about the future, and many of these predictions sound very logical based on the state of affairs at the present time. However, since the future is unknown, all predictions must be considered opinions, not facts.

In order to think logically and critically, you must be able to distinguish fact from opinion. In some types of writing, such as all forms of persuasive writing, opinion is perfectly acceptable and appropriate. An editorial, for example, is supposed to be the writer's opinion. In other types of writing, opinion is inappropriate and even irrelevant. An example of this is an article for the front page of the newspaper. The news stories should be reported factually, and the reader should not be able to determine the writer's opinions or biases. The following examples are a few of the places in which you should read only facts and no opinions:

- News stories
- Police reports
- Most textbook writing
- Official documents
- Court records

When you feel that it is difficult to distinguish between fact and opinion, there are clues to help you with this:

- Look for words that are known to be opinion signal words, such as *better, pretty, ugly, wrong,* and *worst.*
- Look for qualifying words, such as *might, probably, could, perhaps,* and *hopefully.*
- If a statement is given as a fact, ask yourself if there is another side to the issue, especially if the issue is controversial.

Determine whether the author is trying to appeal more to your emotions than to your intellect.

Learn to tell the difference between fact and opinion since many writers use both in the same selection, sometimes in the same paragraph or sentence. Do not be deceived into believing that because some statements are facts, they all are.

Exercise 4.1

Tell whether each of the following statements is a *fact* or an *opinion.*

_____ 1. In twenty years, there will be no uncontaminated water in any U.S. river.

_____ 2. John F. Kennedy was a great president.

_____ 3. No states have laws allowing active euthanasia.

_____ 4. Each state should have the right to pass its own laws regarding abortion.

_____ 5. The acronym, AIDS, stands for Acquired Immune Deficiency Syndrome.

_____ 6. Hopefully, all schools will soon have sex education programs.

_____ 7. By the year 2020, there will be cures for both cancer and AIDS.

_____ 8. The French Revolution began on July 14, 1789.

_____ 9. It is a shame that so many people have lost the work ethic.

_____10. Metacognition means the monitoring of one's own learning.

Point of View and Bias

The **point of view** of any written selection is how the writer looks at a certain subject. A writer's own value system and ideas will determine his or her point of view. Point of view may differ because of gender, age, political party affiliation, religious background, degree of conservatism or liberalism, section of the country, occupation, and many other factors. The list is as varied as the people who write or speak. It is the responsibility of the reader or listener to recognize and evaluate a person's logic while keeping in mind the possible point of view.

Occasionally a writer who is attempting to remain objective allows point of view to cloud the issues and *slant* the writing toward one side or the other. The following examples may clarify this concept:

- A discussion of malls becoming nonsmoking environments from the point of view of smokers (or nonsmokers)

- An account of a crime by the person who was mugged

- Sports teams having names like *Redskins, Braves, Indians,* etc., from the point of view of a Native American

As you read, remember your own point of view as well as that of the writer because your view can affect your comprehension of the material and your ability to remain objective.

Bias is a type of viewpoint that leaves out or alters facts in order to support a certain side of an issue. Bias and point of view are similar in meaning, and, for that reason, the two terms are used interchangeably by some people. However, bias has a more negative connotation because it is often associated with the darker term, *prejudice.* Point of view is a way of looking at the world because of personal experience, while bias interferes with the ability to remain objective. Point of view can, at times, create such a bias that a person cannot objectively evaluate the opposing side of an issue. Consider the following examples of bias:

- A wealthy person does not understand why anyone is homeless.
- An employed person does not believe there is a job shortage.
- A mother says that anyone who does not wish to become a parent is selfish.
- A divorced person feels that marriage cannot work for anyone.
- A victim of crime distrusts everyone.
- A teacher who has always learned new concepts easily cannot relate to the learning-disabled students.

A reader should be able to recognize opposing viewpoints and then evaluate them objectively. A good analogy compares the reader to a judge in a courtroom. The judge has opinions on all subjects but must remain objective and weigh the evidence, giving fair rulings regardless of personal opinions. This is what you have a right to expect in objective writing.

Source and Authority

The source is the publication in which a selection is located. College students have constant contact with various sources—textbooks, newspapers, scholarly journals, magazines, and the Internet (a quick route to all the sources). Regardless of the source, you should read with an inquisitive attitude because all publications are written by people, and people do make mistakes! Obviously, some sources are much more reliable and credible than others.

If you are reading for enjoyment only, any source you select may serve your purpose. However, when you need information that is for a purpose other than pleasure reading, you should select the best sources available. For instance, if you read an article about AIDS prevention, you certainly want the information to be written by top medical personnel, not a teacher or a librarian. If you are thinking of buying a car, you should read research reports in reputable publications, not ads for cars.

EXERCISE 4.2

Consider some of the following reasons for reading, and give a *source* for each that would be appropriate.

1. Reading for fun _____

2. Getting consumer information about VCRs _____

3. Learning about pregnancy _____

4. Locating ads for weekend sales _____

5. Finding recreation in a vacation area _____

6. Deciding on movies and restaurants _____

7. Doing research for a college paper on the subject of Tibet _____

_____

8. Learning about careers in forestry _____

9. Discovering the latest cancer research information _____

_____

10. Finding money for college _____

The authority of an author is as important as the source. An **authority** is an accepted source of information. If someone is proposing to give information on a certain subject, such as anthropology, the person should have special training and education in the field. Remember that everyone has opinions, but when you need *expert* opinion, there are several criteria concerning the authority of the author or speaker:

- Does the author have the proper credentials and expertise in the area?
- If the information is in a constantly changing field, has the expert kept up-to-date?
- Does the author separate the facts from his or her own opinion?
- Does the author seem to present the facts completely, or do you feel that something important is being left out?
- Is the expert biased?

- Is there an ulterior motive, such as fame or money?

- Does the writer take for granted ideas that are not supported by evidence?

- If reporting on an event, did the author give eyewitness or secondhand testimony?

- Do you get the feeling that the author is trying to appeal more to your emotions or your pity than to your reason and intellect?

- Do some of the author's statements seem exaggerated or distorted?

Tone

The author's purpose can often be determined by the tone of the passage. The **tone** can be any conceivable human emotion. Some tones used by authors include *informative, angry, nostalgic, reverent, sarcastic, comical, defensive, respectful, sincere,* and *insulting.*

It is more difficult to determine tone in a written passage than in a spoken conversation or speech. Speaking includes inflections of voice, volume, and even facial expressions, which enable the listener to interpret the mood and meaning. You can learn to determine tone in writing as well, and this is important for overall comprehension.

Note the *sarcastic* tone in the following paragraph:

Of course, school uniforms will transform schools from drug-infested danger zones to institutions of academic excellence. The gang members will automatically want to conform, so they will rush out and buy the uniforms, forever abandoning their gang colors, habits, and activities.

TYPES OF EVIDENCE

When considering the evidence that is presented to support ideas, it is important to look at types of evidence as well as the value of each type. Obviously, some categories of "proof" are more powerful and compelling than others. The following seven types are frequently used as evidence and should be considered and evaluated.

1. Facts and statistics. If used correctly, facts and statistics can be excellent evidence. To evaluate the use of statistics, ask the following questions:

- Are the facts relevant to the issue at hand?
- Were the facts and statistics collected in a way that can be trusted?
- Do the facts really prove a point, or do they just offer one of many possibilities?
- Does the reporter of the facts seem objective and unbiased?
- As you read, do you feel that you are being given *all* of the facts?

2. Personal experience. In most cases personal experience is too limited to be considered, by itself, as proof. In the following situation, the person mentioned may have been the only student having this experience:

> As a foreign exchange student, I can tell you that foreigners are always treated with great respect in the United States because that's how I was treated.

On the other hand, *sometimes* a personal experience *can* prove a point, as in the following example:

> The policy of the company states that no woman will be fired because of pregnancy. I know this policy is not always followed because I was told, when I was four months pregnant, that I could not work there while I was pregnant.

3. Expert opinion. Expert opinion can be very valuable evidence if the person truly is an expert with good credentials. For instance, an article on child abuse quoting a pediatrician would have more credibility than such an article quoting the "man on the street." When the experts are highly qualified, as in the following examples, it helps to create a strong argument:

- The U.S. Surgeon General states that smoking is injurious to health.
- A child psychiatrist states that children should not air their sexual problems on television talk shows.
- A professor of economics from a good university gives an opinion about the financial effects of welfare reform.
- A psychologist with a successful practice gives an opinion about the psychological effects of welfare reform.

4. Testimonial. The testimony of people who are not experts in the field under discussion is not as effective as expert opinion. However, occasionally the testimony of an ordinary person is relevant and powerful, especially in the case of eyewitness testimony of an event.

Testimonials are frequently used in advertising. Movie stars, singers, and sports celebrities sell everything from cereal to luxury cars. When asked if testimonials from famous people are influential, most students say they are not. However, the technique must be effective with millions of people because the celebrities are highly paid for their endorsements.

5. Analogy. An **analogy** is a resemblance in essentials between things or statements otherwise different. When used, the analogy should be accurate and correct. Some examples of analogies used in controversial issues are given in the following sentences:

- A writer compares the furor and excitement over cloning to the previous furor surrounding test-tube babies.
- A death penalty opponent compares capital punishment to barbarism and calls it "state-sanctioned murder."
- A supporter of gay rights compares the military policy on homosexuals to the Salem witch-hunts.
- An editorial writer argues that some countries will not abide by a treaty to ban chemical weapons just as some have refused to sign the Nuclear Non-Proliferation Treaty.

6. Historical support. Writers often give examples from history, especially if the examples support the belief that a certain condition has been a tradition, a law, or a way of life. The First Amendment is often quoted and, sometimes, misquoted or misinterpreted. When reading historical references, you should look for accuracy and relevance. Historical evidence can be introduced using signal words or phrases such as those in the following list:

- Since the dawn of creation
- The Constitution has always provided
- Since the days of Columbus
- For over three hundred years
- Learned from past international disputes

7. Common knowledge. Sometimes evidence appears in the form of a claim that certain facts are general knowledge—that everyone knows certain things to be true. In cases like this, it is important to ask yourself if the facts are really believed by *everyone,* or merely by some people. Also ask yourself if there is a sound reason for believing this information. Perhaps the information is merely folklore, superstition, or general misinformation. As you read the following statements, ask yourself if the statements are accurate or if the opinion expressed applies to some people and not to others:

- Everybody in the United States thinks it is perfectly all right for a six-year-old schoolboy to give a friendly kiss to a female schoolmate.
- People agree that lowering the crime rate is worth any price.
- We all know that dress codes in schools cause behavior to improve.

 ## DETERRENTS TO CRITICAL THINKING

In order to think critically, people must acknowledge that other opinions exist, instead of thinking only of their own opinions. Here are six reasons that critical thinking might *not* occur.

1. Failure to listen. In a discussion process, you must really listen to the opposing viewpoint. Sometimes you may be so eager to make your point that you fail to hear what the other person is saying. In addition to listening, ask the other person specific questions to gain a better understanding of opposing views.

2. Insufficient prior knowledge. The more experiences you have, the better your thought processes will be. You will already possess the idea or the knowledge that people have varied opinions. A knowledge of different cultures, religions, and ways of thinking precedes critical thinking.

3. Belief in stereotypes. A **stereotype** is a fixed idea about a group of people, an idea that attributes the same or similar characteristics to everyone in the group. Some examples of stereotypes are well known and often used:

- The mother-in-law
- The absentminded professor
- The male hairdresser
- The high school jock
- The nerd
- The dumb blonde

A person who believes in stereotypes will not see people as individuals. This failure to individualize will block the path to critical thinking.

4. Rigid belief system. Everyone has and should have values and beliefs, but many people fail to examine their values and the reasons supporting them. Subsequently, an opposing belief comes to someone's attention and is dismissed automatically as being "wrong" or, at least, inferior. An example of this inflexibility is often expressed by parents intent on disciplining their children in whatever fashion their parents used on them, whether or not it proved effective.

5. Wishful thinking. People often believe what they want to believe. Surely everyone is guilty of wishful thinking at one time or another. This is why the mother of a convicted felon will insist on her son's innocence or why a man refuses to believe that his favorite uncle has betrayed him. Wishful thinking also relates to controversial issues because people wish for their view to be the correct one. Many people find it quite troublesome to admit to being wrong.

6. Use of authority figures for decision making. Certain people in society have been endowed by the population with permission to make important decisions for everyone else. Who these people are may vary from one culture to another but may include doctors, teachers, and religious leaders. Of course, people in authority deserve respect and recognition, but each person must ultimately make his or her own decisions about a great number of issues.

ERRORS IN LOGICAL REASONING

You may have heard or read statements that caused you to respond that the statement "did not make sense." Were you able to explain or pinpoint exactly why the statement did not make sense? There was obviously something illogical about the argument, but perhaps you did not understand how to explain it because you did not know about specific errors in reasoning. You need to learn to recognize good and poor logic so that you can evaluate a selection, even in textbooks. You also need to be able to compose a counterargument in some cases. There are several significant reasoning errors.

Testimonials from people who are not actually experts. In both advertising and other forms of persuasion, famous people are presented, along with their opinions, as experts. In most cases like this, expert testimony could be found, but the celebrity status often sells products and ideas more successfully than the real experts could. Following are some examples of such testimonials:

- A movie star endorses a brand of dog food.
    (The argument would have more validity if a veterinarian endorsed pet food since the veterinarian is an expert on the nutrition of animals.)
- In an editorial, a U.S. president is quoted concerning his views about the medical dangers of abortion.
    (The president is a political expert, but he is not a medical expert.)

Overgeneralizations. A **generalization** is the drawing of a conclusion based on an experience, and it is one of the ways people learn. A baby who has never seen a dog is told by the parent that the animal is a "dog." Although the particular dog may be a dachshund, the baby learns that all canines are "dogs" through the process of generalizing.

An **overgeneralization** is a conclusion that has been reached with inadequate and incomplete evidence. Some examples of overgeneralizations follow:

- A college student meets two Swedish exchange students and bases her opinion of people from Sweden on these two examples.
- Your sister tells you that college is boring and difficult because her first instructor, Professor Wise, was boring and difficult and your sister dropped out.
- Your home is burglarized by an Asian man, so you conclude that all Asians are dishonest.

It is easy to understand how overgeneralizations can lead to such serious errors as unfounded bias and prejudice.

Card stacking. If someone presents only one side of an issue, giving only the facts that support the favored argument, this is called **card stacking.** There may be vital facts that would support the opposing side of the issue, but these facts are ignored or omitted. Consider the following:

- An opponent of welfare reform states that many families include generations of welfare recipients, without including facts about those who remain on welfare for a temporary period and then stop using the service.
- A writer states that women and men are equal under the law, omitting such information as statistics indicating that women still earn only about 74 cents for every dollar earned by men.
- A restaurant advertisement claims that the restaurant is the most popular place in the city, ignoring the statistics that prove that other restaurants have more customers.

Misuse of statistics. One of the most powerful forms of evidence, when used correctly and accurately, is statistics. However, often serious errors are made in the reporting, whether intentional or not. In some cases, studies are incorrectly done, nullifying the results. Sometimes the mathematical calculations are also in error. Sometimes the reporting contains accurate numbers, but the numbers are not appropriate, as in the following example:

- City X has one thousand murders a year, while City Y has only twenty-five, proving that the punishment methods in City Y are more effective. (The statement neglects the fact that City X has 2.5 million people while City Y has a population of only two thousand.)

False cause. Two events often occur at the same time, leading some to conclude that one caused the other. All superstitions are examples of this, such as, "I broke a mirror, so I had seven years of bad luck." The fact that both events happened does not mean that one caused the other. It is easy to see the fallacy involved in believing superstitions, but false cause is also found in these types of persuasive writing:

- The political candidate states that inner-city crime has increased because his opponent is soft on criminals. (Although this may have been a contributing factor in the crime increase, many other factors could have contributed, such as drugs, unemployment, or poverty.)
- The writer of a letter to the newspaper editor states that homosexuality is caused by the absence of fathers in modern families. (First, many scientists believe homosexuality may be genetic in origin. Second, many homosexual children had fathers in the home and many heterosexual children did not have fathers in the home.)
- A speaker says that mothers of small children work because they want "extras" like luxury vacations and expensive homes and cars. (Mothers may work to furnish necessities such as food, rent, and medical care.)

In some cases, the statement of one event causing something in the future is predicted. One event is supposed to lead to another, such as the following:

- An opponent for euthanasia for the terminally ill fears that it will lead to euthanasia of mentally or physically challenged children.

Oversimplification. This problem with logic gives only two choices, and they are the two extremes on an issue; there is no room for a middle ground or other alternatives. This is frequently used in both advertising and discussion of controversial issues:

- A commercial claims, "Use Glamour Girl cosmetics or be ugly." (This claim ignores the dozens of other skin care products.)
- A bumper sticker reads, "America: Love it or leave it!" (Many people love America but want to correct some of the problems.)
- A proponent of school prayer states that without school prayer, the children will have no respect for religion at all. (This ignores the possibility of the children being indoctrinated at home or at church.)

Everybody is doing it. Advertisers endeavor to sell products by creating the impression that if everyone, or even most people, use a product, it must be the best one. They ignore the possibility that all of the people could be deceived for some reason. Consider these examples:

- Nine out of ten homeowners have Insurance X.
- This soft drink is the most popular in America.
- Everybody knows that this brand is the best toothpaste on the market.

Often controversial issues are defended by an assertion that a large percent of people feel a certain way. This is not a problem with logic unless it is misused or misleading.

Circular reasoning. **Circular reasoning** is actually a restatement of the original assertion. There is a rewording, but the new statement adds no new information or evidence to support the claim. If you were asked to locate the types of evidence in an argument like this, you would not have any to report, as in the following:

- A gun control proponent states, "Guns should be outlawed because it should be illegal for citizens to own guns."
- An opponent of school prayer says, "School prayer should remain illegal because children should not pray at school."
- A pacifist says, "Killing in any situation is wrong because it is immoral."

Inaccurate analogy. An **analogy** is a comparison of two or more things, people, or situations. An analogy, used correctly, can be both convincing and logical. For example, Gandhi and Martin Luther King, Jr. have often been compared because of their similarities in philosophy and humanitarian work. However, analogy is often used in a way that is misleading. Consider this analogy:

- An editorial writer compares illegal aliens with slaves who were abducted and brought here from Africa. He proposes that the U. S. government owes the children of illegal aliens an education because the descendants of slaves are being given an education.

Emotional manipulation. When a speaker or writer is using a very strong appeal only to pity or to some other emotion, it is probably because there is little or no evidence to support the side being presented. **Emotional manipulation** is an attempt to sway someone else's opinion by causing that person to feel strong emotions, not by presenting evidence or sound reasons. You should always be suspicious of an attempt to control your thinking through the use of emotional manipulation. Some examples of this technique follow:

- A speaker introducing a political candidate urges you to vote for the underdog.
- A company asks you to buy its product before the company goes bankrupt.

- A charitable organization appeals to you to pity a group of people and send as much money as you can spare.

- An encyclopedia salesman says you will purchase the encyclopedias if you are concerned about your children's education.

Making inaccurate assumptions. An **assumption** is a statement or an idea that is taken for granted. The assumption may or may not be true or accurate. A writer may begin a statement with the assumption that a certain condition is a fact, without citing any evidence to support the idea. For example, the following contains assumptions:

- Given that most latchkey kids get into trouble with drugs, mothers should not work.

The above statement contains several possible assumptions:

- Most latchkey kids do drugs.
- Children whose mothers do not work avoid drugs.
- Mothers who are at home all the time keep a watchful eye on their children.
- Drug use is caused by lack of supervision.

EXERCISE 4.3

In each of the following statements, the speaker or writer has made at least one assumption. Tell what assumption is being made in each sentence.

1. Pornography should be outlawed.

   _____

   _____

2. No gay people should have custody of children.

   _____

   _____

3. All murderers should be executed.

   _____

   _____

4. Mothers of small children should not work outside the home.

   _____

   _____

5. Television should not be censored by the government because parents should get to censor their children's TV viewing.

   _____

   _____

6. Now that a sheep has been cloned, human cloning is bound to follow.

   _____

   _____

7. Given that pets cause too much destruction, they should not be allowed in apartments.

   _____

   _____

8. Since most people are not good parents, people should have to get a license to have a baby.

   _____

   _____

9. Since abortion is against the teaching of the church, it should be outlawed.

   _____

   _____

10. Since college requires many hours of study a day, college students should not work.

    _____

    _____

SUMMARY

This chapter began with a discussion of the purposes for writing. Since one of the purposes is persuasion, critical thinkers must learn to identify and evaluate the techniques used to cause people to believe or act in a certain way.

Evaluating written material extends to all forms of writing and requires mastery of such critical thinking skills as distinguishing fact and opinion, recognizing point of view and bias, understanding source and authority, and identifying the author's tone as it reveals a particular point of view.

Various types of evidence were presented and discussed as support for arguments. Some types of evidence lend more support than others, and some are appropriate only in certain situations.

Finally, deterrents to critical thinking were presented, along with advice for overcoming each deterrent. The errors in logical reasoning were identified in order to help students characterize logical arguments and illogical assumptions often presented as facts.

Cooperative Learning Activities

Following are three newspaper editorials. Each of the five cooperative learning groups should select one of the editorials and read it for the purpose of evaluating the arguments. To guide the evaluation process, answer each of the following questions under each category:

POINT OF VIEW AND BIAS

1. Did the author recognize opposing viewpoints?
2. Was the author biased? If not, how can you tell? If so, did the bias affect the logic of the author's argument?

TYPES OF EVIDENCE

1. Refer to the chapter contents to review types of evidence. Then list as many types of evidence as you can locate in your editorial. Give examples of each type you list.
2. Which types of evidence were most effective? Why?
3. What additional evidence might have made the argument stronger?

OVERALL EVALUATION OF EDITORIAL

1. Did you find any errors in logical reasoning? Explain.
2. List the writer's strong points made in the argument.
3. Was the argument convincing to the members of your group? Why or why not?

Reading Selection: *Editorial 1*

Title: *Daytime TV Child Porn Fueled by Profit Motive**
Author: Bob Herbert

New York—The shows cost next to nothing to produce, and there are still plenty of parents willing to usher their children onstage for a nationally televised dose of sexual exploitation and humiliation. So it is unlikely anyone will pull the plug on the degrading shoutfests that are known euphemistically as talk shows.

A few local stations have objected and some sponsors have balked, but barring a wholesale reawakening of common decency among advertisers or top network executives, the airwaves will continue to be fouled with shows that use real children to illustrate such rancid topics as the following:

"My Daughter Is a Tramp," "Teen Sex—Better in the House Than in the Back of the Car," and "Mom, I'm a Teen Prostitute" (all hosted by Sally Jessy Raphael); "Deadly Erotic Teen Games" and "Poor Black Teen Buries Her Baby Alive" (Jerry Springer); "Virgins Face Off Against Sexually Active Teens" (Jenny Jones); and "Teens Who Refuse to Practice Safe Sex," "Teen Girls Who Have One-Night Affairs," and "My Teen Son Killed the Man Who Molested Him" (Montel Williams).

Dr. Alvin F. Poussaint, a clinical professor of psychiatry at the Harvard Medical School, said the shows, with their relentless sexual voyeurism (aimed at inflaming the studio audience and titillating those at home), belong on the same sordid continuum as child pornography. "They often dress the young girls very provocatively," he said, "with miniskirts and lots of makeup, trying to make them look highly sexual."

Like pornographers and pimps, the talk-show hosts and their producers found a gold mine in the sexuality of troubled children. There is no mystery involved. Viewers get turned on, the ratings go up, and the cash rolls in. When I tried to reach Raphael for a comment, I was told she was vacationing in Italy.

Poussaint denounced the shows, in which children as young as 12 are encouraged to go before the cameras and, as he put it, "bare their souls" to satisfy the "salacious expectations of the audience." The youngsters have no idea what to expect, but at the urging of adults who ought to know better, they prattle on about the most intimate, and often traumatic, aspects of their lives.

Then, without warning, they find themselves demonized, as the live audience, and sometimes the host as well, turns on them. Booed, cursed, and otherwise reviled, the youngsters frequently are left weeping and bewildered.

Raphael recently hosted a show that featured a 12-year-old who claimed to have slept with 25 guys, and a 15-year-old who said she had been molested by her mother's boyfriend. The host wore a cloak of sanctimony throughout. "With all due respect," Raphael sniffed, "I don't think they need understanding. They need to be told it isn't right. They don't need to be understood."

Poussaint pointed out that no one knows in advance what the consequences will be for the children, either on the show or long term. A child, unprepared and emotionally vulnerable, could come "completely unraveled," he said.

The youngsters must also face the reaction of friends and others in their home communities who may have seen the program, and there remains the question of how to deal with the problem that got them on television in the first place.

Dr. Albert J. Solnit, a child psychiatrist who is Connecticut's Commissioner of Mental Health, agreed that encouraging sexual revelations by children in the overheated and seductive atmosphere of such shows was "completely irresponsible." He, too, warned that the youngsters could easily feel that things were out of control and that they were "uncared for."

Referring to one show, Solnit said the question that came to his mind was: "Who in heaven's name gave permission for these children to do this?"

Television is exactly the wrong remedy for the kinds of difficulties experienced by the youngsters who are lured to these shows. Poussaint and Solnit stressed the importance of putting such youngsters in touch with responsible adults, and assuring them that they can discuss their problems quietly and confidentially, and in a way that is not at all threatening.

"The proper way is first of all to have empathy," said Poussaint. "These are young people who deserve support and help and direction."

Reading Selection: *Editorial 2*

Title: *Guns and "Savage Young Hands"**
Author: Frank Rich

Why did they do it? The bodies of the four young girls and their selfless teacher were still warm in Jonesboro when by local evening news trotted out a shrink to speculate that boys who kill may be under the influence of the TV cartoon "South Park."

Arkansas Gov. Mike Huckabee spoke of a "culture where these children are exposed to tens of thousands of murders on television and movies." The National Rifle Association agreed: "This is not a gun issue, it's a society issue."

I turned to my handiest 13-year-old, who had just finished a virtual shootout, courtesy of a Nintendo video game. Later that night, he planned to watch "South Park." At summer camp, he practices riflery.

When I asked him if I had reason to worry, he rolled his eyes as only adolescent boys can. "Those kids are twisted," he said dismissively of the Arkansas killers. "They're evil." And then—lest I doubt he had mastered his eighth-grade reading—"It's *Lord of the Flies.*"

But couldn't Nintendo be teaching boys your age to kill? I asked. Mightn't those grown-ups on TV have a point?

"No," he answered, "They need to find a solution, because if there isn't a solution, it's anarchy. They can't blame the kids because kids are supposed to be innocent. So they have to blame something else to make an easy solution for themselves."

Of all those with instant hypotheses for what happened in Jonesboro, it's my 13-year-old resident expert who makes the most sense.

Though few Americans like to say so out loud, children can be evil—or, to put it more antiseptically, sociopaths. And, yes, blaming some blanket external force for such evil is a dodge. The responsible question to be asked after the third school massacre in five months may not be the unanswerable "Why?" but "What do we do to prevent a fourth?"

Predictably enough, politicians in both parties are yelling for stiffer penalties for juvenile murderers—a crowd-pleasing panacea that will hardly deter the next shooting spree. The extended incarceration of 11- and 13-year-old killers is most likely to be of therapeutic value only for the many angry Americans who want vengeance.

Rather than act merely out of anger—or in response to airy theories about pop culture—it might make more sense to confront real facts to see what preventive steps might abort the fire next time. For starters, the facts show that we might identify and intercede with these violent kids earlier; the National School Safety Center says that 80 percent of them are victims of neglect and abuse at home.

The facts also show that juvenile homicide arrests are actually *down* in the United States—by 30 percent from 1994 to '96. Not surprisingly, such crime is often most pronounced where gun regulation is the most lax. In its 1997 report card rating each state on the effectiveness of its laws protecting kids from guns, Handgun Control Inc. finds the sites of our three recent massacres at or near the national bottom: Arkansas and Mississippi get a D, Kentucky gets an F.

Is it any wonder that all three (according to the Violence Policy Center's latest figures) have a higher rate of firearm-related deaths among under-18-year-olds than even big, bad C-graded New York? (Arkansas' rate is more than three times New York's.)

Despite the propaganda put out by the NRA and its congressional patrons, it's obvious that the strengthening of gun-control laws might do more to prevent the next schoolyard slaughter than, say, a V-chip blocking "South Park."

Of particular value might be the so-called Child Access Prevention laws that hold adults liable when they enable a child's access to arms. Only 15 states have such laws—neither Arkansas, Mississippi, Kentucky nor, for that matter, New York among them.

Strong laws of this type would at least spare us the spectacle of the 11-year-old Jonesboro suspect's grandfather, who is tearfully making the TV rounds to say how heartbroken he is about the massacre and how sorry he is that the guns that did the killing were stolen from his home. How touching. A man who is either too stupid or too irresponsible to keep his arsenal kid-proof is, intentionally or not, an accessory to murder.

Though no law can prevent youthful evil, we could act right now, if we really cared, to prevent adults like him from letting their guns slip into savage young hands.

Reading Selection: *Editorial 3*

Title: *Cloning Humans Should Be Off Limits**
Author: Laurel Shackelford

What a disturbing development.

Since the dawn of civilization, uniqueness has been the birthright of every person. Now, however, the emergence of a lamb in a Scottish scientist's laboratory raises anew a jarring possibility that the warranty on guaranteed individuality may one day run out.

Then mothers could give birth to their own twins.

Twins could be born years, even generations, apart.

A person could have dozens of identical looking siblings.

Children would grow up knowing exactly what they would look like when they're old and wrinkly, certainly a punishing thought.

As always happens when the possibility of cloning humans surfaces, the announcement of Dolly's arrival tickled the David Letterman gene.

During the last wave of human engineering news, in 1990, there were jokes about winding up with "a thousand Dan Quayles."

This time there are jokes about parent-and-child relationships. "How could you tell the shrink that you hate your parent when you are your parent?"

Ever since Greek mythmakers created the Minotaur, that creature with the head of a man and the body of a white bull, and Mary Shelley plucked Frankenstein's monster from her head, the specter of masters of science tinkering with the essence of life has filled people with horror.

Even when a cloning experiment bears the face of innocence, as it does with the Scottish lamb named Dolly, it inevitably gives rise to gnawing fears of eugenics.

I say let's harness those fears.

Let's put them to noble use by urging officials to draft the international agreements and national policies needed to secure the genetic and social individuality that should be everyone's birthright.

Let's draw a moral line—firm and fast—that prohibits the use of human embryos in research that is aimed at, even tangentially, cloning people.

There is no good reason to clone people. Just vain reasons.

Needless to say, Dr. Ian Wilmut, the Scottish embryologist who engineered Dolly, and others in his field bleat that they wouldn't dream of experimenting with human embryos.

But you can be certain that clandestine research aimed at cloning the human embryo already is underway in private *in vitro* fertilization laboratories throughout this country and is probably occurring abroad as well.

In vitro fertilization is a highly profitable, competitive business, which has developed with stunning speed without federal money or government oversight. And that's the way its practitioners want the playing field to remain—open and unfettered.

Transferring cloning technology from sheep to humans is certain to be difficult and won't happen soon. However, the arrival of Dolly increases the possibility that sooner or later people with a financial stake in companies engaged in genetic research will begin talking up the benefits of human cloning.

Already, some enthusiasts hint at the possibilities.

If ways could be found to clone human embryos, they reason, then doctors could do more to help couples who are desperate for a baby.

However, scientists are exploring many ways to stimulate production of embryos that don't involve cloning human embryos. Helping infertile couples conceive almost certainly will not hinge on cloning people.

Some genetics researchers say that if the human embryo could be cloned, then there would be more organs for dying individuals who desperately need transplants. However, cloning people to produce transplantable organs shouldn't be necessary because scientists seem close to finding ways to graft organs.

Some soothsayers tout embryo splitting as a fabulous new form of health insurance that would "protect" parents against the death of a child. Cloning, they reason, would give parents the wherewithal to create the dead child's twin.

It doesn't take a genius to see through that argument. The two beings wouldn't be the same people at all because people are shaped by their experiences, not just by their genes.

Once again, it appears that science is developing far faster than our ability to understand its implications.

Is this a case in which the genie is already out of the bottle?

Are the consequences wholly beyond our control?

I don't think so. Rather than being a murky ethical situation, thick with ambiguity, this one is fairly straightforward: Cloning experiments that involve human beings should be prohibited.

Just as scientists and politicians throughout the world have moved swiftly to contain some other aspects of human engineering, so must they move to contain this one. There already are about forty-five international resolutions aimed at restricting efforts that involve making genetic changes that would pass from generation to generation.

Human cloning should be nipped in the bud, too.

Reading Selection: *Essay*

Title: *Someone Is Listening**
Author: Michael Holguin

Activation of Prior Knowledge and Interest

1. What are some of the problems experienced by young people today?

   _____

   _____

   _____

2. Do you have any friends who are gay? Do they discuss any problems they experience because of their sexual orientation?

   _____

   _____

3. Have you ever had a problem you felt no one could understand? If so, what person did you discuss the problem with?

   _____

   _____

In today's society there is a form of child abuse that not even Oprah talks about. Unlike some other forms of abuse, it knows no limitations—no ethnic, no religious, no educational, and no socioeconomic boundaries. Lives are destroyed by parents who act in fear and ignorance. Dreams are shattered by the cruel and hurtful words of friends. Every day, hundreds of gay youths hide in their rooms and cry from pain caused by the mean and careless behavior of those who claim to love them.

In a Judeo-Christian society it is common for families to attend church with their children. The pastor in many of these churches stands at the podium and announces, "Homosexuals are an abomination unto the Lord." The church walls shake from the resounding "Amen" from the congregation. The pastor continues, "Homosexuals are sick. Perverted. They are a danger to our children." In agreement the congregation once more says, "Amen." I know how this feels. As a gay person, I recall the pain of many such Sundays during my childhood. I prayed extra hard for God's cure before someone would find out my secret and embarrass me and my family, because I remembered what had happened to Jason the year before. So I kept answering the altar call every Sunday when the unwanted feeling wouldn't go away. The fear of rejection and eternal damnation made me too terrified to confide in anyone or to ask for help. After all, my parents seemed to tell me I deserved such a fate every time they said, "Amen."

Every day became more difficult to endure. I faced the jokes in the locker room. Even my best friend told some, and sometimes, to keep from being discovered, I told some. At this point, how much self-esteem could I have had? I cringed when my coach urged us to "kick those faggots' asses" but I still kicked. Yet every day my feelings were denied. My health teacher told us, "Someday you will all grow up and get married and have children." I couldn't understand why I had no such desire. I would turn on the television, and there would be a cop show on. This week's criminal was a gay child molester—again. I think "Baretta" had the same story the week before. I changed the station to "Barney Miller," where there was an old man wearing a polyester jumpsuit and a silk scarf around his neck, and talking with a lisp. Couldn't they drop the lisp just once? I wonder. I cringe, thinking this is my inevitable fate, my curse.

By the time I reached my teen years, I'd heard and seen so much negativity toward my "condition" that my life became plagued with constant fears. I became afraid of rejection. I knew my Christian family would think I was sick, perverted, and dangerous to children. Dad would be disappointed, even though I had six brothers to carry on the family name. Mom would not want me around because she'd worry about what to tell Grandma and Grandpa. My brother would pretend he didn't know me at school.

My fears were reinforced by close-up examples. Once I had a friend named Daniel, who was the son of a local preacher. I don't know where Daniel got the nerve at the age of twelve to tell his parents he was gay, but that's what he did. It was also at the age of twelve that his father put him out on the street after all the beatings failed to cure him. Daniel managed to stay alive on the streets as a prostitute. He's in prison now, dying of AIDS. The fear of rejection was real.

I learned how to fit in out of fear of humiliation, but especially out of fear of physical abuse. I had seen Daniel's father and brothers beat him up almost daily. An even earlier memory from when I was very young involved a boy named Terry, who everyone knew was different. Some kids had figured Terry out. One day behind the school, way out in the field, four kids beat Terry up. Kicking and slugging him as he fell to the ground, they called out "Sissy" and "Queer" as they swung at him. We had only heard the word *queer* from the older boys, and no one was sure what it meant exactly. We hadn't encountered the word *faggot* yet. I suppose I didn't like Terry much either, but I felt bad as I watched in terror, knowing that the next time it could be me that they considered "different."

After years of living with low self-esteem, a battered self-image, and a secret life, one's psyche tends to give out. The highest rate of teen suicide is among gay youths. In a recent five-year study, it was determined that fear of rejection was the number one cause of suicide among gay teenagers. After losing the loving environment of friends and families, many gays turn to other means of comfort. Drug and alcohol abuse is high among gays. Many turn to multiple lovers, looking for acceptance and emotional support. The result of this has been the devastating spread of AIDS. With nowhere to go, suicide often seems to be the only option. My friend Billy, when visiting his younger sister at his mother's home, would have to stay on the front porch and talk through a screen door at his mother's request. Last February, at the age of 19, Billy drove up to the mountains and there took his own life. Before he died he wrote on the hood of the car, "God, help me." I recall my own suicide attempt, which was the result of my inability to deal with a life-style everyone close to me was unable to accept. It was only my self-acceptance that eventually saved me from being a statistic.

When planning a family, people should ask themselves, "Will I love my children for who they are, or will I love them only if they're what I want them to be?" If people answer the latter, they shouldn't be parents. The same kind of thing might be said for others who are responsible for helping children develop. Abuse comes in many forms, and ignorance and self-centeredness are usually its foundation. Parents, preachers, teachers, clergy, friends—please be cautious of what you say. The children are listening.

Critical Thinking Questions

1. What proof is offered by the essay that gay youth suffer severe discrimination?

   _____

   _____

   _____

2. Why did the author feel that his own parents would not accept and understand his sexual orientation?

   _____

   _____

   _____

3. Compare and contrast the discrimination against gays with other forms of discrimination.

   _____

   _____

   _____

REFERENCES

Barry, V. E. (1989). *Invitation to Critical Thinking* (2nd ed.). New York: Holt, Rinehart.

Brookfield, S. (1987). *Developing Critical Thinkers: Challenging Adults to Explore Alternative Ways of Thinking and Acting.* San Francisco: Jossey-Bass Publishers.

Chaffee, J. (1991). *Thinking Critically* (2nd ed.). Boston: Houghton Mifflin.

CREDITS

Herbert, B. (1996, March 3). Daytime TV child porn fueled by profit motive. *Louisville Courier-Journal,* p. D1.

Holguin, M. (1995). Someone is listening. In L. Brandon (Ed.), *Celebrating diversity: A multicultural reader.* Lexington, MA: D. C. Heath.

Rich, F. (1998, March 31). Guns and "savage young hands." *New York Times News Service.*

Shackleford, L. (1997, March 2). Cloning humans should be off limits. *Louisville Courier-Journal,* p. D1.

MASTERY OF COLLEGE TEXTBOOKS

This section provides strategies to help you study outside of the classroom. As you process your textbooks, your goals are to understand, to evaluate, to process, to recall. Although your short-term goal may be to discern which facts are important and may, therefore, be test questions, your longer-term goal may be to retain and use relevant information. This section will help you accomplish both your short- and long-term goals. You will learn to locate and comprehend main ideas, interpret graphic illustrations, recognize and understand the patterns of textbook writing, master new terminology, and in general acquire effective methods for studying textbooks and other learning materials.

In Section II:

CHAPTER 5

Main Ideas

CHAPTER OBJECTIVES

▪ To distinguish between topics and main ideas

▪ To locate both stated and implied main ideas

▪ To comprehend different types of supporting details

▪ To locate main ideas in longer passages

Students often have difficulty locating the main ideas in lectures and in written material. They may have an academic history of answering only detail questions instead of being asked to state main ideas. The ability to locate main ideas is vital in college for several academic tasks:

▪ Comprehending textbook material

▪ Synthesizing research information and writing papers

▪ Taking notes from lectures

▪ Underlining and annotating textbooks

▪ Studying for tests

HOW TOPICS AND MAIN IDEAS DIFFER

A **topic** is a word or phrase that is the subject of a paragraph or a series of paragraphs. The following are all examples of topics:

- Video games
- Teenagers
- College athletics
- New findings in science
- Allergies

EXERCISE 5.1

In each of the following paragraphs, write the topic on the line provided.

1. The move was unpredictably hard on everyone in the family. Mrs. Miller had to give up the best job she had ever had. Her husband was changing jobs after his former company went out of business, but he harbored the depressing thought that the new position was a step down. The two teenagers were having to leave the only friends they had ever known and were acting out in self-destructive ways their parents had never witnessed before.

Topic: _____

2. National parks have long provided outdoor activities and beautiful scenery for vacationers. Adults and children alike can find interesting things to do and can learn about nature at the same time. The national parks are also more economically reasonable as vacation spots, in sharp contrast to the ever-popular amusement parks. Some families enjoy camping out in the parks instead of staying in nearby motels, so they save even more money. Children can learn how to have a good time without televisions, video games, or any other modern diversions.

Topic: _____

3. If you want to increase your reading speed, you should practice with books you are reading for fun. Don't stop and look at every single word because this practice slows your silent reading to the speed of oral reading. Instead, practice looking at several words per fixation. You can obtain books that have timed readings, or you can time yourself while you are reading magazines or novels. For example, see how long it takes you to read five pages and

then attempt to read the next five pages faster. If you practice daily, you will soon be able to read faster.

Topic: _____

4. Everyone in the family is looking forward to the vacation. This will be the first time the kids have been outside the United States. The parents have not returned to England since they were students there one summer. They plan to remain in England for one week to tour the entire country. Then a side trip to Scotland is planned to visit a few of that country's one thousand castles. The family members can hardly contain their excitement about their anticipated vacation.

Topic: _____

5. The man who bought the neighboring farm seemed very outgoing and friendly at first. He introduced himself and explained his reasons for moving from New Hampshire to Iowa. After he got settled in the new place, Dad asked him to come for dinner one night when it was convenient. He quickly said he did not socialize with the neighbors and wished to be left alone. Mom went over and invited the new neighbor for dinner, thinking the invitation should come from both her and Dad. Again the man refused, although this time not so politely. He was visibly irritated and asked that none of us ever bother him again.

Topic: _____

A **main idea** is the most important point an author is trying to make about the topic. The main idea may also be called the **topic sentence,** but do not confuse that term with the topic. A main idea, unlike a topic, cannot be only a word or a phrase because the main idea must express a completed thought. It will be expressed as a complete sentence. The previously listed topics might have the following sentences as their main ideas:

- Video games are so popular with children that some parents have to force their kids to go outside and play.
- While many teenagers get into trouble with drugs and the law, even more are law-abiding, productive members of society.
- College athletics have come under close scrutiny in the past ten years.
- New findings in science include many ideas, such as cloning, which were previously considered science fiction.

- Many people believe that allergies are more prevalent today because of the higher incidence of air pollution.

HOW TO LOCATE MAIN IDEAS

Stated Main Ideas

You can look for the main idea of a paragraph in several places where main ideas are most likely to be stated. Most main ideas are probably located in **the first sentence** because the author wants to get the reader to focus on the idea. Then the author guides the reader through the remaining sentences. In the following paragraph, notice the main idea:

> **Married couples decide to have children for a variety of reasons.** Some truly love children and want to provide the best possible home for them. Others respond to peer pressure and have children because all of their friends do. Some are pressured by their own parents who wish to become grandparents. Still others believe that the children will be there to care for them in their declining years.

The second most common place to find the main idea is **the last sentence.** The author may write several informative sentences and then summarize or conclude in the last sentence of the paragraph. This technique is often used in court when an attorney states five pieces of evidence that were introduced and then concludes that the defendant is guilty. The following paragraph has the main idea last:

> If a college freshman says she wants to be a nuclear physicist when she barely graduated from high school and still does not like to study, it is highly unlikely that this goal will be realized. Such a student needs to determine her own strengths and weaknesses. She also needs to ask herself what sacrifices she is willing to make to achieve a goal. She may also need to think about her family responsibilities and her financial situation. **People should always set goals that are both practical and realistic.**

The main idea may also be found in **both the first and last sentences.** The first sentence is reiterated or restated in the last to make an impact on the reader, to make sure that the reader does not miss the important point:

Most colleges provide access to tutors. Some may simply have names of qualified tutors, while others will find the tutor for you. In the typical situation, a student goes to a learning lab or the office of a tutorial coordinator and requests a tutor for a particular subject. The personnel at the office locate a tutor, and the student and the tutor arrange a convenient time for tutoring sessions. If you feel that you need this type of help, don't wait too long before applying. If there is little time left in the course, there may not be time for adequate improvement. **Providing access to tutors is a very valuable service of most colleges.**

The main idea may even be in **the middle of the paragraph,** although this is more unusual. There will be supporting details leading to the main idea, followed by more details after the main idea is stated:

Most people who have pets probably have a dog or a cat, both of which have long been considered "the family pet." Others do not want the trouble of a dog or a cat, so they opt for something that requires less time. They may have a parakeet or a bowl of goldfish, both low-maintenance pets. **People enjoy a wide variety of pets.** Some even own exotic pets such as lions, tigers, or skunks. I once lived on a street with a family who had an ostrich, which they kept in the backyard.

When you are trying to locate the main idea of a selection, remember the grammar exercise of finding the simple subject and simple predicate. Those elements would represent the main idea of a sentence. The other words would be details in the sentence:

The extremely large, young gray <u>horse was running</u> aimlessly through the city streets at noon.

The underlined parts are the main idea of the sentence. The other words are the supporting details.

In the same way, you must find the main idea and supporting details of paragraphs and then longer passages. Ask who or what something is about (topic), and then ask what about it is important or what about it is being communicated (main idea).

You may have questioned why it is necessary to identify both the topic and the main idea. There are many possible main ideas for a single topic, so you must read a paragraph to determine the major point that is being made about a topic. For instance, if you know that the topic is football scholarships, all of the following main ideas could be derived from that topic:

- More scholarships are given for football than for any other sport.
- High school seniors often attempt to earn football scholarships for college.
- A group of female students at George Washington High School are petitioning to be considered as recipients for football scholarships.

If you are still having trouble finding the main idea, ask yourself the following questions:

1. What are the key words?
2. To what do most of the key words refer?
3. Besides the key words, what other words occur frequently?
4. To what do the frequently occurring words relate?
5. What do the details in the paragraph have in common? (For example, are all of the sentences about *South American animals*?)
6. Does it appear that the main idea is stated, or will I have to put it in my own words?
7. Have I checked the most common places for main ideas to see if one of those sentences could be the main idea of this paragraph?

When you think you have located the main idea but are not sure, try using a graphic illustration. Then check to see if all the details really have anything to do with the sentence you have written as the main idea. See the following example:

Main Idea Sentence	People attend college for different reasons.
Detail 1	Some really want to learn.
Detail 2	Some want to please their parents.
Detail 3	Some want to meet people.
Detail 4	Some want to get a good job.

If one of the details had not belonged under the main idea sentence, you should have noticed that it was logically out of place, such as in the following example:

There are many reasons for dropping out of college.

Some lose their financial aid.

Business is a popular major.

Some students lose interest in college.

Many drop out to go to work.

After you read the second supporting detail sentence, you would know that either your main idea was incorrect or you had misunderstood the paragraph in some other way. You should reread and draw another diagram. Going through the process again may clarify your understanding.

EXERCISE 5.2

All of the following paragraphs have a main idea stated in the paragraph. After reading each paragraph, underline the sentence that is the main idea. All of the paragraphs in Exercise 5.2 are taken from *Cultural Anthropology* (8th ed.), by Ember and Ember.*

1. People are likely to resort to violence when regular, effective, alternative means of resolving a conflict are not available. Some societies consider violence between individuals to be appropriate under certain circumstances; we generally do not and call it crime. When violence occurs between political entities such as communities, districts, or nations, we call it warfare. The type of warfare, of course, varies in scope and complexity from society to society. Sometimes a distinction is made among feuding, raiding, and large-scale confrontations.

2. Disasters can have greater or lesser effects on human life, depending on social conditions. And therefore disasters are also social problems, problems that have social causes and possible social solutions. Legislating safe construction of a house is a social solution. The 1976 earthquake in Tangsham, China, killed 250,000 people, mostly because they lived in top-heavy adobe houses that could not stand severe shaking, whereas the 1989 earthquake in Loma Prieta, California, which was of comparable intensity, killed only 65 people.

3. One might think that floods, of all disasters, are the least influenced by social factors. After all, without a huge runoff from heavy rains or snow melt, there cannot be a flood. But consider why so many people have died from Yellow River floods in China. (One such flood, in 1931, killed nearly 4 million people, making it the deadliest single disaster in history.) The floods in the Yellow River basin have occurred mostly because the clearing of forests nearby (for fuel and farm land) has allowed enormous quantities of silt to wash into the river, raising the river bed and increasing the risk of floods that burst the dams that normally would contain them. The risk of disastrous flooding would be greatly reduced if different social conditions prevailed—if people were not so dependent on firewood for fuel, or they did not have to farm land close to the river, or the dams were higher and more numerous.

*CULTURAL ANTHROPOLOGY 8/E. by Ember and Ember, © 1996. Reprinted by permission of Prentice-Hall, Inc., Upper Saddle River, NJ.

4. People in the past, and even recently in some places, viewed disasters as divine retribution for human immorality. For example, the great Flood described in the Old Testament was understood to be God's doing. But scientific research increasingly allows us to understand the natural causes of disasters, and particularly the social conditions that magnify or minimize their effects. To reduce the impact of disasters, then, we need to reduce the social conditions that magnify their effects. If humans are responsible for those social conditions, humans can change them. If earthquakes destroy houses that are too flimsy, we can build stronger houses. If floods caused by overcultivation and overgrazing kill defenseless people directly (or indirectly by stripping their soils), we can decide to grow new forest cover and provide new job opportunities to flood-plain farmers. In short, we may not be able to do much about the weather (or other physical causes of disasters), but we can do a lot (if we want to) about the social factors that make disasters disastrous.

5. It is often assumed that wife beating will be common in societies in which males control economic and political resources. In a cross-cultural test of this assumption, David Levinson found that not all indicators of male dominance predict wife beating, but many do. Specifically, wife beating is most common when men control the products of family labor, when men have the final say in decision making in the home, when divorce is difficult for women, when remarriage for a widow is controlled by the husband's kin, and when women do not have any female work groups. Similarly, in the United States, the more one spouse in the family makes the decisions and has the power, the more physical violence occurs in the family (wife beating is even more likely when the husband controls the household and is out of work).

Unstated Main Ideas

The main idea may be **unstated,** also called **implied.** The main idea is not stated or written *anywhere,* so the reader must determine what the main idea is and then must put the main idea into his or her own words. The following example from a social situation has no main idea sentence because the main idea is merely implied:

> I was walking down the corridor when I saw my best friend, Jane, approaching from the opposite direction. I immediately smiled and started walking toward her. When I got nearer, Jane frowned deeply, stared at me for a long minute, and then turned and walked away.

The main idea of the paragraph is, "Jane is angry with me for some unknown reason." However, this is not stated anywhere in the paragraph. The reader must take clues from the paragraph and draw a conclusion. Textbooks and lectures also contain unstated main ideas, so students must learn to locate them. The following paragraph also contains an unstated main idea. Read the paragraph, and try to state the main idea in your own words:

Many students at the large university come from the Middle East, and a large percentage of these students are studying engineering. About 10 percent of the university student body is composed of young men and women from South America, especially Colombia and Argentina. Roughly 15 percent of the students are from Great Britain, France, and Germany. In recent years, more and more students have been coming from Africa, especially from several countries on the western coast of the continent. In addition, numerous other countries are represented by smaller numbers. About 10 percent of the students are native to the United States, so they are in the minority in their own country.

The main idea of the preceding paragraph is that the university is composed of a very diverse population, but the idea is not stated as a sentence anywhere in the paragraph. You must make an inference based on the facts.

If you have difficulty paraphrasing an implied main idea, remember four simple guidelines.

1. Read all the statements carefully, trying to find what they have in common. All of the ideas must refer to or relate to some topic. Decide what that topic is, and then ask what the different sentences are saying about the topic.

2. Compose a sentence that names something, and then tell something about whatever is named. You should name the topic to which you feel the sentences refer. When you tell something about that topic, get your clues from what all of the sentences are discussing. For example, do all of the sentences refer to some type of tropical plant?

3. Read all of the sentences again, and determine whether or not you wish to revise the sentence you wrote. Get your thoughts down first. Then, when you reread the passage and reread your own sentence, it will become clearer. You will see that your sentence expresses the main idea, or you will understand how to revise your statement.

4. In your revised sentence, be specific enough to get the main idea stated accurately. If you have a topic like *football*, you may need to be more specific, using a phrase like *girls playing football*. The second sentence in the following example is more specific:

- Girls are sometimes interested in playing football.
- Girls at 8 percent of the state's high schools have petitioned the principals for the right to play football on the same team as boys.

It will not always be necessary to be that specific. Every paragraph must be evaluated individually.

EXERCISE 5.3

Each of the following paragraphs contains an unstated main idea. Read each paragraph, and write the main idea on the line provided. All of the paragraphs in Exercise 5.3 are taken from *Cultural Anthropology* (8th ed.), by Ember and Ember.*

1. The Subanun of the Philippines have an expensive bride price—several times the annual income of the groom *plus* three to five years of bride service. Among the Manus of the Admiralty Islands off New Guinea, a groom requires an economic backer—usually an older brother or an uncle—if he is to marry, but it will be years before he can pay off his debts. Depending on the final bride-price, payments may be concluded at the time of the marriage, or they may continue for years afterward.

_____

2. We are accustomed to thinking of marriage as involving just one man and one woman at a time *(monogamy),* but most societies known to anthropology have allowed a man to be married to more than one woman at the same time *(polygyny).* At any given moment, however, the majority of men in societies permitting polygyny are married monogamously; few or no societies have enough women to permit most men to have at least two wives. Polygyny's mirror image—one woman being married to more than one man at the same time *(polyandry)*—is practiced in very few societies. Polygyny and polyandry are the two types of *polygamy,* or plural marriage. *Group marriage,* in which more than one man is married to more than one woman at the same time, sometimes occurs but is not customary in any known society.

_____

3. Among the Tiv of central Nigeria, the patrilocal extended family consists of the "great father," who is the head of the household, and his younger brothers, his sons, and his younger brothers' sons. Also included are the in-marrying wives and all unmarried children. (The sisters and daughters of the household head who have married would have gone to live where their husbands lived.) Authority is strongly vested in the male line, particularly the eldest of the household, who has authority over bride price, disputes, punishment, and plans for new buildings.

4. The members of the same patrilineage address each other affectionately, and within this group law and order are maintained by a headman. Killing within the lineage is considered a serious offense, and any fighting that takes place is done with sticks rather than lethal weapons such as spears. The sublineage headman tries to settle any kind of grievance within the sublineage as quickly and as peacefully as possible. If a sublineage mate commits a crime against outsiders, all members of the sublineage may be considered responsible and their property seized, or a member of the sublineage may be killed in revenge by the victim's kin.

5. Among the Lepcha of the Himalayas, a man was believed to become homosexual if he ate the flesh of an uncastrated pig. But the Lepcha said that homosexual behavior was practically unheard of, and they viewed it with disgust. Perhaps because many societies deny that homosexuality exists, little is known about homosexual practices in the restrictive societies. Among the permissive ones, there is variation in the pervasiveness of homosexuality. In some societies homosexuality is accepted but limited to certain times and certain individuals. For example, among the Papago of the southwestern United States there were "nights of saturnalia," in which homosexual tendencies could be expressed. The Papago also had many male transvestites, who wore women's clothing, did women's chores, and, if not married, could be visited by men. A woman did not have quite the same freedom of expression. She could participate in the saturnalia feasts only with her husband's permission, and female transvestites were nonexistent.

SUPPORTING DETAILS

Details, also called **supporting details,** serve the purpose of explaining or supporting the main idea. It is necessary to be able to recognize the main idea before finding supporting details, although the details can point toward a main idea.

There are both major and minor details, with the major details being the most important. You can look for signal words in order to decide which details are most important. Some of the signal words follow, but there are many other possibilities:

- First, second, third, etc.
- Next
- Furthermore
- Another
- Also
- Finally
- Ultimately

Look again at the paragraph about pets you read earlier. This time some minor details have been added. Notice them, and think about why they are not as important as the other detail sentences:

> Most people who have pets probably have a dog or a cat, both of which have long been considered "the family pet." Dogs and cats are often seen as pets on television. Others do not want the trouble of a dog or a cat, so they opt for something that requires less time. They may have a parakeet or a bowl of goldfish, both low-maintenance pets. Parakeets and goldfish do not seem as affectionate as dogs and cats. **People enjoy a wide variety of pets.** Some even own exotic pets such as lions, tigers, or skunks. Some of these exotic pets seem dangerous. I once lived on a street with a family who had an ostrich, which they kept in the backyard.

In some paragraphs, especially those that are not very long, all of the supporting details may be very important.

Types of Supporting Details

In a well-constructed paragraph, every sentence (besides the main idea sentence) should, in some way, support the main idea. There are many types of details, and the supporting details serve the purpose of supplying different types of information.

Facts. These can also include statistics. Often the writer of the paragraph will give credit to the source where he or she got the facts or statistics. The facts themselves would be the more important supporting details, but the source statements would also be details:

The city of Elmwood is distinct because it has the state's highest concentration of medical doctors. The city is small in comparison with the other leading cities, but Elmwood contains more physicians than the largest city in the entire state, according to the newspaper, the Southeast Tribune. The Tribune reported on August 15, 1997, that there are more physicians than there are patients in Elmwood, with 54 percent of the residents being doctors. The newspaper article added that all of the doctors seem to prosper, although the source of their prosperity remains a mystery. The question remains: Where do the doctors get their patients? The reporter speculated that the likely place is the neighboring town of Glendale as well as surrounding counties. Another question ponders the reason the doctors do not move away from Elmwood to locations where there is not so much medical competition. The reporter offered no explanation for this piece of the puzzle.

Examples. Frequently a main idea statement is given, followed by several examples to clarify a concept or idea. Most students find examples helpful when studying new concepts and information. In the following example, a term is defined and followed by examples of that term:

A felony is defined as a crime more serious than a misdemeanor. Murder is the most serious crime. Rape is also a felony. Another felony is armed robbery.

Description. A writer may relate how a scene looks, how a person acts, how members of a group interact, or many other types of descriptions. A description is usually thought of as telling how someone or something looks, but there can also be a description of events, activities, or ideas. The following example is a description of a family:

A **family** is a group of people who live together and care for each other. This definition is not the same as in the past, when family was likely to be described as "mother, father, and children" (the typical nuclear family). In many modern homes, only one parent will be present, due to death, divorce, or other circumstances. There may be adult children who have returned home after living away for several years. There are many modern couples who no longer wish to be parents. Others prefer to adopt children to give a home to a child who otherwise would not have a family. There may also be members of extended families who live in the home with the parent and the children. Same-sex couples also head families in some places, and this trend seems to be growing. A family may also include a friend who shares the home for economic reasons or who helps raise the children in the absence of one of the parents. The family may be ever-changing, but most people still prefer to share their homes and their lives with others.

Reasons. These supporting details should be easy to locate because the author will sometimes ask a *why* question and then enumerate the answers to the question. Other times the question is implied and then answered. The following example has the question explicitly stated, followed by reasons that answer the question:

Why do many people choose teaching children as a profession? Many feel that they should contribute to society in a meaningful way, and they explain that children are the citizens of tomorrow. They feel that it is very important to get young children off to a good start with their education. Other people who choose to be teachers report that their love of children is the main reason for their chosen profession. Still others enjoy a particular academic discipline and want to impart their knowledge to as many people as possible.

Steps. Many textbooks must list or give steps in a process or an event. The steps may be numbered or simply introduced by signal words, such as *first, next,* and *then.* In most cases, when steps are the supporting details, the main idea will be stated first so that there is no confusion about the nature of the steps.

Steps often comprise the supporting details in many types of textbook writing. The following are only a few examples:

- Instructions for math calculations
- Processes for how a bill becomes a law
- Directions on tests
- Evolutionary processes
- Events leading to a revolution

Definitions. Definitions are often thought of as one sentence, but the entire paragraph may be an extended definition. The word being defined will be introduced in a main idea sentence; the remainder of the paragraph will be the definition. The following examples represent main idea sentences that are likely to be developed as definition paragraphs:

- *Sleep terrors* are extremely frightening experiences that occur during sleep.
- What is *postpartum psychosis?*
- *Affirmative action* refers to remedial actions that have the function of overcoming the effects of both societal wrongs and discrimination against minorities.
- What are *concurrent powers?*

EXERCISE 5.4

In the following paragraphs, the main idea is in *italics*. There are several supporting details, some more important than others. In each paragraph, underline only the most important detail sentences. Then discuss your responses with a classmate. If you and your partner did not underline the same supporting sentences, determine which should have been underlined.

1. *The issue of capital punishment has always been strongly debated.* Those who are opposed to the practice feel that the ultimate punishment is not a deterrent to crime, while those who are in favor of it state that it is a deterrent when done consistently. Some opponents feel that "murder by the state" is morally wrong and sends the wrong message. A well-known Senator recently made this point. Advocates of capital punishment often state that serious and heinous crimes must be punished by death. Some victims' rights organizations hold this view. Some states have capital punishment but rarely enforce it. Others, like Florida and Texas, practice it more often than most other states.

2. *Many people have tried low-fat diets in an attempt to lose weight.* Some people have made the mistake of believing that counting fat grams is all that really matters in the weight loss program, so they consume large amounts of foods that are low in fat but are still high in calories. I know someone who ate all of the sugar she wanted because she knew that sugar has no fat. However, she gained weight rapidly and did not understand the reason for the gain. Some people who diet count all calories and attempt to eat fewer calories per day than they ever have before. Others who want to lose weight eat the same foods as usual but exercise vigorously every day. They maintain that they can eat all they want if they exercise. Still others try fads such as liquid diets or a fruit-only diet. Some celebrities even share their diet secrets with the public. *It is obvious that many people are attempting to lose weight, and there are many methods being used to achieve this goal.*

3. When you initially find yourself experiencing difficulty in a course, the first person you should consult is the instructor. Schedule a conference and explain your problem in detail. It will help if you write down the points you want to make, in advance, to avoid omitting anything important. Another helpful resource when you are having trouble with academics is your academic advisor. Many colleges assign a certain faculty member to each student to give advice about courses to take, problems with courses, and information about majors. The college catalog is another valuable academic resource, containing all of the requirements for all majors. *There are many places where students can get help in solving academic problems.*

4. *There are many reasons a student might visit a learning skills center.* Some may lack valuable study skills, such as note taking or underlining textbooks. Some may be afraid they will fail certain tests. Others might like a professional to look over a returned test to help evaluate the types of errors. The centers are staffed by professionals who have expertise in areas in which students may sometimes need assistance. For example, many of the centers are staffed by instructors from study skills classes. Still other students visit the centers to take ability tests in reading or math.

5. *Homes reflect the personalities of the people who live in them.* One way this is demonstrated is through the use of color. Some very energetic, active people decorate their homes with a blaze of color. Some even paint large words, such as "love," on the wall, or they draw whimsical pictures. More reserved people would rarely feel comfortable in such surroundings. The more reserved might maintain a sedate color scheme of neutrals or lighter colors and shades. Another way personalities are reflected in homes is in the presence or absence of clutter. The more organized among us find a place for everything and keep everything in its rightful place, while some people feel at home in rooms strewn with books, newspapers, and belongings. Personalities are also evident in the photographs, collections, and types of furnishings. *Decoration can tell us much about the people who live in the homes.*

LOCATING MAIN IDEAS IN LONGER PASSAGES

Once you have mastered the skill of locating main ideas, you must extend this skill to longer passages, such as newspaper and magazine articles and sections in textbook chapters. Although most paragraphs contain a main idea, there is an overall main idea of an entire selection. Sometimes the overall main idea is called something else, such as *thesis, major point,* or *argument.* You will need a strategy to find the major idea of an entire selection.

In longer passages, as in paragraphs, the main idea may be either stated or unstated. If stated, it may be in all of the places that a main idea in a paragraph is found. The most common places are at the beginning and the end of the selection, but the major point may be somewhere else. Especially with longer selections, authors are likely to state the major point at the beginning of the passage in order to focus the attention of the reader and guide the reader through the rest of the passage. At other times, the author may wish to make an impact by placing the major point at the end of the passage. Either place can be very effective, depending on the author's purpose.

Since you have already learned how to find the main idea of an individual paragraph, you can extend this skill to longer passages. You should follow these five steps to determine the major point of an entire selection:

1. Find the main idea of each paragraph in the selection.
2. Write the main idea in the margin beside each paragraph.
3. Reread all the main ideas you have written in the margins.

As you reread, you should try to determine whether or not the main ideas seem cohesive or seem to fit together in a way that makes sense. You must constantly monitor your comprehension as you do this. Ask yourself, at several different points, if that sounds like a main idea of a paragraph, if the successive main ideas seem to come in logical order, and if the various main ideas come together as a whole, making sense to you. If something seems wrong, reread and recheck the main ideas.

4. If all of the conditions in step 3 are met, reread the main idea statements again, this time without pausing, to determine the overall major point the author is trying to make.
5. After stating a major point, look back at the individual main ideas and make sure each individual main idea supports the major point.

SUMMARY

The chapter began with an explanation of why the ability to locate main ideas is so important to college students. There are many assignments and tasks that require this vital skill.

Topics and main ideas were explained, and strategies were discussed for finding each and for distinguishing between the two. Additional information was given to help find the main ideas and important supporting details of both paragraphs and longer passages, such as textbook chapters.

Frequently, the main idea of a paragraph or a passage is not stated. It is implied, but the reader has clues and supporting details that lead to the main idea. The student must then paraphrase the unstated, or implied, main idea.

Cooperative Learning Activities

GROUP 1. By all reports, Janice is one of the hardest-working students in the class. She knows that she has learned a great deal of information throughout her school years. However, she does not seem to study and learn "the right things." The information she studies is never what is on the test. Obviously, she is not selecting the main ideas to learn for tests. Considering lectures, textbook study, and test preparation, advise Janice on how to get better grades.

GROUP 2. Mason reads and processes his textbook information very effectively. However, he never knows what the professors are talking about. He feels that he might as well not attend class. What could be the reason for this discrepancy between his textbook learning and his classroom learning? What plan of action will help Mason?

GROUP 3. Find some material you have been collecting and/or studying for an upcoming test. Realizing these may be potential test questions, locate all of the main ideas and mark them in the material. Try to guess which main ideas will be test questions.

GROUP 4. Everyone in the group should get a content area textbook he or she is currently using. Turn to a section of a chapter that has been assigned. Locate and write in the margins the main ideas for an entire section of the chapter. (Review the material in this chapter if necessary.) If there is difficulty in finding the main ideas, discuss the problem in the group and find a solution.

GROUP 5. Everyone in this group should write four or five topics that could be developed into compositions. Pass around the individual lists until each person has selected a topic for a one- to two-page informal essay. Remembering good paragraph construction of main ideas and supporting sentences, write essays to be shared with the group.

Reading Selection: *Essay*

Title: *Disabledness as a Violation of the Ideal**
Author: Nancy Mairs

Activation of Prior Knowledge and Interest

1. What do you first think about when you hear the word "disabled"?

   _____

   _____

   _____

2. How many people do you know who are mentally or physically disabled? Are any of these people your close friends?

   _____

   _____

   _____

3. How have the disabled been portrayed on television and in movies?

   _____

   _____

   _____

Because I hate being crippled, I sometimes hate myself for being a cripple. Over the years I have come to expect—even accept—attacks of violent self-loathing. Luckily, in general our society no longer connects deformity and disease directly with evil (though a charismatic once told me that I have MS because a devil is in me) and so I'm allowed to move largely at will, even among small children. But I'm not sure that this revision of attitude has been particularly helpful. Physical imperfection, even freed of moral disapproba-tion, still defies and violates the ideal, especially for women, whose confine-ment in their bodies as objects of desire is far from over. Each age, of course, has its ideal, and I doubt that ours is any better or worse than any other. Today's ideal woman, who lives on the glossy pages of dozens of magazines, seems to be between the ages of eighteen and twenty-five; her hair has body, her teeth flash white, her breath smells minty, her underarms are dry; she has a career but is still a fabulous cook, especially of meals that take less than twenty minutes to prepare; she does not ordinarily appear to have a husband or children; she is trim and deeply tanned; she jogs, swims, plays tennis, rides a bicycle, sails but does not bowl; she travels widely, even to out-of-the-way places like Finland and Samoa, always in the company of the ideal man, who possesses a nearly identical set of characteristics. There are a few exceptions. Though usually white and often blonde, she may be black, Hispanic, Asian, or Native American, so long as she is unusually sleek. She may be old, provided she is selling a laxative or is Lauren Bacall. If she is selling a detergent, she may be married and have a flock of strikingly messy children. But she is never a cripple.

Critical Thinking Questions

1. What is the topic of this selection? The main idea?

_____

_____

_____

2. What supporting details provide evidence for the main idea?

_____

_____

_____

3. Why does the author feel that discrimination against the physically disabled is sexist in nature?

_____

_____

_____

4. Compare discrimination against the disabled with any other group.

_____

_____

_____

REFERENCE

Smith, B., & Chase, N. (1991). The frequency and placement of main idea topic sentences in college psychology textbooks. *Journal of College Reading and Learning, 24,* 46–54.

CREDITS

Ember, C. R., & Ember, M. (1996). *Cultural Anthropology* (8th ed.). Upper Saddle River, NJ: Prentice-Hall, Inc.

Mairs, N. (1995). Disabledness as a violation of the ideal. In L. Brandon (ed.), *Celebrating Diversity: A Multicultural Reader.* Lexington, MA: D.C. Heath and Company.

Graphic Illustrations in Textbooks

CHAPTER OBJECTIVES

- To understand the purposes and guidelines for reading graphic illustrations in textbooks
- To learn the common types of graphics used in textbooks
- To learn how to interpret the different types of graphics

A uthors of textbooks have two ways to explain facts and concepts: words and various types of illustrations. You have probably heard the saying, "A picture is worth a thousand words." Certain kinds of information can be understood more fully by looking at graphic illustrations. Many students gain insight from studying the graphics found in their textbooks, while others ignore them or fail to understand them. Your total comprehension of the material may depend on becoming competent in the interpretation of graphic illustrations.

Different types of graphics are used throughout the academic disciplines. Following are only a few examples:

THE PURE SCIENCES

- Table depicting the levels of organization of matter on Earth
- Linear graph showing progress of a reaction

- Process diagram of cell division
- Geologic map showing the Earth's strata

THE SOCIAL SCIENCES

- Table showing patterns in the division of labor by gender in different societies
- Geographic map of medieval trade routes
- Diagram of checks and balances in the U.S. government
- Bar graph of drug-related arrests by age group

THE FINE ARTS

- Chart used as a musical listening guide
- Map of Renaissance Italy
- Time line of visual art and architecture of the Middle Ages
- Diagram of the color spectrum

ENGLISH AND FOREIGN LANGUAGES

- Circle graph of the world's major languages and the percentages who speak them
- Table of irregular verbs
- Flowchart of steps in the process approach to writing
- Process diagram of language origins

MATHEMATICS

- Table of trigonometric functions for each quadrant
- Graphs to be matched to polar equations
- Table listing degree and radian measures of common angles
- Statistical tables of significance

BUSINESS

- Table of corporate tax rates
- Line graph showing the cost of capital
- Bar graph comparing stocks of different firms
- Diagram of a convertible bond

This chapter will examine the various purposes of graphics, present some guidelines for reading them, and give examples of different types of graphics along with practice in interpreting and using their information.

 ## PURPOSES OF GRAPHIC ILLUSTRATIONS

1. Graphics present material in another form, accommodating more learning styles.
2. Graphics sometimes present *additional* information.
3. Graphics often *stress* important information.
4. Graphics can summarize large amounts of material.
5. Graphics may reinforce ideas already described in the text paragraphs.
6. Graphics allow you to view trends and patterns.
7. Graphics are frequently used to introduce or reinforce new terminology.

 ## SIX GUIDELINES FOR READING GRAPHICS

1. Read the title and any subtitles. Titles and subtitles will give you the purpose of the graph or the topic of concern of the graph.

2. Read any accompanying information on or around the graphic. Bar graphs have important information written on both the vertical and the horizontal axis. Without this information, understanding the bar graph would be impossible. Some graphs have footnotes below the graphics, telling where the information was obtained. This is important because you can often judge the reliability of the information by the source. Many graphics are accompanied by problems or questions that you will have to study carefully.

3. Read any legend that is part of a graphic display. Some graphics have a **legend**, which is a caption that explains how certain symbols, drawings, or abbreviations are to be used. For example, on a typical road map, there are different types of lines for interstate highways and various other roads. There are also designations for landmarks, hospitals, and other points of interest.

4. Realize that different types of graphics are used for different purposes. Circle graphs are excellent for depicting budgets, but they could not easily show trends over a period of time. Sometimes you can get the needed information only on maps; certain types of maps (such as ones depicting the inner layers of the Earth) are very specialized.

5. Observe markings used on some graphics. An example of markings is the use of arrows in process charts. You should know or find out what the arrows mean so that you can follow the train of thought. Some graphs will use both solid and broken lines, each having a different function.

6. Be able to draw conclusions after processing a graphic display. If you follow the preceding steps, you should acquire enough information to make some judgments about trends, causes, and implications. Practice doing this because college professors will expect you to go beyond literal questions and answer higher-level interpretation questions.

TYPES OF GRAPHICS

There are four types of graphs: pictographs, circle or pie graphs, bar graphs, and line graphs. Each type has variations, depending on the purpose and academic discipline.

Pictographs use pictures to represent amounts. For example, a little stick-man may represent one thousand people on the graph. As long as you read the legend, you should have no trouble with pictographs. Indeed, they are considered the easiest to read.

Bar graphs may have either vertical or horizontal bars. Observe Figure 6.1 and answer the questions that follow.

Figure 6.1   *Sample bar graph.*

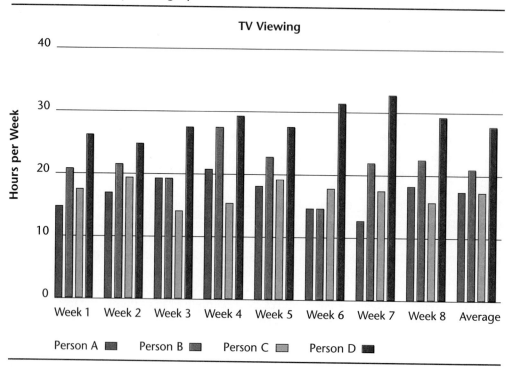

TV Viewing

Hours per Week

Week 1 Week 2 Week 3 Week 4 Week 5 Week 6 Week 7 Week 8 Average

Person A ▪   Person B ▪   Person C ▫   Person D ▪

Answer the following questions by responding *T* (true) or *F* (false):

_____ 1. Person D watched more TV on the average than the other three people.

_____ 2. Person B watched more TV on two of the weeks than did Person D.

_____ 3. The week that had the total highest number of hours watched was Week 5.

_____ 4. You can determine the age of the viewers by this bar graph.

_____ 5. Person A always watched less TV than the other three people.

Line graphs, or **linear graphs**, are graphs that show points representing the frequency of relations or connections among data by using lines, dots, or dashes to connect points. Line graphs may have a single line or several lines (called a **stacked line graph**). Figure 6.2 is a simple line graph, while Figure 6.3 is a stacked line graph.

Figure 6.2 *Sample line graph.*

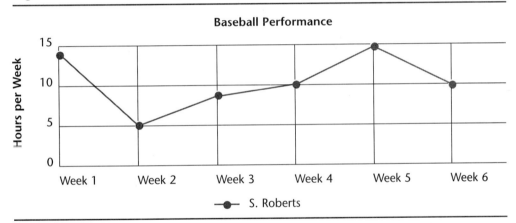

Answer the following questions with *T* (true) or *F* (false):

_____ 1. The line graph compares S. Roberts with another player.

_____ 2. The graph shows the player's hits, runs, and errors.

_____ 3. Week 5 was the best week for this player.

_____ 4. You can tell from the graph that the player is consistently improving over the weeks.

_____ 5. During Week 1, S. Roberts got approximately 17 hits.

Figure 6.3 *Sample stacked line graph.*

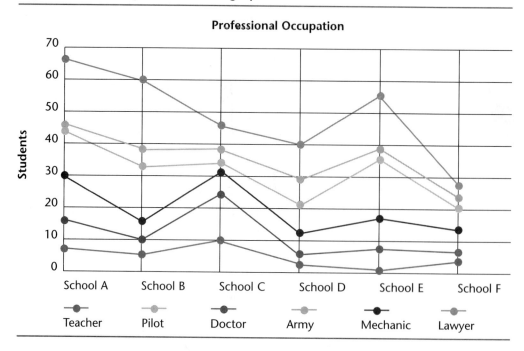

Answer the following questions about the stacked line graph:

1. Which is the most popular occupation at all six schools? _____
2. Which is the least popular? _____
3. Approximately how many students in School C preferred to be doctors?

   _____

4. Look at all of the responses on the graph and predict a reason for the trend you observed. _____

A **circle graph**, also called a **pie graph**, is a circle that is divided in the manner of a pie to show the size of the parts and the relationship among the parts. Other information, such as numbers and percentages, can also be included. Figure 6.4 is a circle graph.

Answer the following questions about the circle graph:

1. In which industry are there the fewest job opportunities? _____
2. What societal trend could explain the situation in Question 1? _____

   _____

3. What percentage of opportunities is in the hotel and restaurant businesses combined? _____

Figure 6.4   *Sample circle graph.*

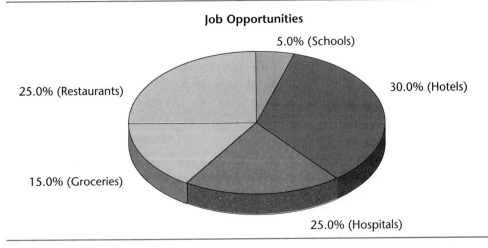

Job Opportunities

5.0% (Schools)

25.0% (Restaurants)

30.0% (Hotels)

15.0% (Groceries)

25.0% (Hospitals)

4. Choose one of the industries on the graph, and predict whether the trend will continue in the same direction. Give a reason for your answer. _____

A **table** is a systematic listing of data in rows and columns. Tables are sometimes preferable to graphs because tables can contain much larger amounts of information without becoming difficult to read and interpret. The orderly arrangement of rows and columns makes the task of locating information easy despite the amounts of data. See Figure 6.5 for an example of a table.

Figure 6.5   *Sample table.*

Vacation Preferences in Poll

	Age Group				
	13–18	19–30	31–45	46–60	60+
Disney World	85%	65%	35%	30%	60%
Yosemite	1%	5%	6%	5%	0%
New York City	4%	2%	15%	5%	5%
Miami	5%	5%	0%	10%	5%
Key West	0%	0%	4%	10%	0%
Colorado	2%	8%	18%	16%	0%
Yellowstone	1%	5%	12%	0%	10%
Grand Canyon	2%	5%	4%	24%	10%
Niagara Falls	0%	5%	6%	0%	10%

Answer the following questions after studying the table:

1. With which age group is Niagara Falls the most popular? _____

2. What is the most popular vacation spot for all age groups surveyed?

   _____

3. What is the least popular vacation spot for the 31–45 age group?

   _____

4. Which age groups had 0% choosing Key West as a vacation destination?

   _____

Maps are most frequently used in social studies books but may be used in any academic discipline. In fact, a map may appear in a textbook in which you would not expect to find maps. An example of this is a map of Renaissance Italy in an art book. Many people have trouble with maps, but five hints can make the comprehension of maps an easier task:

1. Read the title of the map, which can be in any location on the page—the top of the map, beneath the map, or on either side.
2. Familiarize yourself with the legend and the general layout of the map.
3. Understand the purpose of the map.
4. Carefully read the **scale**, the relationship of a distance on the map to the distance on the Earth; for example, one inch may equal one hundred miles.
5. Before attempting to comprehend a map, look up the definitions of any map terms you observe on the map but do not know. For example, you may encounter words like *longitude, latitude, equator, hemisphere*, and various others.

Study the map in Figure 6.6, and then answer the questions that follow.

1. What is the purpose of the skull and crossbones symbol? _____

   _____

2. What is the overall purpose of the map? _____

   _____

3. What is the scale of the map? _____

4. Compose three questions you need to answer, from reading the text chapter, which would help you understand the map. _____

   _____

Diagrams are used to help students understand processes, relationships, a sequence of events, or for some other reason. The type of diagram can be as

Figure 6.6 *Sample map.**

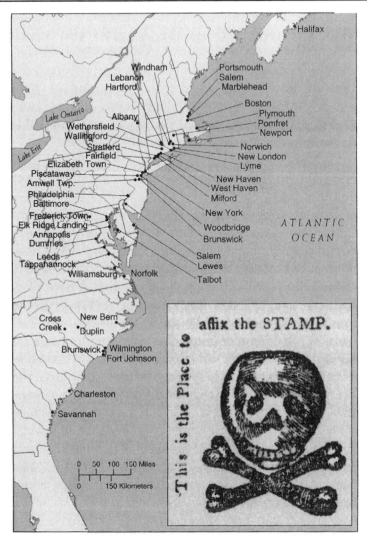

Demonstrations against the Stamp Act, 1765 *From Halifax in the North to Savannah in the South, popular demonstrations against the Stamp Act forced the resignation of British tax officials. One newspaper editor cynically proposed that the stamp itself be in the form of a skull and crossbones (inset).*

**OUT OF MANY: 2/E, A HISTORY OF THE AMERICAN PEOPLE—COMBINED EDITION by Faragher/Buhle/Czitrom/Armitage, © 1997. Reprinted by permission of Prentice-Hall, Inc., Upper Saddle River, NJ.

Figure 6.7 *Sample diagram.*

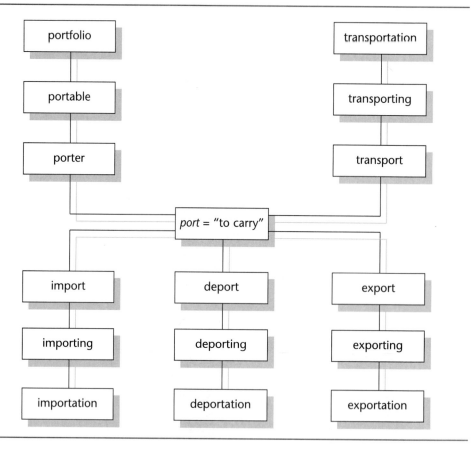

varied as the academic disciplines; for example, a diagram in science can show the muscular system with all of the muscles pinpointed and labeled. The diagram in Figure 6.7 shows how numerous English words can be derived from a single Latin root word.

SUMMARY

Textbooks in all academic disciplines illustrate, clarify, and provide additional information through the use of graphic illustrations of many types. Students should learn how the graphics are used and how to interpret them. This chapter presented the most common forms of graphics and gave guidelines to aid in interpreting them, thereby enhancing textbook learning. Examples of the most common forms of graphs, tables, maps, and diagrams were accompanied by practice questions.

Cooperative Learning Activities

ALL GROUPS. Each group should select one form of graphic illustration that was presented in this chapter. Using a textbook from a course you are now taking, graphically represent one section of a chapter. (If necessary, review the uses of the different types of graphics.) Be prepared to explain your graphic to the other groups, and be able to defend your choice of a particular graphic illustration for your textbook section.

Reading Selection: *Humor*

Title: Excerpt from *Family: The Ties That Bind — and Gag!**
Author: Erma Bombeck

Activation of Prior Knowledge and Interest

1. What humorous books or articles have you read and enjoyed?

   _____

   _____

   _____

2. Have you ever taken a car trip with your family? If so, relate something about your experiences.

   _____

   _____

   _____

3. What seemingly serious episode from your past experience now appears to be funny?

   _____

   _____

   _____

---

*Bombeck, Erma, FAMILY: THE TIES THAT BIND—AND GAG!, 1987. Reprinted with permission of The Aaron M. Priest Literary Agency, Inc., New York, NY.

In truth, I stopped reading road maps in 1977 when my husband accused me of moving the Mississippi River over two states.

It wasn't the first time he yelled at me for tampering with locations. We once quarreled over whether a prominent arch was a McDonald's or the gateway to St. Louis. Another time we had an ugly scene when I wrapped my gum in the Great Lakes and we couldn't find our way to the Canadian border.

Reading road maps is like being a vice president. You wear navy and keep your mouth shut. The only time you are consulted is when the driver is approaching a fork in the road at 55 mph and shouts, "OK, you wanted to drive—now which way do we turn?"

It's funny, but the anatomy of our life together can be summed up in the road map experience.

The first year of our marriage, I told my husband I got nauseated when I read in a moving car and he laughed and said, "Sweetheart, I don't want you to do anything but just sit there and talk to me. Just leave the driving to me."

A few years later, when we had three children fighting over two car windows, he started to delegate things for me to do. One was to "keep those kids from killing one another."

A few years later, he added, "Entertain them or give them a sedative."

Then one day he said, "Start looking for the turnoff." When I said I didn't know what turnoff he was talking about, he said, "Look in the glove compartment for the map. It's marked."

"You know I get nauseated when I read in a moving car," I said.

For the next ten years, I was never to see another monument, scenic wonder, Stuckey's, cathedral, sunset, or spacious sky. I sat for hours hunched over a mural of wavy lines, little circles, numbers too small to read, and distances too long to care.

I was to discover road maps made people say things they did not mean.

"We missed Fort Lauderdale. That's what I'd expect from a woman whose mother swims out to meet troop ships."

"Oh sure, I'll get in the left lane—when you get out of the sack in the morning and make my breakfast, I'll get in the left lane."

"So which way do I go, Erma? Left or right? I'll give you a hint. You pat the dog with your left hand. You dry your fingernails out of the car window with your right."

It's been ten years since I stuffed a road map up his nose. Ten years of riding in silence. That is not to say there is peace in the backseat of the car. Children do not go on a vacation to have a good time. If parents really wanted them to have a good time, they would leave them at home. Each rebels in his or her own way.

No self-respecting family would think of going on a vacation without the "Seat Kicker." The Seat Kicker is a forerunner of the bionic leg. He positions himself just behind Daddy's seat and has been clocked at 200 kicks per minute for as long as 400 miles. The motion affects his hearing.

And not to be missed is the child we call the "Hysteria Connection." You have just turned onto the freeway when she leans over to where Daddy is smiling in anticipation of a week without pressure and says, "Did you mean to leave the garden hose running, Daddy?" Daddy will not smile again on the trip.

She hears a strange knock in the engine that was the same knock her friend, Robin, heard just before the transmission went out of their car. She hears a newscast issuing tornado warnings for the place you are headed. She notes that the farther you go, the higher the price of gasoline gets, and her asthma seems to be getting worse and she probably will not be able to breathe in the cabin you have rented.

Occasionally, she turns to her brother and asks, "Did you tell Mom about the cat you have hiding under your bed?" or to her sister, "Everyone who's been accepted to State next fall has been notified by now."

She hears sirens before anyone else in the car and smells burning rubber. She reassures her mother that the Ryans' dog had a hysterectomy and she got fat, too!

And just when you think the Hysteria Connection has dispensed all the good news a family can stand on a vacation, she says, "I didn't want to mention it, but when Daddy was hiding the key under the flowerpot by the door, I saw a man watching him from a parked car across the street." Then she adds cheerfully, "I wouldn't worry. I've been exposed to measles and if I'm on schedule, the rash should appear tonight and we should all be coming home tomorrow."

All of this makes you wonder why you cleaned out the fireplace, sucked the dust out from under the freezer, glued the tile down in the bathroom, fluffed up all the pillows, bought new underwear for the entire family, and ate three black bananas before the housesitter came. Maybe to give your kids something "interesting" to remember.

Critical Thinking Questions

1. Humorous writing contains many clues that the events depicted are not to be taken seriously. Name as many clues as you can from this selection that would identify the writing as humor.

   _____

   _____

   _____

2. What strategies could be used to master the art of reading road maps? Refer to this chapter if necessary.

_____

_____

_____

3. Who would be more annoying to you, the Seat Kicker or the Hysteria Connection? Why?

_____

_____

_____

CREDITS

Bombeck, E. (1987). *Family: The Ties That Bind—and Gag!* New York: Ballantine Books.

Faragher, J. M., Buhle, M. J., Czitrom, D., & Armitage, S. H. (1997). *Out of Many: A History of the American People* (2nd ed.). Upper Saddle River, NJ: Prentice-Hall, Inc.

Organizational Patterns in Textbooks

CHAPTER OBJECTIVES

■ To understand the ways a student can benefit from knowledge of organizational patterns in textbooks

■ To identify the most common organizational patterns

■ To comprehend and organize textbook material according to organizational patterns

■ To take notes and create graphic illustrations for the common patterns

Research indicates that students who can recognize and identify the most common organizational patterns of textbook writing can comprehend the material better and can also recall the information better. The performance of these students on summarizing and other comprehension tasks is superior to that of students who are not knowledgeable about text structure (Shannon, 1986). Other research shows that learning to recognize organizational patterns increases students' understanding of the main idea (Readence, Bean, & Baldwin, 1981). A knowledge of main ideas is essential to comprehending, note taking from lectures, processing textbooks, summarizing, and writing research papers—all vital college skills for the successful student.

This chapter covers the eight most common organizational patterns: simple listing, order/sequence, comparison/contrast, cause and effect, problem and solution, classification, definition, and example. All of the patterns are found in all disciplines, so examples are provided from a variety of college textbooks.

SIMPLE LISTING

Textbooks provide lists of people, places, theories, reasons, causes, mathematical operations, scientific elements, and so forth. Any group can be placed in a list. With the pattern called *listing* or *simple listing*, sequential order is unimportant—the list could be rearranged without affecting meaning. The list may or may not be numbered. Textbooks often list within paragraphs without any numbers or other divisions. In this case, you must look for signal words that indicate a forthcoming list, such as those below:

afterwards	during	meanwhile
before	first, second, third, etc.	then
by the time	later	while

You are already familiar with lists used in everyday situations, such as *lists of foods needed to prepare a recipe, lists of current movies, lists of best-selling books*, and *lists of places to spend a vacation*. Your next task is to learn to locate and comprehend lists in textbooks, such as the following examples:

- List of famous theorists in psychology
- Layers of the Earth
- Planets in the solar system
- Physical illnesses
- World religions
- Countries in Europe
- Occupations in the pure sciences

In all of the above examples, order is unimportant. For instance, a list of the countries in Europe could be named and discussed in any order.

When organizing material that is a simple list, you can take notes and number the items as you encounter them in the text or the lecture. You can also make a graphic representation. The graphic forms of organizing material that are included throughout this chapter will be developed for the paragraphs immediately preceding, unless otherwise noted. The following two examples were taken from college textbooks:

A trigonometry textbook lists the following important functions: linear function, constant function, identify function, square function, cube function, square root function, reciprocal function, and absolute function. [*Trigonometry,* by Sullivan & Sullivan, 1996]

Trigonometry Functions
Linear function
Constant function
Identify function
Square function
Cube function
Square root function
Reciprocal function
Absolute function

Today, four main rationales for abolishing capital punishment are heard:

1. The death penalty can and has been inflicted on innocent people.

2. Evidence has shown that the death penalty is not an effective deterrent.

3. The imposition of the death penalty is, by the nature of our legal system, completely arbitrary and even discriminatory.

4. Human life is sacred, and killing at the hands of the state is not a righteous act, but rather one that is on the same moral level as the crimes committed by the condemned.

The first three abolitionist claims are pragmatic; that is, they can be measured and verified by looking at the facts. The last claim is primarily philosophical and therefore not amenable to scientific investigation. [*Criminal Justice Today* (4th ed.) by Schmalleger]

Reasons for Abolishing Capital Punishment
1. Wrongly accused person
2. Not effective as deterrent
3. Arbitrary and discriminatory
4. Killing immoral

pragmatic { 1–3 }   philosophical — 4

ORDER/SEQUENCE

This organizational pattern is called by several different names: *order, chrono-logical order, time order,* and *sequence.* **Order/sequence** is very similar to simple listing except that, unlike listing, order is very crucial. The steps could not be placed in a different order and remain as logical. The signal words may be the same as with simple listing, but some additional words may indicate that the sequence must be followed. Some examples of these words are *next, eventually,* and *ultimately.* Following are some examples of books or other written material whose content must be sequential:

- How-to books
- Directions on recipes
- Instructions for assembling products
- Directions for locating specific places
- Sequence of courses leading to a particular major
- Medical instructions given to a patient on how to clean a wound
- Instructions for planting and growing vegetables

Some examples of order/sequence from textbooks will illustrate the widespread use of this organizational pattern:

- Development of language in children
- Order of events in history
- Steps in teaching a child to read
- Steps in evolution of life forms
- Order of operations in mathematics
- Events leading to a major war

The two examples that follow are taken from college textbooks; note the orderly mention of dates as well as the signal words used:

Unique among the seventeenth-century colonies in North America, Massachusetts built an impressive system to educate its young. In 1647 the colony required that towns with fifty families or more support a public school, those with one hundred families were to establish a "grammar" school that taught Latin, knowledge of which was required for admission to Harvard College, founded in 1636. Connecticut enacted similar requirements. Literacy was higher in New England than elsewhere in the colonies, or even much of Europe. Far fewer New England women than men could read and write, however, because girls were excluded from the grammar schools. By 1639 the first printing press in the English colonies was in operation in Boston, and the following year it brought out the first American English publication, *The Bay Psalm Book*. [*Out of Many: A History of the American People* (2nd ed.) by J. M. Faragher et al.]

In the evolution of most landforms, mass wasting is the step that follows weathering. By itself, weathering does not produce significant landforms. Rather, landforms develop as the products of weathering are removed from the places where they originate. Once weathering weakens and breaks rock apart, mass wasting transfers the debris downslope, where a stream, acting as a conveyor belt, usually carries it away. Although there may be many intermediate stops along the way, the sediment is eventually transported to its ultimate destination, the sea. [*Earth Science* (8th ed.) by E. J. Tarbuck & F. K. Lutgens]

In the last paragraph, notice that none of the common signal words are used. However, the words *steps* and *follow* are clear indicators that the activity being described is a process that occurs in a sequential manner.

If you benefit from taking notes graphically, time lines can be constructed for any material that shows a series of events occurring in a particular order or for a process involving a series of steps. This is especially helpful for students who are visual and/or spatial learners. If you prefer, you may even use arrows to indicate the order in a process.

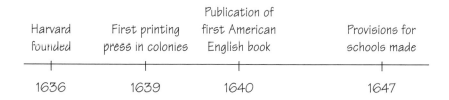

Harvard founded	First printing press in colonies	Publication of first American English book	Provisions for schools made
1636	1639	1640	1647

Weathering >>> Products removed from where they originated. >>> Wasting transfers debris. >>> Stream carries away debris. >>> Sediment transported to sea.

COMPARISON/CONTRAST

A **comparison** tells how two or more things are alike; a **contrast** tells how two or more things are different. The two forms of writing may be used either together or separately. In everyday life, people compare and contrast *restaurants,* *movies, television programs, books, potential vacation spots, sports teams*, and many other people, places, and things. Some of the signal words for comparison/contrast follow:

like	unlike	both
contrasted with	similarly	on the other hand
same	different	opposite
as with	as opposed to	likewise

The organizational pattern is widespread in textbooks. A few examples are given:

- Different forms of government
- Differences between a neurosis and a psychosis
- Various methods of teaching reading
- How certain diseases are alike and/or different
- Similarities of two U.S. presidents
- Different note-taking methods

What clues help you identify the following paragraphs as being of the comparison/contrast pattern of organization?

Union membership is optional in states whose laws permit the **open shop**, where union membership cannot be required as a condition of employment. (In states that permit the **closed shop**, all workers can be required to join the union.) In an open-shop setting the union represents only those workers who choose to affiliate when it negotiates for its members, but any concessions it gains from management are shared by all employees—union and nonunion. Many workers choose not to affiliate with the union when they can secure the same pay without incurring the costs associated with union membership. [*Government by the People* (16th ed.) by J. M. Burns et al.]

There were genuine differences between the Whigs and the Democrats, but they were not sectional differences. Instead, the two parties reflected just-emerging class and cultural differences. The Democrats, as they themselves were quick to point out, had inherited Thomas Jefferson's belief in the democratic rights of the small, independent yeoman farmer. As most of the country was rural, it is not surprising that the Democrats had nationwide appeal, especially in the South and West, the most rural regions. As a result of Jackson's presidency, Democrats came to be identified with independence and a distaste for interference, whether from the government or from economic monopolies such as the Bank of the United States. They favored expansion, Indian removal, and the freedom to do as they chose on the frontier. In the politics of the time, these were conservative values. They expressed the opposition of most Democratic voters to the rapid social and economic changes that accompanied the transportation revolution.

The Whigs were more receptive to economic change, in which they were often participants. Heirs of the Federalist belief in the importance of a strong federal government in the national economy, they supported Henry Clay's American System: a strong central government, the Bank of the United States, a protective tariff, and internal improvements. [*Out of Many: A History of the American People* (2nd ed.) by J. M. Faragher et al.]

If you had any trouble identifying the comparison/contrast patterns, ask yourself three questions to help with comprehension:

1. What two things, people, or ideas are being discussed and compared?
2. Why are they being compared?
3. How are they alike and/or different?

When you are taking notes on material written by comparison/contrast patterns of organization, there are several ways you might display the material. Two popular methods follow, corresponding to the two paragraphs used to illustrate this pattern. The first is called a **Venn diagram**: In one circle, you note everything important about the first thing being compared, in this case the "open shop," and in the second circle, you note important facts about

Figure 7.1 *Sample Venn diagram.*

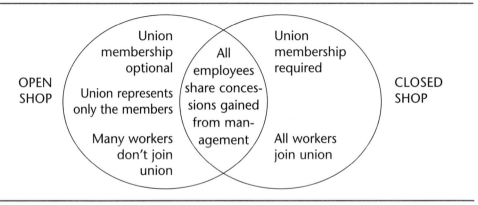

the second thing being compared, the "closed shop"; in the smaller space in the middle, shared by both circles, you write the things the two have in common. Of course, if you are reading a comparison/contrast selection in which there are more similarities than differences, you may draw the middle portion of the diagram much larger. All graphic aids can be modified to help you learn most effectively.

The next display is simply a two-column chart; it could also be modified in any way you choose (for example, if you are comparing/contrasting three or more things, you can use more columns):

Figure 7.2 *Sample chart.*

Whigs	Democrats
Receptive to economic change.	Supported rights of small, independent yeoman farmer.
Believed in strong federal government in national economy.	Disliked government interference.
Supported Bank of the U.S.	Supported by those in South and West.
Supported protective tariff.	Favored expansion.
Wanted internal improvements.	Favored Indian removal.

CAUSE AND EFFECT

The **cause** is the person, thing, or event responsible for something; the result of the cause is the **effect**. Some students prefer to call this organizational pattern "cause and result." Following are some of the signal words for this pattern:

because	causes	creates
since	leads to	stems from
produces	results in	hence
consequently	for this reason	therefore
due to	affects	thus

As you read, study, or take notes, remember that any of the following four combinations of causes and effects are found in textbooks:

1. *Single cause and single effect.*
   Example: Reviewing on a regular basis caused me to earn a good grade.
   Cause: reviewing on a regular basis
   Effect: earning a good grade

   review >>> good grades

2. *Single cause and multiple (two or more) effects.*
   Example: The power failure caused the kids to be late for school, the parents to be late for work, and the whole family to be very grouchy.
   Cause: power failure
   Effects: kids late for school, parents late for work, everyone grouchy

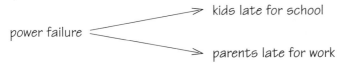

3. *Multiple causes and single effect.*
   Example: Lance failed all of his courses after a semester of partying and missing classes.
   Causes: partying and missing classes
   Effect: failing all courses

4. *Multiple causes and multiple effects.*
   Example: Eating healthy foods, getting enough exercise, and getting yearly medical checkups can lead to lower cholesterol levels, a healthier heart, and more stamina.
   Causes: eating healthy foods, getting enough exercise, and getting yearly medical checkups
   Effects: lower cholesterol levels, a healthier heart, and more stamina

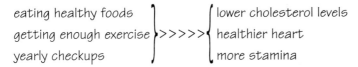

The following are examples of ways in which the cause and effect pattern is used in textbooks:

- Mathematics—What step was missed, resulting in an incorrect answer?
- Psychology—What causes psychotic behavior?
- Sociology—What causes criminal activity?
- Political science—What effect does a candidate's personal life have on the outcome of an election?
- Science—Why did the dinosaurs become extinct?
- Communication—How can language be inflammatory?

As you read the following textbook examples of the cause and effect pattern, look for clues that help you determine the organization of each paragraph:

> What have been the effects of recent campaign-finance reforms on interest groups? Ironically, that impact was not to decrease or restrict such groups but to enlarge their number and importance. The strategy of the 1971 law was to authorize direct and open participation by both labor and corporate organizations in elections and lobbying in the hopes that a visible or proper role for interest-group activity, backed by effective enforcement, would be constitutional under the First Amendment and effective in the world of practical politics. The 1971 act allowed unions and corporations to communicate on political matters to members or stockholders, to conduct registration and get-out-the-vote drives, and to spend union and company funds to set up "separated segregated funds" (PACs) to use for political purposes. [*Government by the People* (16th ed.) by J. M. Burns et al.]

In the preceding paragraph, there is a single cause, which is *recent campaign-finance reforms*. The effect or result was given generally as *to enlarge the number and importance of interest groups*. Further in the paragraph, this effect is explained in more specific terms: *to authorize direct and open participation by both labor and corporate organizations in elections and lobbying*. As the paragraph continues to the end, the effect becomes even more specific: *allowed unions and corporations to communicate on political matters to members or stockholders, to conduct registration and get-out-the-vote drives, and to spend union and company funds to set up "separated segregated funds" (PACs) to use for political purposes.*

One way of graphically illustrating the paragraph follows:

campaign-finance reforms >>> enlarging of number & importance
of interest groups

↓

authorized open participation
by labor and corporations in
elections and lobbying

↓

could

communicate   conduct   set up
politics to   voter   PACs
members   registration

Look for the cause(s) and effect(s) in the following paragraph from an anthropology textbook.

> It is apparent that the preagricultural switch to broad-spectrum collecting was fairly common throughout the world. Climate change was probably at least partly responsible for the exploitation of new sources of food. For example, the worldwide rise in sea level may have increased the availability of fish and shellfish. Changes in climate may have also been partly responsible for the decline in the availability of big game, particularly large herd animals. In addition, it has been suggested that another possible cause of that decline was human activity, specifically overkilling of some of these animals. The evidence suggesting overkill is that the extinction in the New World of many of the large Pleistocene animals, such as the mammoth, coincided with the movement of humans from the Bering Strait region to the southern tip of South America. [*Anthropology* (8th ed.) by C. R. Ember & M. Ember]

If you experienced any difficulty locating causes and effects, reread the paragraph, this time marking and underlining the events that you think are causes and effects. Some students like to draw an arrow from the cause to the effect in their notes or in their textbooks. Try to explain the material in the paragraph by using the following graphic display:

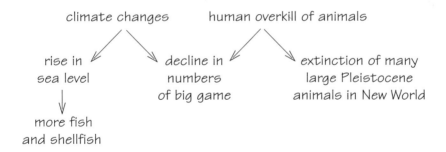

PROBLEM AND SOLUTION

The problem and solution pattern follows cause and effect in this chapter because it is a logical extension of cause and effect. Frequently a cause will be some type of **problem**, or dilemma, and after giving the effect, the paragraph may evolve into some **solution**, or answer. Thus, the next paragraph will be on the problem and solution pattern.

The signal words for problem and solution patterns are the same as for cause and effect, but here a solution is presented, so there may be additional signal words such as *solve, solution,* and *remedy.* In the following textbook paragraphs, read to locate the problem and its solution:

> Rehabilitation seeks to bring about fundamental changes in offenders and their behavior. As in the case of deterrence, the ultimate goal of rehabilitation is a reduction in the number of criminal offenses. Whereas deterrence depends upon a "fear of the law" and the consequences of violating it, rehabilitation generally works through education and psychological treatment to reduce the likelihood of future criminality. [*Criminal Justice Today* (4th ed.) by F. Schmalleger]

In the above paragraph, the problem is changing behavior in criminals so that they will no longer commit criminal acts; the solution is rehabilitation. In this paragraph, you could simply mark the problem and solution in your notes by the use of some abbreviation. If you had a long selection with multiple problems and multiple solutions, you might prefer to chart your notes in columns marked *Problems* and *Solutions*. Find the problem and the solution in the following paragraph:

> The central military issue facing the administration was how to raise and deploy U.S. armed forces. When war was declared, there were only about two hundred thousand men in the army. Traditionally, the United States had relied upon volunteer forces organized at the state level. But volunteer rates after April 6 were less than they had been for the Civil War or the Spanish-American War, reflecting the softness of prowar sentiment. The administration thus introduced the Selective Service Act, which provided for the registration and classification for military service of all men between ages twenty-one and thirty-five. Secretary of War Newton D. Baker was anxious to prevent the widespread, even violent, opposition to the draft that had occurred during the Civil War. Much of the anger over the Civil War draft stemmed from the unpopular provision that allowed draftees to buy their way out by paying $300 for a substitute. The new draft made no such allowances. Baker stressed the democratic procedures for registration and the active role of local draft boards in administering the process. [*Out of Many: A History of the American People* (2nd ed.) by J. M. Faragher et al.]

In the preceding history paragraph, the problem is getting enough people to serve in the armed forces; the solution is the Selective Service Act. Details are then given about the plan to make the draft more democratic than it had been during the Civil War.

 **CLASSIFICATION**

Classification is a method of placing things, people, or ideas into categories. For example, various household items are classified as furniture, appliances, bedding, and so on. People are classified by gender, race, occupation, nationality, religion, economic standing, and so forth. Some common signal words are listed below:

kinds	types	composed of
comprises	classified as	grouped as
arranged	indexed	classed

In everyday life, people read the classified ads in the newspaper to locate jobs (classified by occupation), pets, furniture, cars, and services. Movies are classified as appropriate for children, teenagers, or adults. Books are classified as fiction or nonfiction. The following are a few examples of how classification is used in college textbooks:

- Classification system for the animal kingdom
- Types of mental illnesses
- Schools of thought in psychology
- Types of marriages in anthropology texts
- Types of operations in math
- Types of literature
- Types of government
- Classification of crimes as felonies and misdemeanors

Read the next paragraphs and be able to tell both what is being classified and in what way:

Taxonomy (from the Greek word *taxis*, meaning "arrangement") is the science by which organisms are classified and placed into categories based on their structural similarities and evolutionary relationships. Taxonomic categories form a hierarchy—that is, a series of levels, each more inclusive than the last. There are seven major categories: **species, genus, family, order, class, division** or **phylum** (divisions are used for plants and plant-like microorganisms; phyla for animals and animal-like microorganisms), and **kingdom**. Each category from species to kingdom is increasingly more general and includes organisms whose common ancestor was increasingly remote in its evolutionary relationship. [*Life on Earth* by T. Audesirk and G. Audesirk]

In the preceding science paragraph, living things are being classified in a way that is familiar to all science students. You could organize your notes by placing the categories in the hierarchy in order from specific to general or from general to specific, and then write representatives under each category.

Read the following paragraphs:

> Violations of the criminal law can be of many different types and vary in severity. Five categories of violation will be discussed in the pages that follow. They are: misdemeanors, felonies, offenses, treason, and inchoate offenses.
>
> The general features of crime are: the criminal act, *mens rea,* concurrence, harm, causation, legality, and punishment. [*Criminal Justice Today* (4th ed.) by F. Schmalleger]

In the above selection, crime is categorized or classified in the first paragraph. The general features of crime are categorized in the second paragraph. The text then continues to explain and elaborate on each part of the two categories. The graphic display following is a beginning of this classification selection; you could continue to read the text and place such information as subcategories or details under each category:

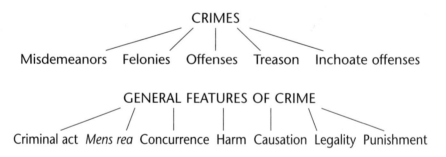

CRIMES

Misdemeanors   Felonies   Offenses   Treason   Inchoate offenses

GENERAL FEATURES OF CRIME

Criminal act   *Mens rea*   Concurrence   Harm   Causation   Legality   Punishment

DEFINITION

Definitions, the meanings of words, are probably most prevalent in introductory courses where a vast number of new terms are introduced. You should devise some special way to record and study all of the terms you will have to remember.

Do you always think of a definition as one sentence? Many of them are only one sentence but may be considerably longer. For instance, a definition of the psychology term, *manic depression,* might be an entire paragraph, an entire chapter, or a whole book—in fact, many books have been written to explain that one term. Instead of signal words, definitions usually are composed of two parts: (1) the general class and (2) characteristics. In the longer definitions, such as entire paragraphs or more, there is also much elaboration. Read the following paragraphs, which contain definitions:

> **Lobbyists** are the employees of associations who try to influence policy decisions and positions in the executive and especially in the legislative branches of our government. They are experienced in the ways of government, often having been public servants before going to work for an organized interest group or association or corporation. They might start as staff in Congress, perhaps on a Congressional committee. Later, when their party wins the White House, they gain an administration post, often in the same policy area as their Congressional committee work. After a few years in the administration, they are ready to make the move to lobbying, either by going to work for one of the interests they dealt with while in the government or by obtaining a position with a lobbying firm. The salary for a lobbyist who has extensive contacts in Congress and the administration can be two to three times what a member of Congress earns. [*Government by the People* (16th ed.) by J. M. Burns et al.]

> The nonreproductive cells of many organisms contain *pairs of chromosomes* that are the same length and that stain in the same pattern. Breeding and biochemical experiments show that the chromosomes of each pair also have similar, although usually not identical, genetic content. Therefore, the members of a pair are called **homologues**, meaning "to say the same thing" in Greek. Cells with pairs of homologous chromosomes are called **diploid**. The 46 chromosomes of the nonreproductive cells of human beings occur as 23 pairs of homologues. [*Life on Earth* by T. Audesirk and G. Audesirk]

Lobbyists

　Employees of associations who try to influence legislature

　　Experienced in government

　　Work for special-interest groups

Homologues

　Members of a pair of chromosomes

　　Similar genetic content

　　Usually not identical content

EXAMPLE

Examples, which are illustrations or instances, are very useful in learning new or difficult concepts. An example, like a definition, may be an entire paragraph or more, such as a case study in psychology. Some of the more common signal words for examples follow:

for example	for instance	such as
to name a few	to mention a few	in the manner of
to illustrate	to demonstrate	to show

The following examples are longer than one sentence (notice how the entire paragraph helps you to understand the ideas being presented):

> Physical differences, too, may be seen as results of adaptations to the environment. For example, in our society we admire people who are tall and slim. If these same individuals were forced to live above the Arctic Circle, however, they might wish they could trade their tall, slim bodies for short, compact ones because stocky physiques appear to conserve body heat more effectively and may therefore be more adaptive in cold climates. [*Anthropology* (8th ed.) by C. R. Ember & M. Ember]

> Finally, federalism permits the benefits and costs of government to be spread unevenly across the nation. For example, some states spend over twice as much on the education of each child in the public schools as other states. Welfare benefits in some states are more than twice as high as they are in other states. Taxes in some states are more than twice as high per capita as in other states. Competition among states may keep welfare benefits low in order not to encourage the immigration of poor people. Federalism obstructs uniformity in policy. [*Politics in America* (2nd ed.) by T. R. Dye]

In most cases, there is no need to make special notes on the examples. You would do this only if the concept being introduced is particularly difficult for you. In that case, marking an example might serve as a trigger for your memory.

MIXED PATTERNS

As you have probably noticed, paragraphs are frequently a combination of two or more different organizational patterns. One pattern may take precedence, but you should be able to recognize and comprehend all patterns. The following paragraph combines five organizational patterns: cause and effect, example, classification, definition, and listing. Read the paragraph and locate the different patterns:

> Religious beliefs and values may also shape political opinion. *Which religion an individual identifies with* (for example, Protestant, Catholic, Jewish) affects public opinion. So does *how important* religion is in the individual's life. It is difficult to explain exactly how religion affects political values, but we can observe differences in the opinions expressed by Protestants, Catholics, and Jews; by people who say their religious beliefs are strong versus those who say they are not; and between fundamentalists (those who believe in literal interpretation of the Bible) and nonfundamentalists. Religion shapes political attitudes on a variety of issues, including abortion, drugs, the death penalty, homosexuality, and prayer in public schools. Religion also plays a measurable role in political ideology.*

EXERCISE 7.1

Read each of the following paragraphs. Decide which organizational pattern is used, and write your answer on the line provided. If you think more than one pattern is used, tell all of the patterns you find. All of the paragraphs in the exercise are taken from the textbook, *Politics in America* (2nd ed.) by T. R. Dye.*

1. Throughout the centuries, thinkers in many different cultures contributed to the development of democratic government. Early Greek philosophers contributed the word **democracy**, which means "rule by the many." But there is no single definition of *democracy*, nor is there a tightly organized system of democratic thought. It is better, perhaps, to speak of democratic traditions than of a single democratic ideology.

2. The Constitution provides a number of arrangements designed to *limit the power of majorities*, including:

   a. *Representative democracy* (which the Founders called **republican government**), in which elected leaders rather than the people themselves decide public issues.

*POLITICS IN AMERICA: 2/E by Thomas R. Dye, © 1997. Reprinted by permission of Prentice-Hall, Inc., Upper Saddle River, NJ.

b. A *separation of powers* system, in which each decision-making body—the Congress, the president, and the Supreme Court—is selected by different means for different terms, so that a majority cannot change the nation's leadership easily or quickly.

c. A system of *checks and balances*, so that each branch of government can restrain actions of other branches.

d. *Federalism*, in which the national government shares power with state governments.

e. *Judicial review*, by which courts can declare laws and government actions that violate constitutional rights to be null and void. This arrangement is not made explicit in the Constitution but is implied from Article VI, declaring the Constitution to be "the supreme Law of the Land."

---

3. *Authoritarianism* is a form of government in which the rulers tolerate no public opposition and there are no legal means to remove these rulers from power. Some authoritarian regimes are *dictatorships* in which power is held by a single individual; others are *juntas* in which power is held by a small group of military officers. While authoritarian governments permit no challenges to their political rule, they generally allow people to go about their religious, social, business, and recreational activities relatively undisturbed. *Totalitarianism* is a form of authoritarian government in which the rulers recognize no limits to their authority and try to regulate virtually all aspects of social and economic life. The term *totalitarian* derives from the "totality" of the rulers' ambitions; they tolerate no opposition in any sphere of life and aim for complete control of the society and its future.

---

4. Following the Civil War, many of the women who had been active in the abolitionist movement to end slavery turned their attention to the condition of women in the United States. As abolitionists, they had learned to organize, conduct petition campaigns, and parade and demonstrate. Now they sought to improve the legal and political rights of women. In 1869, the Wyoming territory adopted women's suffrage; later several other Western states followed suit. But it was not until the Nineteenth Amendment was added to the U.S. Constitution in 1920 that women's right to vote in all elections was constitutionally guaranteed.

---

5. Hispanics—a term the U.S. Census Bureau uses to refer to Mexican Americans, Puerto Ricans, Cubans, and others of Spanish-speaking ancestry and culture—now comprise over 10 percent of the U.S. population. The largest Hispanic subgroup is Mexican Americans. Some are descendants of citizens who lived in the Mexican territory annexed to the United States in 1848, but most have come to the United States in accelerating numbers in recent years. The largest Mexican American populations are found in Texas, Arizona, New Mexico, and California. Puerto Ricans constitute the second-largest Hispanic subgroup. Many still retain ties to the Commonwealth and move back and forth from Puerto Rico to New York. Cubans make up the third-largest subgroup; most have fled from Fidel Castro's Cuba and live mainly in the Miami metropolitan area.

SUMMARY

Nonfiction materials, such as most textbooks, are written in common organizational patterns that students can learn to identify. This skill leads to greater comprehension, better recall of the information, and better performance on other reading tasks. The chapter included an explanation of each of the eight organizational patterns: simple listing, order/sequence, comparison/contrast, cause and effect, problem and solution, classification, definition, and example. Signal words were given for help in locating each pattern. Examples from everyday life as well as from textbooks were provided, along with explanations for how to locate and comprehend the organizational patterns.

There was also an emphasis on note taking by graphic illustrations, which serves as an alternative to the note-taking strategies offered in another chapter. Graphic displays can often further the student's understanding of the expository text.

Practice is required in this and any other study skill. This practice would be most effective if done while studying content area textbooks currently being used.

Cooperative Learning Activities

GROUP 1. Miguel does well on essay tests because he likes to write about causes of events, outcomes, and comparison/contrast issues. His problem is taking tests on which he must learn many details, such as names, dates, and places. His history grade is presently D, and he does not know how to improve the grade during the last half of the semester. Using what you know about organizational patterns, outline a study plan for Miguel that would help him in courses like history. Also include ideas on how he might create some interest in the many facts and details.

GROUP 2. Consider all of the organizational patterns used in textbooks. As a group, select three patterns and compose paragraphs *about study skills* using those three patterns of writing.

GROUP 3. Using any information you have covered in this textbook so far, list two study skills that would be effective when studying material written in each of the eight organizational patterns.

GROUP 4. Poll the members of the group to determine which organizational patterns they find:

1. Difficult to comprehend
2. Easy to comprehend
3. Most prevalent in the courses in which they are currently enrolled

Look through some of your current textbooks to support your answers.

GROUP 5. Each member of the group should use one of his or her content area textbooks. Sharing the textbooks, locate and note one example for each of the eight organizational patterns.

Reading Selection: *Political Science*

Title: *The Politics of Voter Turnout**
Author: Thomas R. Dye

Activation of Prior Knowledge and Interest

1. Why do you think so many people fail to vote?

   _____

   _____

   _____

2. Predict some types of organizational patterns that may be used in this selection. Tell why you predict certain patterns.

   _____

   _____

   _____

3. Do you vote? Why or why not?

   _____

   _____

   _____

Politics drives the debate over easing voter registration requirements. Democrats generally favor minimal requirements—for example, same-day registration, registration by mail, and registration at welfare and motor vehicle licensing offices. They know that nonvoters are heavily drawn from groups that typically support the Democratic Party, including lower-education, lower-income, and minority groups. Republicans are often less enthusiastic about easing voting requirements, but it is politically embarrassing to appear to oppose increased participation. It is not surprising that the National Voter Registration

*Politics in America: 2/e by Thomas R. Dye, © 1997. Reprinted by permission of Prentice-Hall, Inc., Upper Saddle River, NJ.

Act of 1993, popularly known as the "Motor-Voter Act," was a product of a Democratic Congress and a Democratic president.

The Stimulus of Competition. The more lively the competition between parties or between candidates, the greater the interest of citizens and the larger the voter turnout. When parties and candidates compete vigorously, they make news and are given large play by the mass media. Consequently, a setting of competitive politics generates more political stimuli than does a setting with weak competition. People are also more likely to perceive that their votes count in a close contest, and thus they are more likely to cast them. Moreover, when parties or candidates are fighting in a close contest, their supporters tend to spend more time and energy campaigning and getting out the vote.

Political Alienation. People who feel that politics is irrelevant to their life, or who feel that they cannot personally affect public affairs, are less likely to vote than people who feel that they themselves can affect political outcomes and that these outcomes affect their life. Given the level of **political alienation** (two-thirds of respondents agree with the statement "Most public officials are not really interested in the problems of people like me"), it is surprising that so many people vote. While alienation is high among voters, it is even higher among nonvoters.

Intensity. The general decline in U.S. voter turnout over the last several decades has generated a variety of explanations. This decline has occurred despite an easing of registration requirements and procedures over time. It may be a product of increasing distrust of government, which is related to political alienation. People who distrust the government are likely to feel that they have little influence in politics. They are therefore less likely to go to the trouble of registering and voting. The focus of the media, particularly television, on corruption in government, sex scandals involving politicians, conflicts of interest, waste and inefficiency, and negative campaign advertising may add to popular feelings of alienation.

Another explanation focuses on the expansion of the electorate to include young people eighteen to twenty-one years of age. Young people do not vote in the same proportions as older people. After the electorate was expanded by the Twenty-Sixth Amendment to include persons eighteen years of age and over, voter turnout actually dropped, from 60.9 percent in the 1968 presidential election to 55.2 percent in the 1972 presidential election, the largest turnout decline in successive presidential elections.

Still another explanation focuses on the declining role of party organizations in the political system. Strong party organizations, or *machines*, that canvassed neighborhoods, took citizens to the courthouse to register them, contacted them personally during campaigns, and saw to it that they got to the polls on election day have largely disappeared.

The rise in voter turnout in the 1992 presidential election is generally attributed to the presence in the race of a well-financed independent candidate, Ross Perot, and to popular concerns about the state of the economy. The Perot candidacy added interest and competition, as well as some uncertainty over the outcome. Perot also appealed to many people who tended to be distrustful of government and of the Democratic and Republican parties and to those who had not voted in recent elections. Moreover, slow recovery from recession worried many people during the election year, further motivating many to go to the polls and vote for change.

Critical Thinking Questions

1. Using information in the selection as proof, what do you think would improve voter turnout?

_____

_____

_____

2. Describe the significance of the Twenty-Sixth Amendment, and give a possible reason for the voting statistics that followed its passage.

_____

_____

_____

3. Do you think Ross Perot really contributed to the rise in voter turnout? Support your answer.

_____

_____

_____

_____

)f organization was most prevalent in the selection?

_____

_____

_____

REFERENCES

Audesirk, T., & Audesirk, G. (1997). *Life on Earth.* Upper Saddle River, NJ: Prentice-Hall, Inc.

Burns, J. M., Peltason, T. E., Cronin, T. E., & Magleby, D. B. (1995). *Government by the People* (16th ed.). Upper Saddle River, NJ: Prentice-Hall, Inc.

Ember, C. R., & Ember, M. (1996). *Anthropology* (8th ed.). Upper Saddle River, NJ: Prentice-Hall, Inc.

Faragher, J. M., Buhle, M. J., Czitrom, D., & Armitage, S. H. (1997). *Out of Many: A History of the American People* (2nd ed.). Upper Saddle River, NJ: Prentice-Hall, Inc.

Readence, J. E., Bean, T. W., & Baldwin, R. S. (1981). *Content Area Reading: An Integrated Approach.* Dubuque, IA: Kendall/Hunt Publishing Company.

Schmalleger, F. (1997). *Criminal Justice Today* (4th ed.). Upper Saddle River, NJ: Prentice-Hall, Inc.

Shannon, D. (1985). Use of top-level structure in expository text: An open letter to a high school teacher. *Journal of Reading, 28*(5),426-431.

Sullivan, M., & Sullivan, M. (1996). *Trigonometry.* Upper Saddle River, NJ: Prentice-Hall, Inc.

Tarbuck, E. J., & Lutgens, F. K. (1997). *Earth Science* (8th ed.). Upper Saddle River, NJ: Prentice-Hall, Inc.

CREDIT

Dye, T. R. (1997). *Politics in America* (2nd ed.). Upper Saddle River, NJ: Prentice-Hall, Inc.

Vocabulary Acquisition Strategies

CHAPTER OBJECTIVES

- To use context clues to determine the meanings of unknown words
- To employ structural analysis and knowledge of word parts to define words
- To learn common Latin and Greek roots, prefixes, and suffixes to build English vocabulary
- To use etymology as a vocabulary tool
- To learn specific vocabulary-building strategies
- To understand and use the dictionary

This chapter is dedicated to helping you increase your vocabulary. Methods will be explained that you can use to increase your general vocabulary and your specialized vocabulary. A **general vocabulary** consists of those words that can be shared by everyone and are not part of a particular academic discipline. A **specialized vocabulary** consists of those words belonging to a specific discipline. As you become an educated person, you should build both your general and your specialized vocabularies.

Take a minute to informally assess your present general vocabulary. Is your vocabulary sufficient only to read newspapers, everyday reading materials, and light novels, or can you read more complicated materials and comprehend them? If you have a rich vocabulary, you are not limited by difficult materials, and you will experience more and varied opportunities instead of encountering stumbling blocks.

Every academic discipline has its own terminology, just as various occupations have their own esoteric terms, those understood by members of the profession but not necessarily by those removed from the profession. College courses generally introduce a large amount of vocabulary, especially in the survey courses or introductory courses. For example, when you are enrolled in an introductory psychology course, you will be expected to learn most of the terminology used in that field. Subsequent psychology courses will seem easier if you master that vocabulary.

This chapter will stress many techniques to increase your vocabulary. These suggestions are presented in sections on context clues, structural analysis and derivatives, etymology, some deliberate vocabulary-building strategies, and dictionary methods. As you read each section, consider which techniques will benefit you most, according to your personal study preferences and your learning styles. However, you must actively develop *some* strategies to build a good vocabulary and to master the terminology presented in each of your college courses.

CONTEXT CLUES

One of the best ways to unlock the meaning of an unknown word in a sentence is to get clues from the other words in the sentence or the surrounding sentences; clues received in this way are called **context clues**. The context of the words and sentences around the unknown word provides hints about the meaning of the unfamiliar word. For example, a person who does not know the meaning of the word *apiary* could determine the meaning if the word appeared in the following sentence:

- Many people were stung when hundreds of bees flew out of the apiary.

The sentence makes it clear that the definition of *apiary* is *a place where bees are kept and raised for honey*.

Many students report that they are constantly looking up words in the glossary of textbooks when, in fact, most of the words are defined in the chapters. There are many kinds of context clues, some of which you may never have noticed.

Definitions stated in text. Often there is no need to search for context clues as you did in the example containing the word *apiary*. Definitions of words that are important terms in a chapter are often simply defined in the chapter discussion, although many students do not take note of this and proceed to look up words in the glossary. For example, a text may contain a sentence like the following:

- **Plasmids** are self-replicating parasites normally found in the cytoplasm of many bacteria.

Definitions set off by punctuation. Frequently the definition is set off by some type of punctuation, as in the following sentences:

- This is **natural selection**: the process by which the environment selects for those individuals whose traits best adapt them to that particular environment.
- Kendall is a **Rhodesian ridgeback**—a large dog having a smooth brown coat and a one-inch ridge of stiff hair running down its back along the spine.
- The group was used as a **scapegoat**, someone to blame for everything that goes wrong.
- We are going to study the **density** (number of people in a given area) of the population.

Restatement clues. The word being introduced may be restated, using some word or term like *that is*:

- That was John's personal **credo**, or belief.
- The country's form of government is an **autocracy**, that is, government by a single person having unlimited power.

Example clues. Examples are obviously helpful to many students because most textbooks contain numerous examples for important terms and concepts. In some cases, there may be extended examples, such as case studies in psychology. An example, like a picture, helps people to recall information they might otherwise have forgotten:

- "He is as sharp as a tack" is an example of a **simile**.
- He never reads a book but does enjoy **periodicals**. For example, he reads *Reader's Digest*, *Newsweek*, and *Sports Illustrated* every week.

Clues in sentences appearing before or after the sentence containing the unknown word or term. It is true that there are some sentences, when taken alone, which provide no context clues. Such a sentence is: *Tom got a Rhodesian ridgeback.*

From that sentence alone, the reader would not know if the Rhodesian ridgeback was a foreign car, an unusual rug, or some type of animal. In such cases, you should read the preceding sentence and/or the following sentence to get clues. This is illustrated in the following paragraph:

> Dad really enjoyed his trip to South America. Since it was his first visit there, he bought lots of souvenirs to remember his wonderful vacation. His favorite souvenir was the **serape** he bought the last day of his trip. The serape is a bright red and blue wool, and Dad plans to wear it as soon as the weather is cold enough.

After reading the preceding paragraph, you will know that the serape is a colorful garment that is worn to keep warm. Because of personal experience or observation, you may even conclude that it is a poncho. At the very least, you will know that it is some type of garment to wear when it is cold.

Comparison and contrast clues. In some sentences, you can determine the meaning of a word by the way it is being compared to another word, as in the following sentence:

- Like her **supercilious** sister, Phyllis is also haughty and snobby.

In the same manner, you may determine the meaning of a word because of a contrast, telling how two or more things are different, as in the following sentence:

- Maria is not at all like her **taciturn** mother; Maria is very talkative.

Familiar experience or prior knowledge. Other chapters in this book have included discussions about the benefits of having a wide range of experiences. This rich background can also help with vocabulary acquisition. You can often determine the meanings of unknown words because you know how you would feel or react under similar circumstances. All of the following sentences illustrate this point:

- Jan felt very **intimidated** by the poised, intelligent, and beautiful girl who seemed to be so popular.
- The **cacophonous** shrieking and cursing of the parrot made Luis want to put his head under a pillow to drown out the noise.
- Denise felt very **timorous** in the house, which was reportedly haunted.
- **Artificial respiration** saved the little boy who almost drowned in his aunt's pool.

Association. Similar to past experiences, making associations with something or someone familiar is a good way to determine meanings of unknown words. You may not know a word in the sentence, but you can use the other words and associate the new word with something familiar, as in the following examples:

- The **gargantuan** man looked like a professional football lineman.
- Although he was middle-aged, the man was as **effervescent** as a hyper-active two-year-old.
- The **pugnacious** pair seemed more like opposing members in a family feud than brothers.

Summary. Sometimes the sentence containing the unknown word will be in a paragraph that summarizes an idea or situation in such a way that the unknown word can be identified, as in the following paragraphs:

- Bob volunteers two afternoons a week at the nursing home because he believes the residents need someone with whom to talk. He often donates money to charity, and he heads a drive to raise money for the homeless. He enjoys helping all those who are less fortunate than he. Bob is very **altruistic**.
- The interior decorator was famous for her **polychromatic** decorating. The living room was done in blues, greens, and grays. The bedrooms were done in combinations of pinks, yellows, purples, and greens. The kitchen can best be described as a "riot of color." Once again, she has lived up to her reputation.

EXERCISE 8.1

The following sentences contain context clues of the types described above. Using the context of the other words in the sentence or sentences, write the definition of the italicized word on the line provided.

1. He was as *cantankerous* as an old grizzly bear that had been awakened from a nap.

   _____

2. Hank was very *loquacious*, not at all like his quiet, shy brother.

   _____

3. Since my own home is humble, visiting the million-dollar home of my friend gave me a *vicarious* thrill.

   _____

4. The mayor took bribes from citizens who wanted favors granted. He placed his close friends and family members in influential positions in the city. He engaged in some activities across the state line, once having to bribe another official to stay out of jail. The mayor is the most *disreputable* politician the town has ever known.

   _____

5. Aunt Lena has an appointment with the *ophthalmologist* next Wednesday. For several weeks now, she has been having more and more trouble with her eyes. She cannot see as well as before, and she is afraid she also has some type of eye infection.

   _____

6. The comic strip character, Dennis the Menace, is a *rambunctious* little boy.

   _____

7. Terry is very *belligerent*. For example, he has been in a fight or an argument every day this week.

   _____

8. The *omnipotent* king decreed that no citizen in the land could have any rights. The king declared that he, alone, has all the power.

   _____

9. That information is *irrelevant*; it has nothing to do with the case.

   _____

10. Unlike the previous professor, who was unsociable, Dr. Miller is *convivial*.

   _____

STRUCTURAL ANALYSIS AND DERIVATIVES

Many polysyllabic words appear to be ominous to students who have no prior experience in breaking the word down into parts. There are several terms you should learn concerning structural analysis. The term **affix** means a word part that is attached to the root, or main part of the word. An affix changes the meaning of a word in some way. It may only slightly alter the meaning, or it may change the meaning so much that the word becomes an opposite. An affix may be added to the beginning of a word, and this is called a **prefix**; if the affix is added to the end of a word, it is called a **suffix**. The original part of the word is called the **root** or **stem**. See the following examples:

PREFIX	ROOT	SUFFIX	WORD
un	comfort	able	uncomfortable
con	descend	ing	condescending
trans	scrib	er	transcriber

If you learn some of the most commonly used prefixes, roots, and suffixes, you can enlarge your vocabulary very fast. For example, some people try to learn ten new words a week. If they learned ten important *roots* per week, they could be increasing their vocabulary by dozens of words, instead of by just ten. Look at Figure 8.1 and Figure 8.2 to see how many words you can take into your vocabulary by learning a new root word. (There are actually more possibilities than represented in these two tables.)

Figure 8.1

Root word—**port**

porter	portable	porterage
portage	portfolio	portal
portamento	portative	portcullis
import	importing	importation
export	exporting	exportation
deport	deporting	deportation
portly	portmanteau	exportable

Figure 8.2

Root word—**circum**

circumambient	circumambience	circumcise
circumcision	circumduction	circumference
circumferential	circumflex	circumfuse
circumfusion	circumlocution	circumlocutory
circumlunar	circumnavigate	circumnutate
circumpolar	circumrotate	circumscissile
circumscribe	circumscription	circumsolar
circumspect	circumstance	circumvent

Look up any of the preceding words in the dictionary, and you will readily see the influence of the root word. For example, if you know that *circum* means "around," you will be able to define many of the words already. With the others, the knowledge of the root word will make your task much easier.

Most of the common prefixes and roots used in English came from Latin, and some came from Greek. When you learn some of the following, make an effort to learn more derivatives, thereby extending your vocabulary. The list is much too long to be reproduced here, but the following is a partial list of some of the more common word parts:

PREFIX	MEANING	EXAMPLE OF ENGLISH WORD
ab, ex, de	away from	aberration—a deviation from the normal expel—send away deport—send out of the country
ante	before	antecedent—an event prior to another
anti	against	antidote—an agent that works against poison
auto	self	autobiography—life story written by the person the story is about
circum	around	circumnavigate—to sail completely around
com	with	committee—group that works together
inter	between	intercept—to interrupt the progress of
micro	small	microscope—instrument for viewing small organisms
post	after	postscript—note written after closing a letter
pre	before	prerequisite—required as a prior condition
sub	under	subterranean—underground
trans	across	transcontinental—across the continent

Many prefixes can cause a word to become opposite in meaning. For example, all of the following prefixes mean *not,* which would form a word opposite in meaning to the original:

PREFIX MEANING "NOT"	EXAMPLE
a	amoral, amorphous
il	illegal, illegitimate
im	immature, impassable
in	indelicate, inefficient
ir	irredeemable, irrelevant
un	unbelievable, uncertain

Many prefixes refer to *numbers*, as the following examples demonstrate:

PREFIX	MEANING	EXAMPLE FROM ENGLISH
mono	1	monogamy—marriage to one person at a time
bi	2	bilingual—able to speak two languages
tri	3	triangle—-a three-sided figure
quad	4	quadruplets—four siblings born at the same time
penta	5	pentagon—five-sided figure
oct	8	octogenarian—person in his or her eighties
poly	many	polytheism—belief in many gods/goddesses

As an exercise in the usefulness of using prefixes to build vocabulary, use a dictionary to locate as many words as you can that begin with one of the above prefixes. As you read, for pleasure or for your classes, notice the use of prefixes, and use them to unlock the meanings of words you might otherwise skip.

EXERCISE 8.2

Review the prefixes listed, and then define the following words. Try to define the words without using a dictionary. If you do have to consult a dictionary to define some words, notice how knowledge of the prefix helps you learn and recall the definitions.

1. octagon _____

2. bicoastal _____

3. asexual _____

4. antiabortion _____

5. interoffice _____

6. microminiskirt _____

7. predate _____

8. transsexual _____

9. illegible _____

10. undeniable _____

You will find *root* words from Latin and Greek to be very widespread in the English language as well. A few are listed below.

ROOT	MEANING	EXAMPLE FROM ENGLISH
ast	star	astronomy—the scientific study of the stars and planets
aud	hear	audiology—the scientific study of hearing
cap	head	decapitate—to remove the head
cede, ceed	go	proceed—to go ahead
cent	100	bicentennial—200th anniversary or celebration
cide	to kill	homicide—murder
cise	to cut	incision—a surgical cut
dict	speak	contradiction—an asserting of the opposite; denial
fid	faithful	infidelity—act of being unfaithful
geo	earth	geology—scientific study of the Earth
graph	to write	autograph—one's signature
hom	man or same	homonyms—words that have the same sound
		homicide—murder
lib	free or book	liberation—freedom
		library—place to borrow books
milli	1,000	millimeter—1/1000 of a meter
miss, mit	send	transmission—act or process of sending
mort	death	mortician—funeral director
mut	change	immutable—not susceptible to change
nom	name	nomenclature—system of names
ped *(Latin)*	foot	pedestrian—a walker
ped *(Greek)*	child	pediatrician—a doctor for babies and children
port	carry	transportation—means of carrying goods or people
temp	time	extemporaneous—on the spur of the moment
term	end	exterminate—to kill or wipe out
voc	call	vocal—spoken

Even suffixes can help you extend your vocabulary. They change meaning in more subtle ways than many prefixes do, but they can help you extend and enlarge your vocabulary. See the following examples:

SUFFIX	MEANING	EXAMPLE FROM ENGLISH
able, ible	able to be	inexcusable, indefensible
al	relating to	medical, provincial
ance, ence	relating to	governance, dependence
ful	possessing	delightful, wonderful
ion	quality of	communion, communication
ity	quality of	ambiguity, animosity
ment	quality of	entertainment, amazement
ous	possessing	wondrous, laborious
y	possessing	healthy, wealthy

Special Questions or Concerns

Occasionally you may encounter a derivative that does not seem to maintain the original meaning, a situation that may make the definition of the new word more difficult to recall. For example, *cise* means "to cut." Therefore, you may question why a word such as *precise* or *concise* is derived from the root *cise*. The definition of the word *precise* is "clearly expressed." This means that the unimportant or extraneous information is "cut away" or removed, and you are left with the main points, as in the sentence, "Tell me precisely what you mean."

Another source of confusion may be the fact that some words have a history that is not generally known today. You will read more on word histories in the next section, but the word *lunatic* will be used as an example. This word is derived from the Latin word *luna*, meaning "moon." You could question why a lunatic, an insane person, is named after the moon. This comes from an old superstition that people became insane from gazing at the moon too long. A remnant of this idea remains today as some people believe that behavior changes during the time of a full moon.

Still another source of confusion may be the fact that a derivative will often change spelling when the part of speech changes. Observe the following spellings when verbs change to noun forms:

ROOT	VERB	NOUN
cede, ceed	proceed	procession
ceiv, cept	receive	receptacle
clam, claim	proclaim	proclamation

One of the letters in the original word part may also be dropped in some parts of speech; the original meaning of the word part is not altered. For example, the root *cranio* changes to *cranium* in English, with the "o" being dropped.

If you cannot always determine the reason for a derivative, at least you should learn the prefixes, roots, and suffixes that seem logical to you, thereby enlarging your vocabulary considerably. Libraries contain excellent books on word parts that you could consult to learn more prefixes, roots, and suffixes. One of many such books is *English Words from Latin and Greek Elements* (2nd ed.) by Donald M. Ayers, revised by T. D. Worthen in 1986.

EXERCISE 8.3

Based on the word parts presented above, give the definitions of the following words. Try to determine the meanings without using a dictionary. If you do have to use the dictionary, try to decide how the meaning of the English word relates to the original word part.

1. prediction _____

2. submissive _____

3. binomial _____

4. centipede _____

5. immortality _____

6. immutable _____

7. monoplane _____

8. postmortem _____

9. vociferous _____

10. exterminate _____

～ ETYMOLOGY ～

Another word for studying the origins and history of words is **etymology**. This can be a fascinating endeavor, and it will clarify many questions about derivatives. The example of *lunatic* was given previously, with its interesting history. Some of the following will illustrate how much the language is changing and also how etymology can be used to build vocabulary and recall interesting new words. The examples were taken from *Word Mysteries and Histories*, by the editors of *The American Heritage Dictionary,* and from *Word Origins and Their Romantic Stories* by Wilfred Funk. Read the following:

▪ Have you ever wondered why *octo* means "eight" and the tenth month is named October? The reason is that October was the eighth month on the Roman calendar.

▪ Why do the words *testicle* and *testify* both come from the Latin word *testis,* meaning "witness"? Actually there were two Latin words *testis,* with different meanings. It is believed that the second word came from the belief that a testicle was a "witness" to virility or manhood.

▪ Why is an illegal hanging called a *lynching*? Actually the term was named for Captain William Lynch, who decided in 1780 that the courts were too distant to deal with the lawless. It was decided that the lawbreakers would be punished without due process of law. Lynching is always associated with hanging in modern times, but originally, other punishments, both capital and less severe, were used by the group.

▪ Why is a bad dream called a *nightmare*, and does it have anything to do with a female horse (a mare)? In Old and Middle English, *mare* meant an evil spirit that was believed to sit on sleeping people and cause them to feel like they were suffocating.

▪ Why is a snobby person described as *supercilious*? The Latin word *supercilium* meant "eyebrow." A person raising an eyebrow is thought to be stern, haughty, and snobbish.

▪ Did you know that a *girl* could, at one time, be a boy? In Middle English times (from the thirteenth to the fifteenth century), *girl* meant a child of either sex.

▪ Why is an unmarried woman referred to, at least in earlier literature, as a *spinster*? A spinster literally means "one who spins." In earlier centuries, unmarried girls were expected to spend their time spinning yarn into cloth. If a young woman continued to be single, she became known as a spinster.

▪ Why do the words *hysterical* and *hysterectomy* have the same Greek origin? The Greek word from which these two words were derived meant "suffering in the womb." In earlier times, women were considered to be more emotional than men, so the belief that the uterus was the cause came into being.

▪ Why does the English word *chauffeur* come from the French word that means "to heat"? In the early days of the automobile when it was often steam-driven, the French gave the name to the employee who drove the car.

EXERCISE 8.4

Research the origins of the following words or phrases. Then answer the questions.

1. Since *ast* means "star," why is something very bad called a "disaster"?

   _____

2. Where did the term *the iron curtain* originate?

   _____

3. Why is a perfect place called a *utopia*?

   _____

4. The word *gymnastics* comes from *gymnos*, meaning "naked" or "nude." Why is the sport named this way?

   _____

5. What was the depressing origin of *bonfire*?

   _____

SPECIFIC VOCABULARY-BUILDING STRATEGIES

In addition to context clues, structural analysis, and etymology, there are other vocabulary-building methods, which will now be described. Look for methods that will work for you.

Employ the association method. You should use your knowledge of words to learn additional words that are similar in some way. Read the following examples to see how this method works.

WORD ALREADY KNOWN	WORDS TO BE LEARNED
military	militant, militarism, militarize, militia
placid	placate, complacent, implacable
grateful	gratuitous, gratuity, ingratiate
alien	alienation, alienability
credit	credibility, credulous, incredible
gene	genocide, congenital, progeny

Use specialized dictionaries. If you want to increase your vocabulary in a specific field, there are many dictionaries for these special terms, and you can locate them in the reference section of your college or local library. The following are examples of some of the dictionaries:

- *Mosby's Dictionary: Medical, Nursing, and Allied Health*
- *Hammond Barnhart Dictionary of Science*
- *Dictionary of Mythology Folklore and Symbols*
- *Black's Law Dictionary*
- *Dictionary of Clichés*
- *Dictionary of Synonyms*
- *Roget's Thesaurus*
- *The Macmillan Dictionary of Measurement*
- *Words of the Vietnam War*

Develop a course master file. A master file can be developed for one particular course that is difficult or, preferably, for each new academic discipline. Remember that all disciplines have their own terminology; an understanding of these terms is essential. Many textbooks include lists of terms on the first page of each chapter. The texts that do not contain such lists usually have key terms in bold print, italics, underlining, or a different color. You should put all of these terms into your master file.

The file can be organized in several ways, depending on your own personal preference:

- Special notebooks or special sections of the course notebook can be used. Enough space should be provided to enable you to add to the list throughout the course.
- Use the computer to set up files for each course. It is fun and easy to add new words to your computer lists.
- Use a file box filled with cards, like a card catalog, on which you can record your vocabulary words and anything you want to remember about them.

Make semantic maps of all of the terms in each chapter. Semantic maps are especially good because the terms go into categories and must relate to each other. It is much easier to recall information if it is organized in a meaningful way and if there is a connection made than to recall by learning isolated words or bits of information. The brain stores information in units, making it easier to remember. Even a grocery list would be easier to recall if the various items on the list were categorized as *dairy products, meats, fresh vegetables*, and *cleaning products*. Read the following terms and observe the semantic map made of them:

CRIMINAL JUSTICE TERMS

Bureau of Justice Statistics	Uniform Crime Reports	clearance rates
victimization surveys	Part I offenses	Part II offenses
major crimes	violent crime	Crime Index
property crime	murder	forcible rape
larceny	assault	burglary
vandalism	motor vehicle theft	arson
forgery	*Vory v. Zakone*	Cosa Nostra
prostitution	drug law violations	organized crime
robbery	National Crime Victimization Survey	

MAPPING OF CRIMINAL JUSTICE TERMS

PART I OFFENSES	PART II OFFENSES	CRIME DATA
murder	assault (simple)	Uniform Crime Reports
forcible rape	vandalism	National Crime Victimization Survey
robbery	forgery	Bureau of Justice Statistics
assault (aggravated)	prostitution	Crime Index
burglary	drug law violations	victimization surveys
larceny		
motor vehicle theft		
arson		

ORGANIZED CRIME	PROPERTY CRIME	VIOLENT CRIME
Cosa Nostra	burglary	murder
Vory v. Zakone	larceny	rape
	auto theft	robbery
SOLVING OF CRIME	arson	assault
clearance rates		

There are many different ways to correctly map terms, but the categories must be logical, and the information under each category should belong there. Accuracy is important because you may use the semantic maps to study for tests. Sometimes one of the words in the list can be used as one of the categories; other times categories must be devised and named by the student. As in the map above, some terms may be mapped under more than one category.

If you are studying numerous chapters for midterms or finals, mapping terms can serve as a quick review. The terms you recall can be readily placed in the proper categories, so the only terms you will need to look up will be those you have forgotten.

Explore new sources for vocabulary words. Make a deliberate effort to be aware of alternate sources for increasing your vocabulary. As you engage in your regular activities, you can learn new words in many places. When you hear a word that you would like to add to your vocabulary, make a note of the word. If you can determine its meaning from context, note the meaning. If not, look the word up in a dictionary. Add the word to whatever word files you use. Some sources for new words are all around you:

- Vocabulary of your professors
- New words encountered in reading for enjoyment
- News, science, and learning channels on television
- Newspapers and periodicals
- Information from religious and social organizations
- Vocabulary of other college students
- Regular content vocabulary

Use the computer to learn new words. One valuable service you can get from your computer is the *thesaurus* function. When you find yourself overusing some of your favorite words, let the thesaurus give you alternatives that are synonyms. For the word *taciturn*, the thesaurus gives the following synonyms: *reticent, reserved, quiet, closemouthed, uncommunicative, silent,* and *sententious.* The word *predecessor* has the following synonyms: *precursor, antecedent, forerunner, foregoer, antecessor, forefather, ancestor,* and *former officeholder.* In fact, there are several synonyms for most words, and you can quickly build your vocabulary this way. When you discover a new word, use it in your writing, facilitating recall.

Use visualization. There are many words that easily lend themselves to visualization. In some other cases, there may be adjectives that describe people you know or that remind you of someone. Try forming a visual image of the person as you say the word.

Use rhyming if you are talented at creating verse. You have probably heard the rhyme, "I really *lament* the raise in my rent." This rhyme helps because you can imagine that you would feel sorrowful if your rent were raised.

Use some type of deliberate vocabulary strategy.   An example of a deliberate six-step strategy to use after you have isolated some new words follows, but you may make modifications:

1. List the new word.
2. Study the word in the original context.
3. Predict the meaning of the word.
4. Use the dictionary to confirm your prediction.
5. Use the word in a sentence.
6. Use the word several times over the next week after learning it.

The last step cannot be overemphasized. Regardless of the vocabulary acquisition techniques you use, the new words will not be remembered unless you make them a part of your life. There are some words you will use more than others, but reading widely will cause you to encounter the words in print, making them a part of your **receptive vocabulary**, those words you understand when you read or hear them, even if they are not often a part of your **expressive** (spoken) **vocabulary**.

EXERCISE 8.5

Create a semantic map of the following computer terms: alignment, default, field, font, insert mode, merge field, soft spaces, thesaurus, vertical ruler, wizards, word wrap, row, italics, manual page break, and styles tab leaders.

 **USING THE DICTIONARY**

There are many parts to each entry in the dictionary, some of which you may never have noticed. Each part has its own function, which will be briefly described below.

Definition. There are often multiple meanings of a single word. For example, think of the many definitions for the word *run*. The meanings of a word are numbered, with the more common ones first. Sometimes it is necessary to look up a different word to get an adequate definition. An example is the word *professional*. The definition is stated as "of, pertaining to, characteristic of, or engaged in a profession." If you did not know the more basic word, *profession*, such a definition would be of little use.

Pronunciation of the word. Since all dictionaries do not use the same pronunciation guide, you must look up the guide in the dictionary you are using. In some dictionaries, the guide is in the front; in others, it is placed at the bottom of the page.

Part of speech. *The American Heritage Dictionary*, as an example, lists the following abbreviations for the parts of speech:

n.	noun	*pron.*	pronoun
adj.	adjective	*v.*	verb
adv.	adverb	*conj.*	conjunction
prep.	preposition	*interj.*	interjection

The following additional abbreviations are used in the same place in the entry:

pref.	prefix	*suff.*	suffix
pl.	plural	*sing.*	singular
pres. p.	present participle	*p. p.*	past participle
p. t.	past tense	*compar.*	comparative
superl.	superlative		

If you have questions about any of the above terms, consult your English grammar book for a complete explanation.

Etymology of the word. The next element listed is the etymology, or history, of the word. You will be given another abbreviation, this time for the language of origin. The symbol < means "derived from." You will have abbreviations such as *L* for Latin and *Fr* for French. Again consult the dictionary you are using for a complete list of abbreviations. Expect to find a very long list, including some languages that are no longer spoken, such as *OE* for Old English.

Usage. If the word is not considered standard English, is a slang term, is used in certain parts of the country only, or is archaic, that will be noted in this part. For example, the following entry appears in *The American Heritage Dictionary:*

> **ain't** (ant). *Nonstandard.* **1.** Am not. **2.** Used also as a contraction of *are not, is not, has not,* and *have not.*
>
> *Usage:* Even though it would be useful as a contraction for *am not* and as an alternative form for *isn't, aren't, hasn't,* and *haven't, ain't* is still unacceptable in standard usage.

EXERCISE 8.6

Use a dictionary to find the following information, and answer each question on the line provided.

1. What foreign language gave us the expression *faux pas?*

   _____

2. List five words that begin with the word part *syn.*

   _____

3. What is the plural of the word *syllabus?*

   _____

4. What part of speech is the word *sycophant*, and what does it mean?

   _____

5. Find a word in your reading that you have never heard spoken and do not know how to pronounce. Look up the word, and write its pronunciation.

   _____

6. Examine the dictionary you are using to discover whether or not it includes slang words and terms. Does your dictionary contain slang? What word did you look up?

   _____

7. Look up the expression *Achilles' heel*. Why is *Achilles* capitalized?

   _____

8. What is the origin of the term *ad hoc?*

_____

9. What does the abbreviation *v.* represent when it follows a word in the dictionary?

_____

10. How many meanings can you locate for the word *run?*

_____

SUMMARY

A good vocabulary is essential to becoming a successful college student. Each academic discipline introduces numerous content-related terms. In addition, a good general vocabulary is a vital tool of an educated person. This chapter explored the various methods for acquiring a good vocabulary.

The various types of context clues were presented and discussed. The efficient reader uses the context of a passage to determine the meanings of unknown words. Structural analysis—including a knowledge of prefixes, root words, and suffixes—is another very effective and expeditious way to increase vocabulary. Some of the more common word parts were defined, and derivatives were listed. Another vocabulary-building method that was stressed was etymology, or history and origins of words. Many people increase their knowledge of terminology through the study of the origins of interesting words and phrases in the language. Additional specific vocabulary-enhancing strategies were presented and explained. Finally, dictionary usage was covered, and components of the dictionary were enumerated.

It is the responsibility of each person to select strategies that will build vocabulary. Each person has a learning preference and different learning styles. Some of the methods covered in the chapter should be effective for each student.

 **Cooperative Learning Activities**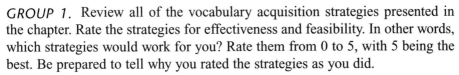

GROUP 1. Review all of the vocabulary acquisition strategies presented in the chapter. Rate the strategies for effectiveness and feasibility. In other words, which strategies would work for you? Rate them from 0 to 5, with 5 being the best. Be prepared to tell why you rated the strategies as you did.

GROUP 2. Each member of the group should use one of his or her content area textbooks. Share the books, and compile a list of all the ways the textbook authors help you learn new vocabulary words. Which ways are most effective?

GROUP 3. Discuss the ways each member of the group learned new vocabulary in high school. Make a group list of the various methods; then evaluate each for effectiveness. Support your answers with reasons.

GROUP 4. Which one of the roots in this chapter do you think has the largest number of derivatives? You may use the dictionary to find out. Which root did you select as being the most useful? How many derivatives did you find?

GROUP 5. Make a list of strange and/or unusual words or expressions you hear in people's everyday language. After completing your list, research the etymology of two of the words or expressions.

 **R**eading Selection: *Art*

Title: *Color Schemes**
Author: H. M. Sayre

Activation of Prior Knowledge and Interest

1. What forms of art do you enjoy, and how do these art forms enrich your life?

   _____

   _____

   _____

2. Name three colors, giving their positive or negative effects on you.

   _____

   _____

   _____

3. What is an example of an artistic work you do not like?

   _____

   _____

   _____

---

*WORLD OF ART by Sayre, © 1994. Reprinted by permission of Prentice-Hall, Inc. Upper Saddle River, NJ.

C olors can be employed by painters in different ways to achieve a wide variety of effects. **Analogous** color schemes are those composed of hues that
neighbor each other on the color wheel. Such color schemes are often organized on the basis of color **temperature**. Most of us respond to the range from
yellow through orange and red as *warm*, and to the opposite side of the color
wheel, from green through blue to violet, as *cool*. Sanford Gifford's *October in
the Catskills* is a decidedly warm painting—just like a sunny fall day. The color
scheme consists of yellows, oranges, and reds in varying degrees of intensity
and key. Even what appears to be brown in this composition is the result of
mixing this spectrum of warm colors. Its warmth is so powerful that even the
blue of the sky is barely perceptible through the all-consuming yellow atmosphere. The painting is a study in atmospheric perspective, though it modifies
Leonardo's formula somewhat, since the distant hills do not appear "bluer,"
only softer in hue. Representing the effects of atmosphere was Gifford's chief
goal in painting. "The really important matter," he would say, "is not the natural object itself, but the veil or medium through which we see it."

Just as warm and cool temperatures literally create contrasting physical
sensations, when both warm and cool hues occur together in the same work of
art, they tend to evoke a sense of contrast and tension. Romare Bearden's *Sheba* is dominated by cool blues and greens, but surrounding and accenting these
great blocks of color are contrasting areas of red, yellow, and orange.
"Sometimes, in order to heighten the character of a painting," Bearden wrote in
1969, just a year before this painting was completed, "I introduce what appears
to be a dissonant color where the red, browns, and yellows disrupt the placidi-
ty of the blues and greens." Queen of the Arab culture that brought the Muslim
religion to Ethiopia, Sheba here imparts a regal serenity to all that surrounds
her. It is as if, in her every gesture, she cools the atmosphere, like rain in a time
of drought, or shade at an oasis in the desert.

Color schemes composed of hues that lie opposite each other on the color
wheel, as opposed to next to one another, are called **complementary.** Thus, on
the traditional color wheel, there are three basic sets of complementary relations: orange/blue, yellow/violet, and red/green. Each intermediate color has its
complement as well. When two complements appear in the same composition,
especially if they are pure hues, each will appear more intense. If placed next
to each other, without mixing, complements seem brighter than if they appear
alone. This effect, known as **simultaneous contrast**, is due to the physiology
of the eye. If, for example, you stare intensely at the color red for about thirty
seconds, and then shift your vision to a field of pure white, you will see not red
but a variety of green. Physiologically, the eye supplies an **afterimage** of a
given hue in the color of its complement. This effect can be experienced in
Leon Golub's *Mercenaries III*. Based on news photos, Golub's painting attempts, in his words, to "have a sense of the contemporaneity of events. They

are poised to be almost physically palpable, a tactile tension of events." The almost neon, electric red and green of the canvas clash dramatically. The color seems as explosive as the situation Golub depicts.

In his *A Sunday on La Grande Jatte*, George Seurat has tried to *harmonize* his complementary colors rather than create a sense of tension with them. With what almost amounts to fanaticism, Seurat painted this giant canvas with thousands of tiny dots, or points, of pure color in a process that came to be known as *pointillism*. Instead of mixing color on the palette or canvas, he believed that the eye of the perceiver would be able to mix colors optically. He strongly believed that if he placed complements side by side—particularly orange and blue in the shadowed areas of the painting—that the intensity of the color would be dramatically enhanced. But to Seurat's dismay, most viewers found the painting "lusterless" and "murky." This is because there is a rather limited zone in which the viewer does in fact optically mix the pointillist dots. For most viewers, Seurat's painting works from about six feet away—closer, and the painting breaks down into abstract dots, farther away, and the colors muddy, turning almost brown.

One of the more vexing issues that the study of color presents is that the traditional color wheel really does not adequately describe true complementary color relations. For instance, the afterimage of red is not really green, but blue-green. In 1905, Albert Munsell created a color wheel based on five, rather than three, primary hues: yellow, green, blue, violet, and red. The complement of each of these five is a secondary. Munsell's color wheel accounts for what is, to many eyes, one of the most powerful complementary color schemes, the relation between yellow and blue-violet. The Brazilian feather mask, known as a *Cara Grande* . . . illustrates this contrast. The mask is worn during the annual Banana Fiesta in the Amazon basin; it is almost three feet tall. It is made of wood and covered with pitch to which feathers are attached. The brilliantly colored feathers are not dyed but are the natural plumage of tropical birds, and the intensity of their color is heightened by the simultaneous contrast between yellow and blue-violet, which is especially apparent at the outer edge of the mask.

Artists working with either analogous or complementary color schemes chose to limit the range of their color selection. In his painting *Filas for Sale*, Charles Searles has rejected such a *closed* or *restricted palette* in favor of an *open palette,* in which he employs the entire range of hues in a wide variety of values and intensities. Such a painting is **polychromatic**. The painting depicts a Nigerian marketplace and was inspired by a trip Searles took to Nigeria, Ghana, and Morocco in 1972. "What really hit me," Searles says, "is that the art is in the people. The way the people carried themselves, dressed, decorated their houses became the art to me, like a living art." A pile of *filas*, or brightly patterned skullcaps, occupies the right foreground of this painting. The confusion and turmoil of the crowded marketplace is mirrored in the swirl of the variously colored textile patterns. Each pattern has its own color scheme—yellow arcs against a set of violet dots, for instance, in the swatch of cloth just above the pile of hats—but all combine to create an almost disorienting sense of movement and activity.

Critical Thinking Questions

1. Compare and contrast analogous and complementary color schemes.

_____

_____

_____

2. Charles Searles said that art can be "in the people." Explain what he meant by this expression, and give an example from your own observation.

_____

_____

_____

3. Other than the bold print or italicized terms, list additional words that were not a part of your vocabulary. Tell which of the methods described in the chapter you used to define these words.

_____

_____

_____

REFERENCES

American Heritage Dictionary: Second College Edition. (1983). Boston: Houghton Mifflin Company.

Ayers, D. M. (1986). *English Words from Latin and Greek Elements* (2nd ed.). Tucson: University of Arizona Press.

Editors of The American Heritage Dictionaries. (1986). *Word Mysteries and Histories*. Boston: Houghton Mifflin Company.

Funk, W. (1950). *Word Origins and Their Romantic Stories*. New York: Bell Publishing Company.

CREDIT

Sayre, H. M. (1997). *A World of Art* (2nd ed.). Upper Saddle River, NJ: Prentice-Hall, Inc.

Study Methods for Textbooks

CHAPTER OBJECTIVES

- To master strategies that aid in processing textbooks
- To acquire specific study methods to use with all assignments
- To learn to use prior knowledge and interest to aid study
- To correct problems of insufficient prior knowledge and inadequate prerequisite skills

Students entering college for the first time often are unaware that there are proven techniques that can enhance study and increase memory. In this chapter, you will learn how to get the most out of a textbook by using helpful text aids and by using specific study methods. You will also learn how to employ information you already know to help learn new information. Perhaps most importantly, you will learn how to monitor your own learning.

STRATEGIES FOR PROCESSING TEXTBOOKS

Reading Flexibility

Reading flexibility means reading different types of material at different rates. If you are reading for fun, you can certainly read as fast as you want. Speed is less of a factor in textbook reading, and you should concentrate on comprehension. However, reading flexibility is essential, even with textbooks, in order to handle all of the reading demands of a college student. Various factors will influence how fast you will want to read your texts: interest in the material, prior knowledge of the subject matter, difficulty of the material, and purpose for reading.

You would benefit from learning to skim and to scan when reading for certain purposes. **Skimming** means reading very fast by paying attention to some parts of a selection and skipping other parts in order to get only the main ideas. When skimming, you are not trying to read for details or in depth. Skimming is appropriate in all of the following situations:

- When doing research, skim articles and tables of contents to get the gist of the material.
- Skim to get a quick review of material you have previously learned.
- Skim to get a general idea of the content of new textbooks and newly assigned chapters.

Scanning means searching for a particular name or topic. It gives you less information than skimming. While scanning, you do not determine main ideas; you simply locate a specific word. Scanning is appropriate in many situations, such as in the following examples:

- While doing research and attempting to locate information on the Egyptian pyramids, look through all of the tables of contents trying to find the word *pyramid*.
- Scan to find words in dictionaries, glossaries, or indexes.
- Scan to locate answers to very specific questions.

Previewing Textbooks

Previewing a textbook, also called **surveying**, is an examination of the textbook to get a general idea of such features as the format, instructional aids, difficulty of material, author's purpose, and type of organization. Since textbooks can vary greatly in all of these aspects, the student, who will be using the book for at least one semester, will need to know how best to use the book and how to get help when it is needed. This should be a process you go through with each and every new textbook you use.

All of the following parts of the book should be included in a textbook preview. The parts of the textbook will be covered from the front of the book to the back.

Title page. In addition to the title, the title page gives the author, the author's title and institution, the publishing company, and the city in which the book was published. When the title of the book is not followed by an edition number, it means that the book is the first edition. When there are several cities listed, the book was published in the first city listed.

Copyright page. This page is very important because you can learn when the book was published. Students need the most up-to-date information in the academic field. It is easy to see the significance of the copyright date in subjects that are constantly changing, such as science, but current books are preferable in all courses.

Table of contents. If students are not accustomed to conducting complete previews of their textbooks, they may at least look over the table of contents, which is the list of chapters and other material included in the book. Reading the table of contents is the best way to determine what is covered in a course and the manner in which the chapters are arranged. Some instructors attempt to cover every chapter in the textbook, while others select only certain chapters. In the latter case, the remaining chapters may be used for class assignments, reports, or reference.

Preface. The preface, also called the *introduction*, states such information as the author's purpose for writing the book, the intended audience, information about how the book is to be used, and often the philosophy of the author.

References. Found in the back of the book, references are the sources to which an author refers during the course of writing the book. Depending on the writing style used, the references may be called by other names, such as *bibliography* or *notes*. This is a good starting place for a student who would like more information on a subject when doing research for a term paper or a project. Like the textbook authors, you also must give credit to all sources you use in your papers; even spoken sources must be cited.

Index. The index is an alphabetized list of all the subjects covered in the book, complete with the exact page numbers where each subject is located. This is a very valuable part of any textbook because you can quickly and easily find any topic while you are studying.

Glossary. A glossary is a mini-dictionary, which is extremely beneficial because it gives only the definitions that apply to the particular course for which the textbook was written. Think of a word such as *matter*. This word has various definitions and uses, but a glossary in a science book will give only the scientific definition. This conciseness causes a glossary to be much shorter than a general-purpose dictionary. It is, therefore, easier to use and more relevant

Appendix. An appendix is a supplement containing additional information that may pertain only to a specific course. Therefore, the information in an appendix will differ from one course to another. For example, an appendix in a science book may contain topographic maps, star charts, or a periodic table of the elements, whereas an appendix in a history book may contain a copy of the entire U. S. Constitution. Some books have no appendix at all, but you may find the appendix helpful in texts that do contain them.

Supplementary learning aids. While conducting a book preview, you should also look for any supplementary learning aids found in some books. Generally, the following features will make a textbook easier to process:

- Pictures and graphic displays
- Lists of key terms for each chapter
- Questions at the beginning or end of the chapter
- Main ideas highlighted (possibly in a different color)
- Chapter summaries
- Typographic differences to emphasize important words or main points

EXERCISE 9.1

Tell which part of the textbook you would use to get information to answer each of the following questions.

_____ 1. Where would you look to find additional sources of information on the same subject as that covered by your textbook?

_____ 2. Where would you find a definition of a term used in the science text?

_____ 3. Where would you locate the page number to find information about *atoms*?

_____ 4. At the beginning of the course, what part of the book could you consult to get an idea of what will be covered in the class?

Health Watch: Sexually Transmitted Diseases

Sexually transmitted diseases (STDs), caused by viruses, bacteria, protists, or arthropods that infect the sexual organs and reproductive tract, are a serious and growing health problem worldwide. The World Health Organization estimates that there are 250 million new cases of STDs each year. As the name implies, these diseases are transmitted either exclusively or primarily through sexual contact. Here we discuss some of the more common of these diseases.

Bacterial Infections

Gonorrhea, an infection of the genital and urinary tract, is one of the most common of *all* infectious diseases in the United States, estimated to infect at least 2 million people each year. The causative bacterium, which cannot survive outside the body, is transmitted almost exclusively by intimate contact. It penetrates the membranes lining the urethra, anus, cervix, uterus, oviducts, and throat. In males, inflammation of the urethra results in a discharge of pus from the penis and painful urination. About 10% of infected males and 50% of infected females have symptoms that are mild or absent. These people often do not seek treatment and become carriers who can readily spread the disease. Gonorrhea can lead to infertility by blocking the oviducts with scar tissue. Treatment by penicillin was formerly highly successful, but penicillin-resistant strains now require use of other antibiotics. Infants born to infected mothers may acquire the bacterium during delivery. The bacterium attacks the eyes of newborns and was once a major cause of blindness. Today, most newborns are immediately given antibiotic eyedrops to kill the bacterium.

Syphilis is a far more dangerous, though less prevalent, disease than gonorrhea. It is caused by a spiral-shaped bacterium that enters the mucous membranes of the genitals, lips, anus, or breasts. Like gonorrhea, it is readily killed by exposure to air and is spread only by intimate contact. Syphilis begins with a sore at the site of infection. Syphilis may be cured with antibiotics, but if untreated, syphilis bacteria spread through the body, multiplying and damaging many organs, including the skin, kidneys, heart, and brain, sometimes with fatal results. About 4 out of every 1000 newborns in the United States have been infected with syphilis before birth. The skin, teeth, bones, liver, and central nervous system of such infants may be damaged.

Chlamydia causes inflammation of the urethra in males and the urethra and cervix in females, but in many cases there are no obvious symptoms, so the infection goes untreated and is spread. Like the gonorrhea bacterium, *Chlamydia* can infect and sometimes block the oviducts, resulting in sterility. Chlamydial infections can cause eye inflammations in infants born to infected mothers.

Viral Infections

Acquired immunodeficiency syndrome, or **AIDS,** is caused by the HIV virus. Because the virus does not survive exposure to air, it is spread primarily by sexual activity and by contaminated blood and needles. The HIV virus attacks the immune system, leaving the victim vulnerable to a variety of infections, which almost invariably prove fatal. Children born to mothers with AIDS sometimes become infected before or during birth. There is no cure, although certain drugs, such as AZT, can prolong life. AIDS is discussed in detail in Chapter 24.

Genital herpes reached epidemic proportions during the 1970s and continues to spread to more than a million new victims yearly. It causes painful blisters on the genitals and surrounding skin and is transmitted primarily when blisters are present. The herpes virus never leaves the body but resides in certain nerve cells, emerging unpredictably, possibly in response to stress. The first outbreak is the most serious; subsequent outbreaks produce fewer blisters and may be quite infrequent. The drug acyclovir, which inhibits viral DNA replication, may reduce the severity of outbreaks. Pregnant women with an active case of genital herpes may transmit the virus to the developing child, causing severe mental or physical disability or stillbirth. Herpes may also be transmitted from mother to infant if the infant contacts blisters as it is born.

Protists and Arthropod Infections

Trichomoniasis is caused by *Trichomonas,* a flagellated protist that colonizes the mucous membranes lining the urinary tract and genitals of both males and females. The symptoms are a discharge caused by inflammation in response to the parasite. The protist is spread by intercourse but can also be acquired through contaminated clothing and toilet articles. Lengthy untreated infections can result in sterility.

Crab lice, also called pubic lice, are microscopic arachnids that live and lay their eggs in pubic hair. Their mouthparts are adapted for penetrating the skin and sucking blood and body fluids, a process that causes severe itching. "Crabs" are not only irritating; they may also spread infectious diseases. They can be controlled through careful hygiene and chemical treatments.

1. What are the three bacterial infections?

   _____

2. Define: gonorrhea, syphilis, and chlamydia.

   _____

   _____

   _____

3. What is the cause of AIDS?

_____

4. When did genital herpes reach epidemic proportions?

_____

5. Has genital herpes been brought under control? How do you know?

_____

6. Define *trichomoniasis* and *crab lice*.

_____

_____

 **SPECIFIC STUDY METHODS**

There are many different study methods available. As you read the following section, contemplate each method and decide which one would help you study most effectively and also be compatible with your learning styles. You will notice that some of the methods are for specific courses, while others may work equally well for all disciplines.

SQ3R

It seems fitting to begin with the most famous study method, SQ3R, from which many other methods have been adapted. SQ3R was developed in the 1940s by Francis P. Robinson, a psychologist at Ohio State University. When SQ3R was originally developed, it was for the purpose of helping military men and women, in special programs at the university, to read and study more effectively. **SQ3R** stands for the following:

S = Survey

Q = Question

R = Read

R = Recite

R = Review

1. *Survey.* The first step is to conduct a chapter survey, or preview, which was explained in the previous section.

2. *Question*. Now that you have an idea of what the chapter will cover, you should convert the chapter headings into questions. Later you will read for the answers. You should make questions one heading at a time. Then read to find the answer before proceeding to the next heading.

3. *Read*. In this step, you should carefully read the section. When you find the answer to the question you made from the heading, you should underline it or make notes on the answer.

4. *Recite*. The recite part of SQ3R can be adapted to your learning style. The traditional way of reciting is to look away from the book and tell the main ideas or give the answer to the question you made. You should always *paraphrase* the main ideas; this means to say the information in your own words. If you simply restate the author's words, you may only be memorizing, not comprehending. If you prefer another method for this step, such as writing the main ideas, do what works for you. *(At this point, Steps 2, 3, and 4 should be repeated for each section of the chapter.)*

5 *Review*. Go over your underlining or your notes on the material. Make sure that the information seems logical and cohesive. If there seem to be gaps or some misunderstanding, reread portions until you can clarify any confusion.

The popularity of SQ3R could be attributed to its feasibility with all subject areas. Since it is for your benefit, you can modify it in any way that suits your needs, such as adding a step or doing the steps in a different order. For example, when studying mathematics, you may want to review first since a new math operation always builds on previous math knowledge. You may also prefer to make more questions than you can construct from a heading or subheading, and you could use other material such as boldface terms and first sentences of paragraphs. SQ3R or a similar method, used conscientiously, is highly effective.

EXERCISE 9.3

Step 2 of SQ3R is to turn chapter headings into questions. Practice this skill by making questions out of the following chapter headings or subheadings.

1. Abstinence as a Form of Birth Control

_____

2. Parts of the Brain

_____

3. Evolution v. Creationism

_____

4. New Insight into Ulcers

_____

5. Cancer Research

_____

6. Fertility Rates of Americans

_____

7. Extinction of Animals

_____

8. The Most Serious Floods of the Twentieth Century

_____

SQ3R, or some of its modifications, can be used for all disciplines. However, if you prefer to use a method that is designed for a particular course, such as one you are finding difficult, the following study methods may appeal to you. The first stresses writing, the second is used with literature, and the last is for mathematics.

ROWAC

Devised by Betty Roe (1993), ROWAC is good for students who like to write. As you may recall, writing is one of the techniques to improve memory. The acronym, **ROWAC**, stands for the following words:

R = READ
O = ORGANIZE
W = WRITE
A = ACTIVE READING
C = CORRECT PREDICTIONS

1. _Read._ In this step, you should read each heading and subheading in the selection. This will give you a general idea about the material and will activate prior knowledge.
2. _Organize._ The headings and subheadings should be organized in some way that you prefer. It can be in the form of an outline, a chart, a semantic map,

or any form that can be used as a framework to place details learned from later reading.

3. *Write*. Based on the organizer you developed in Step 2, you should now write a few paragraphs on your predictions of the material's content.

4. *Active reading*. The key word in this step is "active" because there are many activities occurring besides the reading. As you read, you should constantly be checking your predictions, understanding why variations occurred between your predictions and what you read, and writing information on the organizer, which you made in Step 2.

5. *Correct predictions*. In this step, you must revise your original prediction paragraphs. You do not have to rewrite the paragraphs; you can simply mark them, crossing out information and inserting ideas. Your final corrected version should be accurate.

EVOKER

This study method is very good for studying literature rather than expository writing. It is presented as a method for prose, poetry, or drama (Pauk, 1963). **Evoker** stands for:

E = EXPLORE
V = VOCABULARY
O = ORAL READING
K = KEY IDEAS
E = EVALUATE
R = RECAPITULATION

1. *Explore*. Silently read the literary selection in its entirety in order to get an idea of the message. Unlike other methods discussed previously, EVOKER *does* require a complete reading first, without other previews or initial activities, because literature is best appreciated holistically. The reading may also give you a theme, or message.

2. *Vocabulary.* You should look up any words or terms, as well as unfamiliar people, places, and events. If the literary work is from a time far in the past, you may notice many unfamiliar expressions that are no longer used. These are usually explained somewhere in the literature book, so locate these explanations.

3. *Oral reading*. Read the selection aloud with appropriate expression.

4. *Key ideas*. Locate the key ideas, including the theme of the passage.

5. *Evaluate.* Evaluate the key words and sentences, and judge how they contributed to the key ideas and the overall main idea.

6. *Recapitulation.* Reread the selection.

SQRQCQ

This last method is for the study of mathematics. Many students report having "math anxiety," and the problem may be lack of knowledge about how to approach the task. Research shows that more students have problems with math word problems than with simple calculations, so SQRQCQ was developed to help with word problems (Fay, 1965). **SQRQCQ** is an acronym that refers to the following:

S = SURVEY

Q = QUESTION

R = READ

Q = QUESTION

C = COMPUTE

Q = QUESTION

1. *Survey.* Quickly read the problem to get an idea of what is needed to solve it.

2. *Question.* Question yourself about what is being asked in the problem. You can often clarify difficult material by verbalizing it or thinking it through silently.

3. *Read.* This is a careful and deliberate reading of the problem. Pay attention to all aspects and details.

4. *Question.* In this step, you must ask and then decide what mathematical operations must be performed and in what order. (This seems to be the point where many students experience difficulty, but performing the first three steps should help.)

5. *Compute.* Do the mathematical computations on which you decided in the last step.

6. *Question.* At this point, check your work by reviewing the entire process; determine whether or not your answer is correct.

All of the study methods presented in this chapter illustrate that learning is a multifaceted mental activity. The many different steps involved in the methods indicate that learning takes time and effort.

USING PRIOR KNOWLEDGE TO AID STUDY

It is best to assess your prior knowledge before beginning a new assignment. Remember that learning and memory are enhanced if you can make a connection between new material and the information you already know. Knowing something about a topic usually generates some interest as well, and people find it easier to learn and retain material they perceive as interesting.

An example of the benefits of prior knowledge will illustrate its importance. If you were given an assignment to read a selection about your own state, you would have a rich experiential background. You would already be familiar with many aspects of the culture, which would increase your understanding of the selection. You would have a wealth of knowledge about population, customs, education, religion, climate, and other factors that distinguish a place. Your learning task would thus be less formidable because you would already possess so much information.

On the other hand, if you were given an assignment to read about customs in an ancient country you know nothing about, you would really have to start "from scratch." At least, perhaps the ancient culture would remind you of something in your culture, even if only to contrast the two places, such as thinking about how different the forms of government are.

If you are enrolled in a class where you discover that you have little or no prior knowledge, it is possible that the instructor will supply background information. If the instructor leaves the background information to you, there are sources where you can build your background knowledge.

Consult reference books. You could start by reading entries on the subject in several different encyclopedias. Encyclopedias never go into great detail, but they provide introductory information. Depending on the subject, there are various sources in the reference section of the college library.

View films or videos. College libraries now check out videos as well as books. Learn to use the library, and view a film on the topic.

Talk to knowledgeable people. These people include instructors, students who have completed the course, people in study groups, and tutors.

Ask a reference librarian for advice, or conduct a computer search. Students often hesitate to ask reference librarians for assistance, but that is their job and obligation to the students. It would be well worth the time to learn to search for material through the computer; it is much quicker and more effective than searching through the stacks in the library.

 **BUILDING PREREQUISITE SKILLS**

Another serious problem is lack of adequate or prerequisite skills. This is most problematic in the courses, such as math or foreign language, where each new skill builds on previous learning. College instructors, unlike those in high school, do not make a practice of reviewing previous courses. If possible, you should withdraw from the course, work on needed skills, and reenroll during the next session. If this is not a viable alternative, consider the following four recommended ways to correct missing or inadequate skills:

1. Obtain a review book or an easier text. Most college bookstores and even regular bookstores in malls carry review books, which usually break tasks down into easier steps. You might also be able to obtain a high school book, which usually goes into more detail than college texts.

2. Keep special notebooks for terms. Introductory, or survey, courses are usually considered by students to be more difficult than more advanced courses because of the vast amount of information presented. Much of this introductory information is in the form of terms for that discipline. Even mathematics courses have a large vocabulary component. Know the terms before they are presented in class by reading ahead and writing the terms in a notebook.

3. Get a tutor or a study group from the very beginning of the course. If you experience trouble or confusion in any course, never wait too long to enlist the aid of a tutor. Students often wait until they receive their midterm failure notices and then get a tutor. Most colleges offer tutoring for little or no cost.

4. Follow the instructor's clues to determine what is important. Earlier in this chapter, you read about how to determine what an author thinks is important. Instructors also give clues to help you know what you should recall for future tests. The following is a partial list of clues, since there is great variability among instructors:

- Writing on the board
- Giving special handouts
- Using overhead presentations
- Lowering or raising the voice for emphasis
- Pausing for emphasis
- Actually stating that certain material is important

Basically, you should use a good study method diligently, and never miss class except in extreme emergencies. Anyone who is determined and motivated can become a good student.

SUMMARY

This chapter presented suggestions for processing textbooks, the primary source of learning in college. At the beginning of each course, students should preview the textbook in order to learn what is expected in the course as well as to familiarize themselves with the textbook aids available. Subsequently, with the assignment of each chapter, a chapter preview should be conducted to get the main ideas of the material that will be covered in the chapter.

Various study methods were presented. Some methods can be used with all subjects, while some are designed to be used with a specific discipline. All students should use at least one study method, and they should use the method with all assignments for maximum efficiency and recall.

The importance of prior knowledge and interest in the material was stressed. Suggestions were given to help students learn how to build on and use prior knowledge as well as how to build prerequisite skills needed for classes.

Cooperative Learning Activities

GROUP 1. Discuss the present study habits of the members of the group. Note and report on the following:

- Presence or absence of a specific study method like SQ3R
- Ways the group members approach a new chapter
- Present habits that are not conducive to study
- Plans for study in the future

GROUP 2. Evaluate the study methods presented in this chapter. With *each* method, determine its potential effectiveness, the reasons it will or will not be effective, and some suggestions for how your group thinks it could be improved.

GROUP 3. In this chapter, you learned specific study methods for literature (EVOKER) and for math (SQRQCQ). Devise a study method that you feel would be effective for studying *history.* (*Note:* Remember the vast number of dates, people, and events that must be learned.)

GROUP 4. Select one of the pure sciences, then devise a study method you feel would be effective for studying that subject. (*Note:* Science courses contain numerous advanced vocabulary lists. The study method you create should help with learning all of the terminology as well as other aspects of science.)

GROUP 5. All of the members of the group should select a course that they find more difficult than other courses. This can be a course you are taking now, a course taken in high school, or an earlier college course. Then compile a group list of all the reasons courses can be viewed as difficult, and another list of how each of those problems could have been handled by better study methods.

Reading Selection: *History*

Title: *The Politics of Gender in Massachusetts**
Authors: J. M. Faragher, M. J. Buhle, D. Czitrom, S. H. & Armitage

---

Activation of Prior Knowledge and Interest

1. What do you know about the role of women in the seventeenth century?

   _____

   _____

   _____

   _____

2. Predict what the typical day would be like in those days.

   _____

   _____

   _____

   _____

3. What study methods discussed in this chapter will help you to study a history textbook or the following history selection?

   _____

   _____

   _____

   _____

---

*OUT OF MANY: 2E, A HISTORY OF THE AMERICAN PEOPLE—COMBINED EDITION by Faragher/Buhle/Czitrom/Armitage, © 1997. Reprinted by permission of Prentice-Hall, Inc. Upper Saddle River, NJ.

The Puritans stressed the importance of well-ordered communities and families. Colonists often emigrated in large kin groups that made up the core of the new towns. The Massachusetts General Court granted townships to proprietors representing the congregation, who then distributed fields, pasture, and woodlands in quantities proportional to the recipient's social status, so that wealthy families received more than humble ones. Settlers clustered their dwellings at the town center, near the meetinghouse that served as both church and civic center. Some towns, particularly those along the coast such as Boston, soon became centers of shipping. These clustered settlements and strong, vital communities made seventeenth-century New England quite different from Chesapeake society.

The family farm economy operated through the combined efforts of husband and wife. Men were generally responsible for field work, women for the work of the household, which included tending the kitchen garden (crops for household use), the dairy, and the henhouse, and securing fuel and water. Women managed an array of tasks, and some housewives independently traded garden products, milk, and eggs. One New England husband, referring to his wife's domestic management, said, "I meddle not with the geese nor turkeys, for they are hers for she hath been and is a good wife to me." Indeed, women traders helped to create and sustain many of the bonds of New England communities.

It is mistaken to regard the Puritans as "puritanical." Although adultery was a capital crime in New England, Puritans celebrated the sexual expression that took place within marriage. Courting couples were even allowed to lie in bed together, with their lower bodies wrapped in an apron, a custom known as "bundling," free to caress and pet. In the words of an old New England ballad:

> *She is modest, also chaste*
> *While only bare from neck to waist,*
> *And he of boasted freedom sings,*
> *Of all above her apron strings.*

There were certainly many loving Puritan households with contented husbands and wives. Anne Bradstreet, a Massachusetts wife and mother and the first published poet of New England, wrote about her husband and marriage:

> *If ever two are one, then surely we.*
> *If ever man were lov'd by wife, then thee;*
> *If ever wife was happy in a man,*
> *Compare with me ye women if you can.*

Nevertheless, the cultural ideal of the day was the subordination of women to men. "I am but a wife, and therefore it is sufficient for me to follow my husband," wrote Lucy Winthrop Downing, and her brother John Winthrop declared, "A true wife accounts her subjection her honor and freedom." Married women could neither make contracts nor own property, neither vote nor hold office. The extraordinarily high birth rate of Puritan women was one mark of their "subjection." The average woman, marrying in her early twenties and surviving through her forties, could expect to bear eight children. Aside from abstinence, there was no form of birth control. There was significant cultural suspicion about wives who failed to have children or widows who were economically independent.

These suspicions about women came to the surface most notably in periodic witchcraft scares. During the course of the seventeenth century, according to one historian, 342 New England women were accused by their neighbors of witchcraft. The majority of them were childless or widowed or had reputations among their neighbors for their assertiveness and independence. In the vast majority of cases these accusations were dismissed by authorities. But in Salem, Massachusetts, in 1692, when a group of girls claimed that they had been bewitched by a number of old men and women, the whole community was thrown into a panic of accusations. Before the colonial governor finally called a halt to the persecutions in 1693, twenty persons had been tried, condemned, and executed.

The Salem accusations of witchcraft probably reflected generalized social tensions that found their outlet through an attack on people perceived as outsiders. Salem was a booming port, but although some residents were prospering, others were not. Most of the victims came from the eastern, more commercial section of town, whereas the majority of their accusers lived on the economically stagnant western side. Most of the accused also came from families whose religious sympathies were with sects of Anglicans, Quakers, or Baptists, not Puritans. Finally, a majority of the victims were old women, suspect because they lived alone, without men. The Salem witchcraft trials exposed the dark side of Puritan ideas about women.

Critical Thinking Questions

1. Courtship and marriage customs were very different in the Puritan days. What factors could account for the great changes seen today?

   _____

   _____

   _____

2. What were the advantages and disadvantages of being a wife in Puritan times?

_____

_____

_____

3. You read about the characteristics of the groups victimized by being accused of witchcraft. Why did those particular characteristics cause them to be victimized?

_____

_____

_____

REFERENCES

Adler, M., & Van Doren, C. (1972). *How to Read a Book*. New York: Simon & Schuster.

Fay, L. (1965). Reading study skills: Math and science. In J. A. Figurel (ed.), *Reading and Inquiry*. Newark, NJ: International Reading Association.

Ostrander, S., & Schroeder, L. (1979). *Superlearning*. New York: Dell Publishing.

Pauk, W. (1963). On scholarship: Advice to high school students. *The Reading Teacher, 17,* 73–78.

Robinson, F. P. (1961). *Effective Study*. (4th ed.). New York: Harper & Row.

Roe, B. D. (1993). *ROWAC: A Study Method*. Unpublished paper. Cookeville, TN.

CREDITS

Audesirk, T., & Audesirk, G. (1997). *Life on Earth*. Upper Saddle River, NJ: Prentice-Hall, Inc.

Faragher, J. M., Buhle, M. J., Czitrom, D., & Armitage, S. H. (1997). *Out of Many: A History of the American People* (2nd ed.). Upper Saddle River, NJ: Prentice-Hall, Inc.

CLASSROOM PERFORMANCE

This section concentrates on skills and behaviors needed for success in the classroom. Just as the previous section provided strategies to be used in preparing for class, this section provides key strategies for use in class. Section III will help you take successful notes during lectures and class discussions, understand the requirements of the various types of writing you will encounter in college coursework, and prepare for and take tests.

In Section III:

Chapter 10   Note Taking, Annotating, and Underlining

Chapter 11   Writing in College Courses

Chapter 12   Test Taking Skills

Note Taking, Underlining, and Annotating

CHAPTER OBJECTIVES

- To learn effective note-taking strategies
- To learn the Cornell note-taking method
- To acquire a system for abbreviations and symbols
- To effectively underline textbooks
- To master the skill of annotation for both lectures and textbooks

College students are persistently faced with a vast amount of new information that must be processed and recalled. If you wish to be a successful student, you must develop study strategies that will enable you to comprehend all of the information and retrieve it for the numerous tests you must take. This chapter identifies and discusses some of the most fundamental study skills—note taking, underlining, and annotating.

NOTE TAKING

Note taking is a crucial study skill, one you will need throughout college. You should learn to take good notes on both your class lectures and your textbooks. Many students enter college with limited experience taking notes. They attempt to learn the skill by trial and error. This chapter proposes to set guidelines for taking notes on the important, not the extraneous, information, and for being able to distinguish between the two.

What are the purposes of note taking? First, people have limited capacities to remember information. You learned in Chapter 2 that information will not proceed from short-term to long-term memory, where it may remain indefinitely, without some active strategy. Writing the information in your notes is a very effective method to enable you to remember more material. Another reason for note taking is to record the material that you believe will be included on tests. Regardless of what you think you have learned from a class, you must prove it—by earning a good grade on a test. A third reason for taking notes is to help you remain alert in class because you must be actively listening in order to learn the material presented.

Listening Skills

Effective skill in listening is a prerequisite to effective note taking. Many students complain of being unable to concentrate on a lecture. Some can concentrate at intervals, but not for an entire lecture. The mind begins to wander, things in the room and outside the window draw attention, or worries about real or imagined problems arise. How can you get your mind on the lecture and keep it there for the duration of the class? Here are ten suggestions.

1. Always have some idea about what to expect by reading your assignments before *going to class.* You will recognize information when you hear it, and prior knowledge will generate some interest in the topic.

2. Sit where you can see and hear the lecturer. This will make you feel more involved. When you are not writing notes, make eye contact. If you are taking a class in a large lecture hall, get there early and try to get a seat close to the front. If you have a physical problem with sight or hearing, tell the instructor so that you can be assured of a seat in front.

3. Pay close attention to the lecturer's opening statements and closing remarks. The opening statements will probably contain the main idea of the lecture. The concluding remarks will summarize the important points that were made during that class session.

4. Try to control physical conditions that are distracting to you. If you know that the lecture hall is always going to be too hot or too cold, dress accordingly. If a scene out the window interests you, sit as far away from the window as you can get. Control your physical surroundings; don't let them control you.

5. Be aware of ways in which your attitude can interfere with effective listening. Do you go to class thinking negatively, as illustrated in the following statements?

- "Why do I have to take this boring class in literature when I plan to be a mathematician?"
- "This teacher is so boring that I can't concentrate."

If you sit in class thinking thoughts like those above, your ability to concentrate will be severely inhibited. Are you going to let your opinions about the instructors, the academic requirements, or the subject matter prevent you from achieving your goals?

6. Ask questions and offer answers when invited. If you feel that you are an active participant in the class, you will concentrate better. You will also get more out of the class.

7. Set short-term goals for yourself each class period. For example, decide that you are going to note one page of main ideas from the lecture in a certain amount of time. Then you will have to listen to the lecture closely to locate and record the important ideas.

8. Predict questions that will be answered during the lecture. If you mentally compose some questions and then actively listen for the answers, you will remain more alert. Also see if your questions are those that the instructor says are important points.

9. Purposely attempt to associate the new information with what you already know. If the lecturer is discussing a past president of the United States, associate the acts or behaviors with those of a modern-day president; compare or contrast the two. Make the new information meaningful.

10. Continue to take notes throughout the lecture. The actual process of writing will help you stay awake and alert. The memory process will also be enhanced.

Twelve General Guidelines for Note Taking

1. Keep a separate notebook or a separate section of the notebook for each class. Your notes must be in a place where you can easily locate them, and they should be organized in sequence. Instructors report seeing students take notes in class and then place the notes in their pockets! These students are prone to misplace their notes. Even in the dormitory room or your room where you study at home, you should put materials for different courses in different stacks or places.

2. Always put the date and lecture title on your notes. A test will often cover material presented during a specific time period, or you may need to refer to your notes for a conference with the instructor. Lecture titles may be announced in class or given on the syllabus.

3. Take notes with pen instead of pencil, except in classes in which you are solving problems. This is recommended because notes written in pencil tend to smear. However, if you are comfortable *only* with a pencil, it will work for you.

4. Read the assigned textbook chapter or chapters before *the lecture.* If you have read the chapter, you already have a good idea of the subject matter.

5. Write down the main points, not everything the lecturer says. Some students do attempt to write every word. However, there are many times when a professor will stray from the subject or merely give several examples to reinforce a point being made. Sometimes a professor will relate an anecdote to get the students' attention or to "break the ice."

6. Learn lecturers' cues that signal important information. Perhaps you know you need to record only the important points, but you do not know how to determine what is important. The lecturer, depending on lecture style, may give any of the following cues:

- Writing information on the board
- Using an overhead or computer presentation
- Changing voice volume or rate of speech when making an important point
- Walking toward the class when making an important point
- Explicitly stating that something is important
- Repeating information

7. Paraphrase information as long as you do not change the meaning. Writing information in your own words shows a real understanding of the material, an understanding not evidenced by writing word for word as if you were taking dictation. However, it is very important not to change the meaning of the lecture. If you are unable to paraphrase and also keep up with the lecturer, you could paraphrase the notes after class when you have more time.

8. Make associations and ask questions as you take lecture notes. Always attempt to connect the new notes to something you already know so that you will recall the information and so that it will seem important to you. You may want to write the association in the margin. When there is a pause in the lecture, ask any questions you need to have addressed.

9. Early in the class session, try to determine the organizational pattern of the lecture. As you learned in Chapter 7, there are several commonly used organizational patterns in textbook writing; the same is true of lectures. If you can determine that the lecture is of the cause and effect pattern, for example, you can include a useful diagram in your notes. This is very helpful for spatial and/or visual learners. Look at the following examples of lecture topics for different organizational patterns:

- Listing   "Major Imports from the Orient"
- Order/Sequence   "Events Leading to the American Revolution"
- Comparison/Contrast   "Urban v. Suburban Lifestyles"
- Cause and effect   "Reasons for Suicide"
- Problem and solution   "Searching for a Cure for AIDS"
- Classification   "Types of Psychoses"
- Definition   "What Is Fetal Alcohol Syndrome?"
- Example   "A Public High School That Eliminated Grades"

10. Use an abbreviation system and meaningful symbols. You will need to develop your abbreviations and symbols over a period of time, instead of attempting too many at once. Be sure you can comprehend your system days and weeks after your notes are made. Use the same abbreviations and symbols consistently. (See Figure 10.1 for sample abbreviations and symbols.)

11. Leave blank spaces when you know you have not been able to write down all the important information. At times the lecture may be too fast, or there may be so many important facts and concepts introduced that you simply cannot get everything into your notes that day. This is a common complaint in survey or introductory courses. If the lecture corresponds with the textbook material, you can fill in the missing information as you go over the chapter. If the lecture material is entirely different or supplemental, ask a study partner in the class if you can compare notes. You might also ask the instructor if he or she could recommend any reading material on the lecture topic so that you could make more complete and comprehensive notes.

12. Above all, attend all *classes.* Even if your instructor says that attendance is optional, remember that you are *still* responsible for everything that is covered in your absence.

Some students may still feel unable to record everything that is important, even after following these guidelines. Note taking takes much practice; you will get better at it if you consistently attend class and take notes. However, if you are falling further and further behind while you practice your note-taking skills, you might consider asking the professor for permission to record the lectures. You should not do this without asking. If you record the lectures, you will have to listen to the lectures again to fill in the missing information, so consider whether you have twice as much time for the lectures.

Figure 10.1 *Sample list of abbreviations and symbols.*

&	and	b/c	because
=	equals	def	definition
≠	does not equal	ex	example
" " "	repeating information	gen	general
>	greater than	?	question about this or good test question
<	less than	sp	spelling
etc	and so on	*	important
w/	with	vs	versus or against
w/o	without	p, pp	page, pages
@	at	+	plus
–	minus	dept	department

Note Taking and Types of Lecturers

Students have learning styles, and instructors have teaching styles. The style will, in part, determine the way and the ease with which you take notes. Although you will have a preference about teaching styles, there is really nothing you can do about any instructor's style or methods, except to do the best you can to earn a good grade. The characteristics of instructors will be mentioned as they relate to your note taking. The discussion will be divided into class structure and teaching style.

CLASS STRUCTURE

1. *Flexibility.* Some instructors will change the class format often. They will alternate among large group work, small group work, whole class lectures, and class discussions. They may even change the location of the class

at times. Other instructors, being much more rigid, will not alter the format from one day to the next. If you have flexible grouping, you may have more opportunities to clarify misunderstandings about your notes because you can speak in private with the instructor while the students are otherwise occupied. If you have a more rigid instructor, you may need to visit him or her during office hours or schedule a special appointment. Do whatever it takes to get good notes.

2. *Encouragement of questions.* Some instructors welcome many questions, and others may consider them an interruption of the lecture. Some may welcome questions only after they pause or invite questions. When you do ask a question, do it in such a way that you do not interrupt the train of thought for the instructor and the other students.

3. *Class atmosphere.* Some instructors will remain on the topic all or most of the time, while others will digress from the lecture and tell jokes or anecdotes. Sometimes the anecdotes, if related to the class, will help you remember some of the information you might otherwise forget. If you have an instructor who always stays on the lecture topic, you will need to be very careful to take good notes on all the material. You will also have to write more notes if there are no stops along the way.

TEACHING STYLE

1. *Voice characteristics.* Some lecturers are loud enough for a large lecture hall, while others are more soft-spoken. If you cannot hear the lecture well, try to move closer to the front of the room. Some instructors have interesting voice characteristics that give you clues about important points or potential test questions. Some voices have unique traits, such as accents or unusual pitch. As you are taking notes, make every effort to concentrate on the lecture material, not on the lecturer personally.

2. *Lecture speed.* Some lecturers speak very fast, with few pauses. Others are slow and deliberate, pausing often for effect. If you have a lecturer who presents much information and speaks very fast, you may wish to tape-record the lectures.

3. *Mobility.* Some instructors move around the room while lecturing; others remain either behind the podium or desk or in the same place at the front of the class. Different students like different styles. You may prefer that the lecturer remain in one place, or you may think he or she is identifying more with the students when moving around. Again, concentrate on the lecture itself, not on the mannerisms of the one delivering the lecture.

4. *Use of audiovisual teaching aids.* You will have an easier task of writing important information and spelling terms correctly if the instructor does use some audiovisuals. However, some instructors use the strict lecture method, with

none of the aids. You will have to pay very close attention to a lecturer who uses no teaching aids if you are to be successful in recording all of the information.

It is important to remember that different students like different teaching styles. Try not to think of these lecturer differences as inadequacies or problems. You can learn to adapt to all these styles, and your education will be more complete.

A Note-Taking Method—Cornell Notes

The **Cornell note-taking system** was developed by Walter Pauk at Cornell University over forty years ago; it is still considered one of the best ways to take notes from lectures or textbooks and is widely taught in study skills courses. It is an effective method both because of its organization and because of the feasibility of using the notes when studying for tests.

How to take Cornell notes. The steps to Cornell note taking are as follows:

▪ Draw a vertical line down your paper leaving 2.5 inches on the left side. (Figure 10.2 shows how the paper should be lined. Figure 10.3 shows an example of Cornell notes.) The 2.5 inch column is often called a cue column. It will be used to write main ideas or topics, while the majority of the notes will be on the remaining part of the page. While you are taking the notes, you leave the cue column empty. Then when you review your notes, you should devise questions from the notes and write them (or just the topics) in the cue column. The questions or topics will be used later to test your recall.

▪ Draw another margin for the bottom of the page. This margin should be 2 inches at the bottom of each page of notes; this space will be used for a summary. Each page of notes should be summarized concisely in one or two sentences.

▪ The information you write in the large space will vary from student to student and from course to course. You may compose the notes in whatever logical way is best for you. You may compose paragraphs, make lists, or use another method.

▪ Read your notes *soon* after class. Do not let them "get cold," or you may not be able to remember what you meant to write. At this time, you should clarify or fill in any missing information. Also rewrite anything that appears illegible. If you think it is illegible right after class, you will not be able to decipher it at all next week.

▪ After reviewing your notes, you are ready to use the 2.5 inch margin that you left blank on the left side of the page. You should write either key phrases that summarize that part of the notes or questions from the ideas in the notes. This column, when completed, will look like a list of main ideas or a list of questions.

Figure 10.2   *Sample Cornell notes page.*

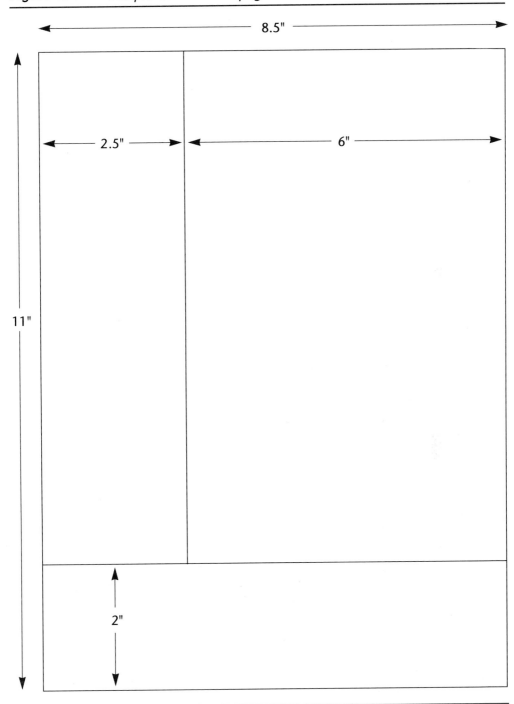

Figure 10.2   *Sample Cornell-style anthropology notes.*

	Oct. 6—Anthropology 205—Dr. Good
	TYPES OF MARRIAGE
4 types of marriage	Some variations but basically 4 types—polygamy (2 kinds), group, & monogamy.
Def—polygamy	polygamy—having more than 1 spouse. "poly" = "many"
2 kinds of polygamy	KINDS OF POLYGAMY:
Def—polygyny	I. (1) polygyny—1 husband & 2 or more wives. "gyn" = "woman" (Greek) as in word gynecologist (Dr. for women).
Sororal vs. nonsororal polygyny	This type of polygamy is more common than #2. In culture having #1, most men are still monogamous (not enough women for many men to have several wives). 2 types of #1 are "sororal" (wives are sisters) & "nonsororal" (not sis.). May be less jealousy w/sororal.
Def—polyandry	(2) polyandry—1 wife & 2 or more husbands. Practiced by only about 1% of world.
Fraternal vs. nonfrat. polyandry	II. 2 types are "fraternal" (husbands are brothers) and "non fraternal" (not bro.). In Tibet were frat. is practiced, no effort made to determine father of children. Fewer kids w/this system.
Def—group marriage	III. Group marriage—2 or more husbands & 2 or more wives. This has happened but is not custom in any known country.
Def—monogamy	IV. Monogamy—1 husband & 1 wife. Some people have practiced "serial" monogamy—several marriages always followed by divorce. Monogamy is only recognized form of marriage in U.S.

There are 4 basic types of marriage in the world: polygyny, polyandry, group marriage, & monogamy.

- When studying, you should cover the 6-inch side of the page to determine whether or not you can recall the important information from the key phrases or questions. If you can, proceed to the next part. If you cannot recall the information, you can uncover the other side and study the information. This is a very effective way to study for tests.

- The summary area at the bottom of each page helps you to understand the overall main ideas. If you can determine what to write in this space, you have a clear grasp of the material and are not focusing too much on details.

Note-Taking Problems and Solutions

Students often report to study skills instructors the problems they are having with content area courses. The following are some of the problems related to taking notes, each followed by some possible solutions for the problems:

Problem: "The instructor talks too fast."

Solutions: Perfect your system of abbreviations and symbols. Get a study partner in the class who can compare notes with you. (Be sure to get a partner who has good attendance.) If two good note-takers compare notes, between the two of them, they should get all of the information. You may have to ask the instructor for permission to tape-record the class. Also be sure to read the corresponding chapter before going to class.

Problem: "The instructor rambles and digresses too much."

Solutions: Record as much as you can. Immediately after class, organize your notes, using the textbook as a guide. Always rewrite your notes in an organized manner, regardless of whether the lecture was organized.

Problem: "The professor tells too many jokes and anecdotes that have nothing to do with the class."

Solutions: This complaint really does not affect your ability to take notes. It merely gives you time to pause between bouts of note taking. In one way, you are fortunate if the professor does this because you can use the time to fill in, expand, or organize your notes.

Problem: "There is no need to take notes at all because the professor goes right by the book."

Solutions: Even if this charge is completely accurate, you should still take notes. It will greatly aid your recall ability if you have been exposed to the same material in more than one way.

Problem: "I begin to daydream during the lecture."

Solutions: Review the listening skills section of this chapter. If you need to sit right in front of the instructor, then arrange to do that. Make eye contact; try to ask questions and make verbal responses as often as possible.

Problem: "I am in a large lecture hall, and people are having conversations around me."

Solutions: If you are not seated according to the instructor's seating chart, get to class early and sit in front. Most conversations in large lecture halls occur in the back, not directly in front of the instructor. If a class immediately before this one prevents you from arriving early, speak with the instructor. You might also ask another student to reserve a seat for you every day. You must be able to hear the lecturer.

Problem: "I can't spell some of the important terminology, and the lecturer uses no audio-visual aids, not even the chalkboard."

Solutions: Write the terms phonetically; look them up in the textbook later. It also helps if you have read the chapter in advance. Make lists of the important terms, most of which are in bold print or some other typographic form that is different.

Problem: "I can't determine the important points, so I don't know what to write in my notes."

Solutions: Before class, read the chapter, noting the textbook clues about what is important. Look at the headings and subheadings, and read the summary if there is one. Read the list of questions the author placed at the beginning or end of the chapter. While in class, write down the instructor's emphases, such as the important concepts written on the board.

Problem: "I try to write everything because I'm in a world history class, and there are so many facts. Everything is a potential test question."

Solutions: Use all of the tips given in the first problem above (the instructor who talks too fast).

Problem: "The information is so boring, but it is a required course."

Solutions: What is "boring" is a matter of opinion. There are some students who will consider that course the most interesting and will major in that area. If the course is required, find a way to build some interest. Speak to some people who earn a living in that field, or talk to some students who are pursuing a major in that subject. Perhaps some of their interest and enthusiasm will motivate you.

Note-Taking Checklist

To assess your note-taking skills, get out the notes that you consider to be your best notes and ask yourself the following questions:

- Are the notes in a subject notebook or a special section of a large notebook?
- Are the notes titled and dated?
- Are the notes legible?
- Are the notes written in pen?
- Were margins left for topics or questions?
- Are all of the main ideas noted?
- Are the notes a *condensed* version of the lecture?
- Were helpful abbreviations and symbols used?
- Are spaces left for information that was not completed?
- Are the notes paraphrased whenever possible?

UNDERLINING

Many first-year college students have no experience with marking or underlining textbooks. Others say that they do not want to make any marks in their textbooks so that they can resell them at a better price. Considering the high cost of college, the price of textbooks is comparatively minimal. You should use your textbooks fully, getting all you can from your college education. Then save money by not having to repeat any classes!

There are several reasons for underlining your textbooks. Done correctly, it helps you to locate and attend to the important ideas in the course. It also gives you a helpful set of ideas and facts to study for tests. For example, you may have a test that covers ten chapters; it would be much too time-consuming to reread all of the chapters. However, you will have enough time to study the underlined parts of the chapters; you will find this to be a valuable way to study a large amount of information in a short time.

Another reason for underlining is to have reference points when you wish to discuss the subject matter with the instructor, the class members, a study group, or a tutor. As you underline, you also endeavor to understand and recall the material. When you experience any difficulty or lack of understanding, you will be able to refer to the material and ask for clarification.

You may also wish to make notes from your underlining. This may be a helpful strategy when you are enrolled in courses you perceive as difficult. Your note taking from the text will be an easier task if you have already located and marked the important information. If you wish to make notes on your textbooks, you can make Cornell notes the way you do during a lecture. Many students report greater recall when they underline their texts and *also* take notes from their underlining.

How to Underline

Have you ever looked through any used textbooks? Some barely appear used at all because nothing is underlined. Frequently the first chapter contains some underlining, and the practice seems to have been abandoned after that. Some textbooks have been so heavily highlighted that the entire page is yellow. Apparently, all of those textbooks were owned by students who did not know the proper procedure for underlining texts.

The term **underlining,** drawing lines under words or phrases, is sometimes referred to as **marking;** some may refer to it as *annotation*. In this chapter, underlining and annotating will be discussed as separate functions, with **annotation** being the phrases, remarks, and symbols placed in the margins or, sometimes, over words in the text.

Three common errors are made while underlining. First, too much can be underlined. Remember that a primary reason for underlining is to have important information to study for tests. If most or all of the page is underlined, you will have to reread the chapter. Second, too little may be underlined. All of the main ideas and some important supporting details should be noted so that they will stand out from the rest of the text. If you are very inexperienced in this skill, begin by looking for a main idea in each paragraph. The third error is underlining the wrong information. For example, instead of underlining the main points, you might underline a minor detail.

The following twelve guidelines will help you master the skill of effective underlining.

1. Use a pen instead of a pencil or a highlighter. A pen is better than a highlighter because students enjoy using a highlighter so much that they tend to get carried away and highlight too much.

2. Develop some system to distinguish main ideas and other important ideas. You might underline the main ideas in one color and the secondary ideas in a different color. Another way to distinguish is by using single underlines for some purposes and double lines for other purposes; perhaps you would use the double underlining for the most important ideas. Develop your own system, but use it consistently.

3. Before you begin to underline a chapter, assess your prior knowledge. Generally, if you know much more about a subject, you will have to underline less. There is no need to underline information that you have known for years. If you have little or no prior knowledge, be careful not to underline too much.

4. Before you begin to underline, preview the chapter. It helps to know something about the topic before marking the text. If you are in the habit of previewing chapters before you read them, you know how much information you can get from parts of the chapter such as headings and subheadings.

5. Read a section first *and then underline.* If you do not follow this guideline, you will not know what to expect by the time you reach the conclusion of the section. Frequently the main idea is the last sentence of the paragraph, in the form of an important conclusion. Sometimes the concluding sentence will negate the previous sentences, such as a conclusion that reads, "Scientists now know that none of this is accurate." If you had not read before underlining, you would have been underlining inaccurate, or outdated, information.

6. Use your knowledge of organizational patterns (Chapter 7) to help you underline effectively. The following are tips for the different patterns:

- Simple listing—Instead of underlining everything in an important list, just write numbers over each item. Underline the title or subject of the list.
- Order/sequence—Again place numbers over the item, and underline the type of list it is. Make a note to yourself in the margin if the list must be in order.
- Comparison and contrast—Identify and underline the two or more things being compared. Underline some of the characteristics that make them alike and/or different.
- Cause and effect—Draw an arrow from the cause to the effect. You can do this even if there are multiple causes or multiple effects.
- Problem and solution—Whenever you are reading about a problem, always search for one or more possible solutions. If one solution is preferred by the author, underline enough to indicate that preference.
- Classification—Search for signal words, such as *types* and *kinds*. Then underline the parts of the classification system. In some cases, numbers can be used also. Underline enough to determine what is being classified and into what parts.
- Definition—Write *def* beside the word being defined, or circle the term. It is not necessary to underline the entire definition as long as your attention is called to the word during later study.
- Example—Write *ex* beside an example that helps you recall a new concept. If multiple examples are given, mark only one.

7. Observe headings and subheadings to help determine what to underline. Since headings and subheadings are the topics of paragraphs or sections, you should underline the main points about those headings. Some headings or subheadings are phrased in the form of a question, such as "Why Did Food Production Develop?" In that case, you need to underline the answer to that question.

8. Underline in telegraphic terms. If you send a telegram and must pay by the word, you shorten the message to the bare essentials, giving the main idea only, such as "Arrive flight 201 July 31 3 P.M." You can also underline just the main ideas, not the modifiers and nonessential elements. In the following examples, the underlined words give you the main idea of the sentences:

> As you underline your textbooks, always be sure that your <u>underlining reflects</u> the <u>main ideas only,</u> not the many less important details.
>
> <u>Many freshmen</u> at any given university are <u>undecided</u> about the course of study they will later pursue as a <u>major.</u>

9. Underline no more than about 15 to 20 percent of the page. You may underline even less if you have a good system of annotation, which will be discussed after underlining. You may also be able to underline considerably less if your prior knowledge is outstanding on the particular topic or subject.

10. If you have trouble determining what supporting ideas are important, first read the main idea; then look for support or evidence for the main idea. If you have trouble locating main ideas and important supporting details, review Chapter 5 on main ideas. Without the ability to locate and understand main ideas, it is very difficult to take notes, underline correctly, or annotate texts for tests.

11. Look for numbers or bullets that are often used to mark important concepts that are in stages or in a list. There are many examples of both numbers and bullets in this chapter. Practice looking for them in your other textbooks as well.

12. Make sure you do not underline in such a way that you change the meaning of the passage. Read the following example, which has been incorrectly underlined. (If you read only the underlined portion of the sentence, you will miss the main point completely.)

> If you wish to be a successful student, <u>you </u>must develop study strategies that will enable you to <u>comprehend all of the information</u> and retrieve it for the numerous tests you must take.

Limitations of Underlining

There are times when underlining is not recommended because of the type of reading material:

1. *Literature anthologies.* Textbooks such as literature anthologies do not lend themselves to underlining because the literary works must be interpreted. There may be no literal information that needs to be underlined because every literal element may represent something else. Instead, you should write your interpretations in the margins.

2. *Supplemental reading.* This is extra reading material that is assigned and that reinforces another discipline. Instead of underlining, you should make associations with the regular material. It would be better to write interpretations and reflections in the margin, if the book is yours, or to make notes on the material if the book is on reserve in the library.

3. *Rarely used textbooks.* Obviously, underlining is of limited use if the textbook is rarely used or is used only for reports and activities. You may still underline if it helps you process and recall the material, but you probably will not find many test questions among the underlined information.

4. *Reference material.* You can never make marks on reference materials that cannot be checked out of the library. On these materials, you should take good notes.

5. *Texts in certain technical courses.* Some courses have texts that may be used more to guide research and lab experiments than for any other purpose. While these texts are necessary tools for the classes, underlining is of little use.

6. *Collections of readings such as essays.* Readings, such as essays, are often assigned in the social sciences; they are valuable both for reinforcing ideas and theories and for elaborating on issues. They are generally read for the overall main idea. You should make reflective notes on these readings.

Read the following passage, which is an example of effective underlining. Notice that the main ideas are underlined according to the guidelines in this section and that no more than 20 percent of the passage has been underlined. The selection is taken from the college textbook, *Cultural Anthropology* (8th ed.), by C. R. Ember and M. Ember.*

*Cultural Anthropology 8/e by Ember/Ember, © 1996. Reprinted by permission of Prentice-Hall, Inc., Upper Saddle River, NJ.

One-Parent Families: Why the Recent Increase?

Not only is the custom of marriage almost universal, but in most societies known to anthropology most people marry. And they usually remarry if they divorce. This means that, except for the death of a spouse, or temporarily during times of divorce or separation, <u>one-parent families are relatively uncommon in most societies.</u>

In many <u>Western countries,</u> however, there has been a <u>dramatic increase recently</u> in the percentage of families that are one-parent families, most of which <u>(about 90 percent) are female-headed families.</u> So for example, in the 1960s about 9 percent of families in the United States were one-parent families, but in the mid-1980s the figure jumped to about 24 percent. Whereas <u>Sweden once led the Western countries in percentage of one-parent families</u> (about 13 percent in the 1970s), the <u>United States now</u> has the highest percentage. Before we try to examine the reasons for the increase, we need to consider that there are a <u>variety of ways to become a one-parent family.</u> First, many one-parent families result from the divorce or separation of two-parent families. Second, many one-parent families result from births out of wedlock. In addition, some result from the death of a spouse and others from the decision by a single person to adopt a child.

① ② ③ ④

<u>Many researchers suggest that the ease of divorce</u> is largely <u>responsible</u> for the increase in one-parent families. On the face of it, <u>this explanation</u> seems plausible. But it is <u>flawed.</u> In many countries during the late 1960s and early 1970s, changes in the law made getting a divorce much easier, and the percentage of one-parent families did rise after that. But why did so many countries ease divorce restrictions at the same time? Did attitudes about marriage change first? <u>A high divorce rate by itself will make for a higher percentage of one-parent households only *if* individuals do not remarry quickly.</u> In the United States, for example, remarriage rates did decline sharply in the mid-1960s, particularly among younger, better educated women, and so the percentage of one-parent households may have risen for that reason. In many other countries, divorce rates stabilized in the 1980s, but the percentage of one-parent families still increased. Thus, easier divorce does not fully explain the increase in number of one-parent families.

<u>Although some parents are clearly choosing to stay single, many might prefer to marry if they could find an appropriate spouse.</u> In (some countries, and among some ethnic groups within some countries, there are many fewer males than females, and sometimes a high proportion of the males have poor economic prospects.) In the former Soviet Union, there are many more women than men; males were more likely to have died from war, alcoholism, and accidents. The United States does not have such a skewed sex ratio, but in some neighborhoods, particularly poor neighborhoods, there are very high mortality rates for young males. And many males in such neighborhoods do not have work. One study by Daniel Lichter and his colleagues estimated that for every 100 African American women between the ages of 21 and 28, there were fewer than

80 available African American men. If we count only men who are employed (full- or part-time), the number of available men per 100 women drops below 50. So there <u>may be</u> considerable <u>merit to the argument that one-parent families</u> (usually headed by women) <u>will be likely when a spouse</u> (particularly an employed one) <u>is hard to find.</u>

<u>Another popular explanation for the rise in number of one-parent families</u> is that, in contrast to the past, <u>women can manage without husbands because of support from</u> the <u>state.</u> This scenario seems to fit Sweden, where unmarried and divorced mothers receive many social supports and allowances for maternity and educational leave. But Iceland has few social supports from the government and yet has the highest rate of out-of-wedlock births of all the Scandinavian countries. <u>In</u> the <u>United States,</u> the <u>welfare argument fails to predict changes over time.</u> The program called Aid to Families with Dependent Children provides aid largely to single mothers. If the theory about government help were correct, increases in such aid would generally predict increases in the percentage of mother-headed households. But, in fact, during the 1970s the percentage of families receiving aid (and the value of aid) decreased, while the percentage of mother-headed households increased. And in the 1980s it was more difficult to go "on welfare," but the percentage of mother-headed households increased anyway. Women might be more able to manage alone if they have high-paying employment, and therefore we might expect more one-parent families by choice, as more women enter the job market. But, although this may explain the choices of some women, recent research finds that <u>employed women generally</u> are *more* rather than less <u>likely to marry!</u>

In any case, there <u>seems to be a general association between commercial economies and the possibility of one-parent families.</u> Is there something about subsistence economies that promotes marriage and something about commercial economies that detracts from it? Although marriage is not universally based on love or companionship, it entails a great deal of economic and other kinds of interdependence, particularly in not-so-commercial economies. Market economies allow other possibilities; goods and services can be bought and sold and governments may take over functions normally handled by kin and family. So the <u>one-parent family</u> is <u>likely to remain</u> an <u>option</u>—either a <u>choice or</u> a <u>necessity</u>—<u>for some people.</u>

ANNOTATING

Annotate means to take notes and, in this chapter, will refer to all of the marks used to call attention to terms or main points and to the remarks written in the margins. You can use this skill in textbooks and in your lecture notes.

Annotating combined with appropriate underlining is a far superior technique to underlining used alone.

Many types of marginal annotation can be used effectively, all of which will increase comprehension and recall, if reviewed properly, and will cause you to be able to underline less material. The following types of marginal annotations are helpful:

- Main ideas and/or summary statements
- Circling unknown words and putting a question mark in the margin
- *Def* to mark an important definition of a word you have marked in the text
- *Ex* to mark an example of a difficult concept
- Parentheses around an example or anything you want to find *if* you need it
- Numbers for important lists of people, theories, reasons, historical events
- Some type of mark (for example, an asterisk) for a possible test item or important point
- Association with other knowledge (for example, "This theory is completely different from Freud's")
- Arrows to show cause and effect relationships
- Reflective comments to help you recall or comprehend
- Questions you want to ask the instructor or something you wish to have clarified
- Reminders to yourself (for example, "Get more references on this")

How and When to Use Annotation

After you have underlined the main ideas and important supporting details, you are ready to annotate. As you will see from a later text example, underlining and annotation together provide much valuable information. Annotating is an activity that requires your active attention because you constantly are deciding what to write. Remember the following five tips to help you master this skill.

1. Never use a highlighter for marginal annotation because it is too bulky. Even if, against previous advice, you continue to use a highlighter to underline, you simply cannot manipulate such a bulky tool while making comments.

2. Annotate only a section at a time. If an entire section is too much for you to process at once, go by paragraphs. You may feel the need to do this in your more difficult subjects. Cover whatever amount of material is comfortable for you, which you can comprehend and recall.

3. Paraphrase when doing marginal annotation. When writing the main ideas, you may be tempted to use the exact words of the professor or of your textbook. Repeating the words in the paragraph, which you have probably already underlined, is futile. You will remember the material better if you do not use the wording of another person either.

4. Remember your list of abbreviations and symbols used for Cornell Notes. These very helpful abbreviations and symbols should be used for annotation as well as for Cornell note taking.

5. Remember: "Practice makes perfect." This old adage is true of all of your study strategies. Continue to work on these skills, and your efforts will be rewarded by good grades.

Annotating in the Various Academic Disciplines

There are different types of learning required in the different academic subjects; you may need some examples of the kinds of information you should locate and annotate. The following lists are possibilities:

LITERATURE

- Symbolism
- Figures of speech
- Connotation and denotation
- Moral or lesson of the literary work
- Outstanding points made
- Your personal reflections (how the work makes you feel)
- Interpretations offered by the instructor

MATHEMATICS

- Important terms and symbols
- Interpretations of graphs
- Applications of mathematical operations
- Questions or points of confusion
- Important review sources (when needed)
- Asterisk beside effective sample problems
- Remarks to help you recall a new operation

FOREIGN LANGUAGES

- New and/or difficult vocabulary
- Translations
- Grammar rules or exceptions to the rules
- Comparison/contrast with your native language
- Questions about pronunciation or grammar
- Customs that explain terms

SOCIAL SCIENCES

- Important theories and theorists
- Cause and effect relationships
- Types of social problems and solutions
- Psychological disorders, causes, and treatments
- Family structures, practices relating to marriage and children, and societal gender roles
- Governing methods, societal taboos, religions, accepted behaviors, and customs
- Important people, dates, inventions, discoveries, leaders, and wars throughout history

PURE SCIENCES

- Important terminology and concepts
- Formulas
- Processes and patterns
- Important scientific principles
- Taxonomy or classification systems
- Significant research

BUSINESS

- Concepts
- Terminology
- Economic trends
- Statistical analyses
- Frequently used symbols and formulas
- Methods

PERSUASIVE WRITING

- Author's viewpoint and opposing arguments
- Evidence offered for each side of an issue
- Your personal conclusion about the logic of the arguments
- Further questions you have on the issue
- Strong or weak sections of the arguments
- Emotionally charged language

COMBINED USE OF CORNELL NOTES, UNDERLINING, AND ANNOTATION

1. Read all of the notes, underlining, and annotation to study for tests.
2. Relate the class material and the text material.
3. Clarify anything you had previously marked with a message that something was unclear.
4. Do something extra (overlearn) with the notes, underlining, and annotation.

Any of the following strategies or activities could be considered overlearning:

- Make semantic maps of the information.
- Write summaries of the chapter's main points.
- Record the main ideas into a tape recorder.
- Make graphic illustrations, such as time lines, bar graphs, or process charts.
- Compose test questions on each chapter and learn the answers.
- Put the information into whatever form you like using a word processor.
- Verbally review the material with a classmate, tutor, or study group.
- Make note cards with questions on one side and answers on the other.

This reading selection illustrates the benefits of *both* underlining and annotation. It is taken from *Politics in America* (2nd ed.), by T. R. Dye.*

*POLITICS IN AMERICA: 2/e by Thomas R. Dye, © 1997. Reprinted by permission of Prentice-Hall, Inc., Upper Saddle River, NJ.

Support Agencies. In addition to the thousands of personal and committee staff who are supposed <u>to assist members of Congress</u> in research and analysis, <u>four Congressional support agencies provide Congress with information:</u> the Library of Congress, the General Accounting Office, the Congressional Budget Office, and the Office of Technology Assessment.

4 agencies provide serv. to Cong.

■ The <u>Library of Congress and its Congressional Research Service (CRS)</u> are the oldest Congressional support agencies. Members of Congress can turn to the Library of Congress for references and information. The Congressional Research Service responds to direct requests of members for factual information on virtually any topic. It tracks major bills in Congress and produces summaries of each bill introduced. This information is available on computer terminals in members' offices.

Roles of CRS:1) Give info on ANY topic

2) Tracks & summarizes bills

① ■ The <u>General Accounting Office (GAO)</u> has broad <u>authority</u> to ② oversee the operations and finances of executive agencies, to evaluate their programs, and to report its findings to Congress. ③ Established as an arm of Congress in 1921, the GAO largely confined itself to financial auditing and management studies in its early years but expanded to more than five thousand employees in the 1970s and undertook a <u>broad agenda of policy research and evaluation.</u> Most GAO studies and reports are requested by members of Congress and Congressional committees, but the GAO also undertakes some studies on its own initiative.

Duties of a GAO

■ The <u>Congressional Budget Office (CBO)</u> was created by the Congressional Budget and Impoundment Act of 1974 to strengthen Congress's role in the budgeting process. It was designed as a congressional counterweight to the president's Office of Management and Budget. The CBO supplies the House and Senate budget committees with its <u>own budgetary analyses</u> and economic <u>forecasts, sometimes challenging</u> those found in the <u>president's</u> annual budget.

CBO's purpose: strengthen Cong.'s role in budgeting

■ The <u>Office of Technology Assessment (OTA)</u> was created in 1972 to provide Congress with its own source of expertise on scientific and technical matters. The OTA responds to requests for information and analyses from Congressional committees rather than from individual members.   *Do scientists work here?*

OTA gives Cong. info on science & technology

Note that both the CBO and the OTA were created at a time when Congress was growing in power relative to a presidency weakened by Vietnam and Watergate. In these same years, Congress encouraged the GAO to undertake a more active and critical role relative to executive agencies. Thus the <u>growth of Congressional staff and supporting agencies is tied to the struggle for power between the legislative and executive branches.</u>

SUMMARY

Students who wish to be successful in college should master the skills of note taking, underlining, and annotating. For note taking to be effective, listening skills are mandatory. The chapter gave suggestions for improving listening skills, general guidelines for note taking, guidelines for using symbols and abbreviations, and some examples of symbols and abbreviations used by many students. There was also a discussion of taking notes during lectures of professors who have varying lecture styles. A specific note taking method, Cornell notes, was explained and recommended, with examples being given. Finally, there was a discussion of some of the common note taking problems, with possible solutions offered for each.

Underlining texts was discussed, with an explanation of how to underline as well as the appropriate amounts to underline. Limitations of underlining were mentioned, some of which can be addressed through the use of effective marginal annotations.

Annotation was discussed separately from underlining, although the two skills complement each other and are most effective when used together. Tips were given for annotating, and types of information to annotate in the various academic disciplines were listed. The chapter concluded with ideas for combining the three skills discussed in the chapter into an effective strategy for test preparation, comprehension, and recall. Examples from different texts illustrated underlining used alone and underlining used in combination with annotating.

Cooperative Learning Activities

GROUP 1. Melanie is enrolled in her first semester in college. She has little experience with note taking and no experience with marking her textbooks. She is having trouble underlining her world civilization history text because there are so many names, dates, and events that are important. She underlines most of every page because everything is an important fact. She has so much annotation in the margins that it is difficult to read it. Her methods are obviously not adequate for this particular type of course. What else would help Melanie, besides underlining and annotating? How could she change her underlining and annotating to make them more effective?

GROUP 2. Michael takes excellent notes in science and math courses, but his note-taking strategy falls apart in courses he does not like, such as literature, psychology, and anthropology. He often makes no notes at all and merely tries to find the material discussed in class somewhere in his textbooks. He says that when courses are boring to him, he cannot concentrate in class. However, he must take all of the core requirements during the first two years. What should he do?

GROUP 3. Ashley has a sociology professor who talks extremely fast and rarely ever pauses. She cannot write all of the information, so she leaves spaces to fill in the information later. However, when she tries to locate the information in the text, she usually discovers that the lecture does not cover the same material as the text. She has tried taping the lectures, but she rarely has time to listen to the tapes. Solve this problem for Ashley.

GROUP 4. Dwayne's professor in history rambles and jumps from century to century and from country to country in his lectures. Dwayne has been told that the tests are derived almost exclusively from the lectures, but his notes are totally disorganized. He feels sure that all of the necessary information is presented in class, but the facts are never in any sort of order that Dwayne can detect. How can he use his notes, or other sources, to prepare for tests?

GROUP 5. Each member of the group should bring in examples of lecture notes. Follow the note-taking checklist in this chapter and assess another group member's notes. Then give the following information:

- List ways your partner could make better notes.
- Decide which one of you has better notes, and discuss the reasons.
- Will your partner's notes be helpful in preparing for tests? If not, what additions or changes could make the notes helpful for test preparation?

Reading Selection: *Cultural Anthropology*

Title: *Body Decoration and Adornment**
Authors: C. R. Ember & M. Ember

Activation of Prior Knowledge and Interest

1. How you do feel about tattoos and body piercing?

    _____

    _____

    _____

2. Would you consider either of the two? Why or why not?

    _____

    _____

    _____

3. What other types of body adornments do you know?

    _____

    _____

    _____

In all societies, people decorate or adorn their bodies. The decorations may be permanent—scars, tattoos, changes in the shape of a body part. Or they may be temporary—in the form of paint or objects such as feathers, jewelry, skins, and clothing that are not strictly utilitarian. Much of this decoration seems to be motivated by esthetic considerations, which, of course, may vary from culture to culture. The actual form of the decoration depends on cultural traditions. Body ornamentation includes the pierced noses of some women in India, the elongated necks of the Mangebetu of central Africa, the tattooing of North American males, the body painting of the Caduveo of South America, and the varying ornaments found in almost every culture.

*CULTURAL ANTHROPOLOGY 8/E, by Ember/Ember, © 1996. Reprinted by permission of Prentice-Hall, Inc. Upper Saddle River, NJ.

However, in addition to satisfying esthetic needs, body decoration or adornment may be used to delineate social position, rank, sex, occupation, local and ethnic identity, or religion within a society. Along with social stratification come visual means of declaring status. The symbolic halo (the crown) on the king's head, the scarlet hunting jacket of the English gentleman, the eagle feathers of the Native American chief's bonnet, the gold-embroidered jacket of the Indian rajah—each of these marks of high status is recognized in its own society. Jewelry in the shape of a cross or the Star of David indicates Christian or Jewish inclinations. Clothes may set apart the priest or the nun or the member of a sect such as the Amish.

The erotic significance of some body decoration is also apparent. Women draw attention to erogenous zones of the body by painting, as on the lips, and by attaching some object—an earring, a flower behind the ear, a necklace, bracelet, brooch, anklet, or belt. Men draw attention too, by beards, tattoos, and penis sheaths (in some otherwise naked societies) that point upward. We have only to follow the fashion trends for women of Europe and North America during the past 300 years, with their history of pinched waists, ballooned hips, bustled rumps, exaggerated breasts, painted faces, and exposed bosoms, to realize the significance of body adornment for sexual provocation. Why some societies emphasize the erotic adornment of women and others emphasize it in men is not yet understood.

In many societies the body is permanently marked or altered, often to indicate a change in status. For example, in the Poro initiation ceremony practiced by the Kpelle of Liberia, newly circumcised boys spent a period of seclusion in the forest with the older men. They returned with scars down their backs, symbolic tooth marks indicative of their close escape from ngamu, the Great Masked Figure, which ate the child but disgorged the young adult (Gibbs, 1965).

The tendency to decorate the human body is probably universal. We have noted some of the various methods people have used to adorn themselves in different societies. We are also aware of body-decoration practices that raise questions to which we have no ready answers. What explains adornment of the body by permanent marking such as scarification, or by bound feet, elongated ears and necks, shaped heads, pierced ears and septums, and filed teeth? Why do different societies adorn, paint, or otherwise decorate different parts of the body for sexual (or other) reasons? And what leads some members of our society to transfer body decoration to their animals? Why the shaped hair of the poodle, the braided manes of some horses, and diamond collars, painted toenails, coats, hats, and even boots for some pets?

Critical Thinking Questions

1. Choose to either defend or refute the following statement: *Permanent and temporary body decoration and adornment serve entirely different purposes.*

_____

_____

_____

2. Give evidence from the selection that both "conservative" and "progressive" cultures practice body decoration and adornment.

_____

_____

_____

3. List as many ways as you can in which members of *your* modern society decorate and adorn themselves.

_____

_____

_____

REFERENCES

Barker, L. L. (1971). *Listening Behavior.* Englewood Cliffs, NJ: Prentice-Hall, Inc.

Pauk, W. (1993) *How to Study in College.* Boston: Houghton Mifflin Company.

CREDITS

Dye, T. R. (1997). *Politics in America* (2nd ed.). Upper Saddle River, NJ: Prentice-Hall, Inc.

Ember, C. R., & Ember, M. (1996). *Cultural Anthropology* (8th ed.). Upper Saddle River, NJ: Prentice-Hall, Inc.

Writing in College Courses

CHAPTER OBJECTIVES

- To understand the writing demands in college classes
- To comprehend the basic requirements involved in the various types of writing assignments
- To understand the writing process and its product
- To have an awareness of the resources available to aid in writing assignments

 **COLLEGE WRITING DEMANDS**

Regardless of academic major, every college student will be faced with numerous writing assignments across the curriculum. You should anticipate the same high assessment standards for compositions done in science and mathematics as for those written in composition classes. The following are examples of the types of writing assignments given in college:

- Literature—Interpret the symbolism in the poem *The Rime of the Ancient Mariner.*

- Psychology—In two pages, compare and contrast a neurosis and a psychosis.
- Statistics—Conduct an empirical experiment, and write a paper on your findings.
- Composition—Write an essay defending a point of view on a controversial subject.
- Sociology—Write a research paper, using at least ten sources, on some aspect of family life in a foreign country.
- Biology—Maintain a content journal, including the results from all lab activities.

As you can determine from the examples, the writing assignments vary in purpose, length, and expectations of the professor. Throughout your college years, you should attempt to perfect your writing skills. Warriner, Ludwig, and Connolly (1977) feel that people learn to be better writers in three ways: (1) by actual study of the elements of writing, such as mechanics and organization; (2) by reading widely; and (3) by the actual process of writing and rewriting. You become good at the skills you practice often, as in sports. This chapter submits suggestions for writing some of the more prevalent types of assignments. Writing is then explained as an ongoing process having several stages. Finally, resources are listed that are available to help college writers.

TYPES OF WRITING IN COLLEGE CLASSES

Summaries

Summary writing is one of the most essential skills needed by college students. It is necessary for many tasks and assignments that you will be given. This skill helps with all of the following: reading comprehension, monitoring reading and learning skills, textbook study, preparation for essay tests, note taking, writing research papers, and recall of information.

Writing a summary is difficult for many students because they do not know what material to include, and they write far too much. Their summary is not concise and is really not a summary as much as a restatement of the original passage. This could be due to the inability to locate main ideas and important supporting ideas. (Refer to Chapter 5.) The following steps will help you write good summaries:

1. Preview the material you will have to summarize.
2. Let your purpose guide you in determining organization and length.
3. Read the material through once for main ideas.

4. Reread, looking for the main ideas of each individual paragraph.
5. Write the opening statement that you think expresses the major idea.
6. Write the ideas that support the major idea.

In addition to the steps in the process of summary writing, remember a few important guidelines:

- Avoid including details, examples, anecdotes, or other material besides the main points.
- Do not repeat any information.
- Do not include your opinion.
- Use your own words.
- Use transition words or expressions to go from one paragraph to another, such as the examples below:

accordingly	another	as a result	at last
at this time	consequently	finally	furthermore
in contrast to	in fact	likewise	moreover
nevertheless	otherwise	on the other hand	

Sometimes you will be told to write a **precis,** a type of summary that is distinctive because it is written from the point of view of the author, not the person writing the precis. In ordinary summaries, you often write, "The author says," but not in a precis. In this case, you would write as though you were summarizing your own writing; you would be very concise and to the point. You should paraphrase with any type of summary, and you may need practice both in rewording sentences and in using synonyms (Bromley & McKeveny, 1986).

EXERCISE 11.1

Use one section of any textbook and summarize it. Review the steps and guidelines if necessary.

Essays

A Dictionary of Reading and Related Terms (Harris & Hodges, 1981) defines **essay** as a relatively brief literary composition, usually in prose, giving the author's views on a particular topic. Students often underrate the effort involved in essay writing since they are giving their own views. However, the views must be supported logically. Here are ten guidelines to consider when writing an essay.

1. Decide in advance the organizational pattern you will use. (See Chapter 7.) If you decide on a pattern before you begin to write, you can then develop your composition according to your plan, affording maximum clarity.

2. Generate ideas by brainstorming. You may be assigned a topic, but if you are allowed to choose, think of all the interesting ideas related to the academic discipline in which you were given the assignment. You may also brainstorm with other students or anyone who might have an interest and some good ideas.

3. Form a thesis statement. The **thesis** is the major point of an essay. For example, the topic *Life in the 1950s* could have the following thesis:

- Life in the 1950s was more satisfying because of strong family ties, strong religious beliefs, and a low crime rate, all of which were related.

You should carefully plan your thesis statement and refer to it regularly to make sure you remain on the subject. If you narrow the topic, the thesis statement will also change. If you have difficulty deciding on a thesis for your essay, remember a few guidelines:

- *Write some potential titles for your paper.* This is easier for most students than writing a thesis. You may derive the thesis from the potential titles.
- *Read your list of ideas to determine what they all describe.* When you are looking for the main idea of a paragraph, you ask yourself what all the sentences have in common or to what they all refer. In the same way, you can find a thesis statement.
- *Practice formulating thesis statements with an easier task.* When you see a controversial newspaper editorial, you probably have an opinion of your own. Formulate a statement that explains your view and for which you could offer reasons. Practice this skill often.
- *After formulating your thesis, be sure that all of the ideas you want to include relate to the thesis.* Feel free to revise either the thesis or the list of ideas if there is inconsistency.

4. In the introduction to the essay, present the purpose of the composition. This will enable the reader to follow your line of thought, and it should stimulate interest in the topic. Always keep in mind your purpose for writing.

5. Make smooth transitions between paragraphs. You may use a pronoun to refer to the preceding paragraph; for example, "*This* arrangement did nothing for the political party involved." You may also use transitional words or expressions, such as those listed above in the Summaries section.

6. Group related ideas together so that your essay will be logical. Paying attention to this guideline will prevent you from rambling as new ideas come to mind. Check over each paragraph to make sure the ideas you put together actually belong together.

7. Give reasons or evidence for your views. Never limit an essay to only your opinions. You should give support for your views because instructors expect you to know enough or research enough to support your ideas with facts, reasons, analogies, examples, or some other information.

8. Be sure that you relate the essay to the course content. Instructors always want to feel that you have learned something in the course. As you support your position in the essay, you should refer to the textbook, lectures, or related material. If your topic has not been specifically discussed, relate it to a topic that *has* been discussed.

9. Write a conclusion that will highlight your major point. A strong conclusion will reiterate your introductory statement of your major point. Before writing the conclusion, reread the essay to make sure you have provided enough evidence for your viewpoint.

10. Proofread the entire essay for both ideas and mechanics. You should make proofreading a practice with any writing assignment.

EXERCISE 11.2

Which organizational pattern or patterns would you use to develop essays on the following topics?

1. Use of Animals in Laboratory Research

   _____

2. Formal Preschool Education

   _____

3. Legalization of Euthanasia

   _____

4. Prison Reform

   _____

5. Causes of Teenage Drug Use

EXERCISE 11.3

Write a concise but complete thesis statement for each of the following topics.

1. Marriage in the 1990s

2. Public Schools

3. College Athletics

4. Independence Day

5. Medical Advancements

Narratives

A **narrative** is a form of writing in which a fictional or nonfictional story is told; it can be either prose or poetry. In a composition class, you might be told to write a narrative poem, or the assignment might specify a short story. A form of writing like a short story may be more fun to read or write, but in some ways it will also be more difficult. This is because it requires creativity, not merely researching the ideas of other people. If you do not feel that you are very creative, the following eight guidelines should help you do your best.

1. Write about what you know. Most of you will remember hearing this advice from a teacher at one or more times during your school experience. It remains good advice. The events about which you write may not have occurred, but you should place the action in a setting with which you are familiar. Your knowledge will be reflected in the story, as will your lack of knowledge if you write about something of which you have little or no prior experience. Even writers of stories in a genre like science fiction have much knowledge about scientific principles, and some of their characters probably remind them of people they have encountered in life or in print.

There are several ways you can write about what you know:

- Write about an actual incident from either your life or the life of someone you know well.
- Write about an interesting person you know.
- Write about an imaginary person or incident in your familiar surroundings.
- Write about an imaginary person embroiled in a controversy about which you have strong feelings.
- Write about a fond daydream or a personal goal.

2. When writing a narrative, be sure that you have an ending in mind. It would be disastrous to write a very interesting narrative only to have no way to end it. For this reason, think of an ending before you plan the sequence of events in the action. The ending should always be consistent with the plot line. For example, if you are writing a mystery story, the pertinent clues should have been included in the sequence of events. The reader should get to play detective while reading the mystery.

3. Determine the viewpoint of the story. Usually the story is told from the viewpoint of a character who has some redeeming qualities. Most readers do not wish to identify with a villain. You may tell a story in first person or third person. The first person ("I") may give the story more of a feeling of intimacy, while the third person ("he," "she," or "they") will seem more objective. The narrator may or may not be a character in the story. Your purpose will help you determine the point of view.

4. Use the appropriate amount of detail. Basically, you need to include enough detail to make a story easy to comprehend but not enough to make the story boring and monotonous. If you like architecture so much that you must describe every corner of a building in minute detail, remember that the reader may not share your interest. It is best to give just enough detail so that the reader can form a clear and lasting impression.

5. If you include dialogue, be sure that it is realistic. This is one of the reasons you should write about things you know. For example, slang is constantly changing, especially that used by young people. If you were writing about high school students while you are closely acquainted with many of them, you could write more realistic dialogue than someone who does not keep in touch with young people. Colloquial expressions also can be a problem. **Colloquial expressions** are those used only in certain areas of the country; you may not be familiar with the current colloquialisms of other parts of the country. If you are insistent on writing about a part of the country that you do not know, either avoid colloquial expressions or get some expert advice.

6. Avoid stereotyping your characters. Since stereotyping, by its very nature, assigns characteristics of a few people to an entire group, it is both inaccurate and insulting. People, unlike stereotypes, are complex and interesting.

7. Keep in mind the basic elements of a story. These include characters, setting, plot, and resolution. A story usually contains a problem, although the conflict may be as simple as attempting to make a decision. The conflict may also involve a change within a character.

8. Consult composition books or the writing center for additional help. The suggestions offered in this chapter are not intended as a substitute for such important references as grammar books and good literary models. After you complete your required English courses, keep your grammar and composition books as a very valuable reference.

EXERCISE 11.4

Answer the following questions about your narrative preferences as if you were required to write a narrative in composition class.

1. What type of short story would you write—human interest, character study, mystery, adventure, love story, science fiction, or other?

   _____

2. Name a person you know from your life experiences who would be an interesting character in a story.

   _____

3. What type of story would you *not* wish to write? Why?

_____

4. Do you prefer stories in first or third person? Why?

_____

5. What recent news event might inspire a good story?

_____

6. What problem have you experienced that might be the basis for a good story?

_____

EXERCISE 11.5

Select one of the following statements, and write a paragraph in which the statement might be made. Be as creative as you can.

1. "I have something to tell you."
2. "How could you do such a thing?"
3. "How long will you be gone?"
4. "This is not as bad as it's going to sound."
5. "This is what I've always wanted!"

_____

_____

_____

_____

_____

_____

_____

Laboratory Reports

Most science classes and some classes in other disciplines have a lab every week. Most professors expect all lab experiments to be accompanied by a written report. Although expectations vary from one professor to another, you will probably be expected to include the procedures used, materials used, the results, and possibly the implications.

Use the following five guidelines in writing your laboratory reports:

1. *If the professor specifies a format, go by it every time.*
2. *Take good notes while you are conducting the experiment; then write your reports from your notes.*
3. *Write your report as soon as possible after the lab.*
4. *Write your reports in clear and concise language.* Unlike composition classes, you should avoid experimenting with language. Do not use flowery phrases and elaboration. Science is more concerned with accuracy than with creative writing.
5. *Some science instructors require you to do your reports in a laboratory manual or workbook.* In this case, you will not have to worry about the format, but you must be careful to complete every part of the exercise.

Experimental Studies

You may be given an assignment requiring you to conduct some type of experiment and report on the results. This may be a simple survey, such as an opinion poll, or it may involve more experimentation and statistical analyses. It will depend on the level and type of class in which you are enrolled. In general, however, with any experimental research, there are several parts to your written product.

1. Introduction. In this opening section, you give information about the nature and purpose of your work. Explain what you were seeking and your reasons for doing the study.

2. Background research. You must research the issue by locating information in scholarly journals in your subject area. All academic disciplines have their own scholarly journals to which researchers contribute articles. For example, if you were enrolled in a teacher preparation course, you could get information in journals like *The Journal of Educational Psychology*. You may use several journals, but you must make notes on all of the articles in your bibliography and then write the conclusions of the research. You will then explain your plan to do additional research in this area or a closely related area.

3. Hypothesis. A **hypothesis** is a tentative assumption that accounts for a fact or set of facts and that can be tested by further investigation (*American Heritage Dictionary*). In other words, you will make an educated guess about the findings of your forthcoming investigation.

4. Description of procedures. You will tell all of the necessary information, such as methods, materials, and subjects. You should describe your procedures in enough detail that another researcher could replicate the study if desired.

5. Results. Relate the findings, including any statistics used. The level of the course will determine the complexity of the statistical procedures that will be required.

6. Implications/Discussion. In this part of your written report, you will discuss the significance of your findings, both practical and theoretical. You might tell how your study would help people, what it will mean, or if further investigation is recommended.

Content Journals

More college instructors are now asking students to maintain content journals, also called *learning logs.* These journals are a student's record of material learned in content areas, but the record is both informal and personal. At times, instructors give guidance on the types of material that should be recorded, such as new ideas the students have learned from specific assignments. The content journals are read by the instructor and assessed for content, not mechanics (Roe, Stoodt, & Burns, 1995).

Research Papers

Research papers are also called *term papers,* and the two terms will be used in this chapter to mean the same type of assignment. The papers may vary with the professor's creativity, but the guidelines presented should be appropriate for all research paper assignments.

You will have to use the library and obtain multiple sources. Often the research paper is assigned the first week of a course and is due around the end of the course because the paper is expected to be a lengthy project. You probably know students who *begin* a research paper the week before finals. It is virtually impossible to do quality work at the last minute.

A research paper may be accompanied by some sort of oral presentation, so you must really know the material well. It is difficult to "fake it" in front of a class where both students and professor will be asking in-depth questions.

Use the following eight guidelines if you are allowed to choose your own topic:

1. *Choose a topic based on your interests and the relevance to the academic discipline.*

2. *If necessary, narrow the topic.* Some topics are obviously too broad; they are more suitable for entire books than for research papers. The following are general topics that have been narrowed to more manageable topics.

- U.S. History—The Bombing of Pearl Harbor
- Juvenile Crime—Effects of Absentee Fathers on the Behavior of Teens
- Women Around the World—The Role of Women in Moslem Society
- Christianity—The Rise of Christian Fundamentalism in the 1990s

3. *Gather information, remembering to find as many sources as required.* Some students do not take this directive seriously. However, using fewer sources than required by the professor will result in points lost.

4. *Form your bibliography.* As you make notes (on note cards, for example), jot down the reference in the same place as the citation or paraphrased material so that you can reference it when you are writing your paper. You must give proper credit in all cases; failure to do so is called *plagiarism.*

5. *Make a formal or an informal outline.* It is much easier to work from an outline, and it will prevent rambling or writing a disorganized paper.

6. *Take notes on your assembled material.* Based on an outline of your proposed paper, you can take notes on one section at a time. This is helpful, especially for the inexperienced writer of research papers. You should always paraphrase, even when taking the original notes. Later you will write the paper from your notes, so be very thorough. It would be better to include too much in the notes and omit it in the paper than not to have enough material noted.

7. *Repeat step # 6 with the remaining sections.*

8. *Write a rough draft from your notes, and revise it later.* (A later section will give information on the various stages of the writing process and the work involved in each stage.)

Deductive and Inductive Writing

You have already been told that you may write your paper by one of the common organizational patterns. Another way some composition teachers approach the subject is to teach their students to write in either a deductive or inductive manner. Both are appropriate for papers of any length.

The derivative of deductive reasoning, **deductive writing** presents the most important points first and the supporting information after that. This type of writing has the effect of getting the reader's attention by stating a viewpoint, a main idea, or a conclusion right away. This form of writing is usually employed in newspaper articles, which are short and must get to the point. The reader's interest is activated right away. It is estimated that about 75 percent of student themes are written deductively (McCall, 1989). The following example is a deductive paragraph:

> John B. Watson was the first student to receive a doctorate in psychology from the University of Chicago. His dissertation was on learning in rats. One of the department's requirements was that he speculate on the kind of consciousness that produced the behavior he observed in his rats. Watson found this demand absurd; he doubted the rats had any consciousness at all. Nevertheless, he complied with the requirement, received his degree, and returned to his laboratory to think about consciousness. [*Psychology: An Introduction* (9th ed.) by C. G. Morris]

Inductive writing gives supporting points first, in a logical manner, and builds to a conclusion. In effect, the main idea is given last. The benefit of this type of writing is to have an impact at the end, but the interest up to that point must be sustained by effective writing. An example that you have probably heard many times in the movies is the detective who gives the clues one by one and then announces, "The butler did it." Use this form when you want to save a striking conclusion, point, or lesson for the end (McCall, 1989). The following paragraph is an example of inductive writing:

> Recently, the American Psychological Association (APA) developed standards that require people in institutions such as clinics and hospitals and in private practice to be supervised by a doctoral-level psychologist. Such regulations limit the opportunities for those with master's degrees to move into higher positions. Therefore, although jobs for people with master's degrees are available, most of them are in business, government, schools, and, to a lesser extent, hospitals and clinics. [*Psychology: An Introduction* (9th ed.) by C. G. Morris]

Exercise 11.6

Tell whether each of the following paragraphs is deductive or inductive. All of the paragraphs were taken from *Psychology* (2nd ed.), by S. F. Davis and J. J. Palladino.*

1. Drugs that block the operation of a neurotransmitter are called **antagonists.** They attach to postsynaptic receptor sites and block the neurotransmitter

*PSYCHOLOGY, 2E by Davis/Palladino, © 1997. Reprinted by permission of Prentice-Hall, Inc., Upper Saddle River, NJ.

from attaching there. By stopping the action of the neurotransmitter, they prevent transmission of signals. For example, the drug haloperidol (Haldol) attaches to dopamine receptors on the postsynaptic membrane. As we shall see in Chapter 14, some psychological disorders are thought to result from high levels of dopamine. Haloperidol is effective in the treatment of these disorders because it reduces the level of dopamine.

---

2. Guilt (or regret) is produced when an individual evaluates his or her behavior as a failure and focuses on the specific features of the self or actions that led to the failure. These individuals are pained by the evaluation of the failure, but they direct the pain to the cause of the failure or the object of the harm. Guilt has always been associated with some corrective action taken to repair the failure and prevent it from happening again. Therefore, guilt is not as intensely negative as shame and does not lead to confusion and loss of action.

---

3. **Stimulants** are drugs that speed up the activity of the central nervous system. Among the most common stimulants are **amphetamines,** also known as "uppers" or "speed," which stimulate the release of dopamine and norepinephrine. In low to moderate doses, they make us more alert, elevate mood, reduce appetite and the need for sleep, and induce euphoria. Larger doses of amphetamines can make us irritable and anxious or bring on a serious reaction that is indistinguishable from paranoid schizophrenia.

---

4. Physicians began to document their patients' symptoms and to note which ones occurred together. The occurrence of groups of symptoms, called *syndromes,* helped physicians identify underlying diseases and develop effective treatments. Approaching abnormal behaviors just as one would approach medical illnesses is known as the **medical model.**

STAGES OF THE WRITING PROCESS

Many educators feel that writing assignments are best accomplished through attention to several stages, so they assess a paper at intervals during its development and give the students feedback concerning revisions. However, some of your instructors will want to read only the finished product, and it will be *your* responsibility to use the process approach to writing (Roe, 1995). The **process approach** means that you complete your writing assignment, either fiction or nonfiction, in several stages. You will probably enjoy doing your assignments this way because the difficult task is broken down into smaller tasks, and you can view your progress and make revisions along the way.

There are only four main stages in the writing process, but several activities must be accomplished in each stage.

1. Prewriting

In the first stage, you should choose a topic if one is not assigned. You could brainstorm with other people, or you can peruse journals and books in the library. You may find that your original topic is too broad, so you may consider only one aspect of the general topic. When you have selected your exact topic, you will need to decide how to organize your paper, for example, by cause and effect organization. Decide how much you already know about the topic, and how much and what particular facts you still need to research.

In the prewriting stage, you should consider the audience for your work. It may be only the professor, or you may also have to share the work orally with the entire class. Knowing who will read or hear what you have written will influence your style. For example, you might want to make your paper more unusual and more upbeat to keep the interest of a class full of students. You should make either a formal or an informal outline (see later section, "Tips on Outlining") and refer to it as you write. (See Figure 11.1 for an example of an outline and Figure 11.2 for an example of the same information on a semantic map.)

If you are working on a term paper, it will require much research, unlike a creative endeavor such as writing your own poetry, short story, or essay. When you have gathered your sources, you are ready to take notes. Although you may take notes on paper, note cards, or the computer, you should take them in such a way that you can go back and sort them into sections, going by your outline. If you use a word processor, you can move material around as needed. Note cards can be sorted and placed in categories. If you prefer note cards, use a section from your outline as the title of the card; also jot down the reference. Then you can write the rough draft from the note cards. Consider the taking of notes to be an ongoing activity for several weeks.

2. Writing a Rough Draft

During the rough draft stage, you will be attempting to get your ideas on paper with only content in mind. At this stage, you do not have to worry about grammar, correct composition, or neatness. You will be revising your paper later, so that will be the time when you correct the mechanics and also refine the content. If you think some parts of your paper need more information, leave spaces until you can consult your research materials or, for nonresearch projects, until ideas come to mind. Write notes to yourself in the margins if this is helpful to you.

Figure 11.1 *Sample outline.*

Effects of Poverty

  I. Health Effects
    A. Infant mortality
    B. Childbirth complications for mother
      1. Infections
      2. Maternal mortality
    C. Malnourishment
      1. Brain damage
      2. Physical retardation

  II. Housing Effects
    A. Substandard housing
    B. Homelessness
    C. Rental conditions
      1. Rural
      2. Urban
    D. Shopping areas

  III. Family Life Effects
    A. Age of marriage and childbearing
    B. Divorce and desertion
    C. Family violence
    D. Personality development of children
      1. Coping strategies
      2. Antisocial behaviors

  IV. Education Effects
    A. High school dropout rate
    B. Family expectations
    C. Quality of schooling

Figure 11.2 *Sample semantic map.*

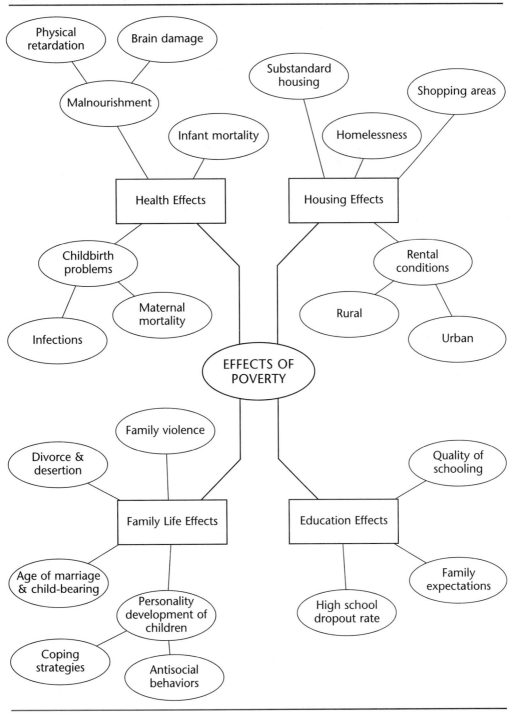

3. Revision

This is a very important stage in the writing process because your revised version will be turned in to the professor for a grade, possibly the only grade on this assignment. Read your paper carefully, perhaps aloud to other people. You may even want to ask someone else to examine the paper as well. You can get feedback from other students or from someone who staffs the university writing center. If your rough draft was written on a computer, now is the time to use a spell checker or a thesaurus if you wish to change words. Examples of some of the things you should look for during the revision stage are listed below (more detailed checklists are found at the end of the chapter):

- Is the major point of the paper obvious?
- Does the introduction call the reader's attention to what you are about to write?
- Do the ideas flow in an organized manner?
- Are the major points well supported with facts, evidence, examples, or other important supporting details?
- Do you have a strong conclusion instead of dropping the reader at a point that is not a good stopping place?
- Should some sentences be reworded for clarity?
- Is the vocabulary level adequate?
- Does the paper conform to grammar and composition rules?
- Is the paper neat?

Always proofread your final paper. It is sometimes obvious to professors that you failed to proofread because words may be omitted or repeated, or because some statements may not make sense when the finished product is read.

Use the appropriate style for citing references. The author of this book is most familiar with three styles, but there are additional writing styles; style manuals are available for specific academic subjects, such as mathematics. Your professor will tell you if you are required to use a certain style; you will lose valuable grade points if you do not use that recommended style. Even if a professor says that you may use any style you wish, you will still be expected to use one style correctly and consistently. The three common styles listed below all have manuals you may purchase or borrow from the library. The three manuals listed below follow the American Psychological Association (APA) style:

- American Psychological Association. (1994). *Publication Manual of the American Psychological Association* (4th ed.). Washington, DC: American Psychological Association.

- Gibaldi, J. (1995). *MLA Handbook for Writers of Research Papers* (4th ed.). New York: The Modern Language Association of America.
- Turabian, K. L. (1996). *A Manual for Writers of Term Papers, Theses, and Dissertations* (6th ed.). Chicago: University of Chicago Press.

You may have a professor who asks for a discipline-specific style; the following is an example of a style manual for physics:

- American Institute of Physics Publication Board. (1978). *Style Manual for Guidance in the Preparation of Papers* (3rd ed.). New York: American Institute of Physics.

4. Publishing or Sharing

While some upper-level classes may require you to submit a paper for publication, most professors will merely read your work for a grade. If the writing is a narrative for a literature class, you may be asked to read it to the class. If the work is the result of an experimental study, you may be asked to share with the class in some other way.

TIPS ON OUTLINING

If the idea of outlining appeals to you but you lack the knowledge to make a good outline, follow the tips below.

1. *Make a simple list of the major points you want to include in the paper.* For example, if you were writing a research paper about life in the 1950s, you might want to include important points about each of the following:

- Roles of men and women
- Divorce rate
- Influence of extended families
- Religious affiliation
- Crime rate

2. *Scrutinize the list to check for ideas that should be added, eliminated, or combined.* It is probable that you might find the above list too long and involved for all of the ideas to be included in one paper. You might, therefore, decide to narrow your topic and write about one aspect of life in the 1950s. If you did this, you would have to begin again with a new list of ideas you want to include in the paper.

3. *Determine the best order for the topics in the list.* The paper will read better if there is a logical flow of ideas. Finish writing about one idea before

going on to the next. Stick to the topic at hand, and you will refrain from rambling, a problem with many college compositions.

4. *Put ideas in an outline form, showing the proper subordination of ideas.* Consult a composition book if you need to review outlining form.

5. *Feel free to revise your outline any time you feel that it is not working.* The outline is made for your benefit, unless the instructor makes it a part of the assignment, so you should alter it to suit your needs.

6. *Always keep your overall topic in mind as you outline or revise your outline.*

 # RESOURCES TO HELP THE STUDENT WRITER

The resources available to help with writing assignments and with becoming a more proficient writer will be categorized according to university resources, computer resources, and library resources.

University Resources

Most universities have a writing center, a place staffed by instructors of English and composition, where you can go for help with writing assignments. In many universities, you can receive individual attention from an instructor, even without an appointment. If appointments are necessary due to numbers of students, make an appointment as soon as you realize your need for help. Students are not charged for this service. Some reasons you might need help from the writing center are listed below:

- Problems with the mechanics of writing
- Questions about correct sentence and paragraph structure
- Lack of knowledge about the process of writing papers
- Lack of knowledge about research
- Questions concerning certain styles for references

Most universities also offer tutoring services at little or no cost to the student. You and a qualified tutor can arrange times when you can conveniently be tutored.

Computer Resources

A computer can be much more efficient than a typewriter because of the ease in editing material you have written. It is easy to rewrite, delete, and move both sentences and whole sections. Computers also contain many helpful aids, such as the spell checker and the thesaurus. Word processing programs can help you create interesting formats and can be used to make graphics.

A word of caution is necessary concerning a spell checker. Some students make the mistake of expecting a spell checker to correct all spelling errors, but it will not do this. If the word you have typed is an actual word, it will not be corrected even if it has been used incorrectly. An example is any homonym: If you type *blue* when you should have typed *blew,* the spell checker will not make a correction since *blue* is a word. Read the following paragraph, which contains many homonyms used incorrectly.

> Eye hate two right two tail yew this news. Ant Nell dyed. Wood yew bee able two come four the funeral? Eye wood appreciate it sew much if yew wood due this four me. Eye have all ready tolled Uncle John yew wood knot dessert me in my our of knead. Eye no its along weigh butt pleas dew catch a plain as soon as yew can. Eye will bee their two mete yew.

After the above paragraph was written, a spell checker was applied to it. No misspellings were reported, but can you imagine the grade you would receive if you turned in work like this?

Library Resources

As soon as you enter a college or university, you should locate and learn to use the library. Some large libraries have training sessions, especially for doing research by computers. You will spend much time in the library if you are to be a successful college student. Become familiar with all of the following library resources.

Reference librarians. The librarians may not know anything about the particular topic you are researching, but they are experts in locating information. It is the duty of the reference librarians to help you find information, but a surprising number of students report being reluctant to ask for their help. Such students spend countless hours looking for information, sometimes with no success.

Interlibrary loans. If your college library does not have a publication you need, the librarians can get the material from another college library. This means that even a small library can provide access to an unlimited supply of books by way of interlibrary loans. You need to be very well organized and plan ahead to ask for an interlibrary loan because it may take awhile to get the book you have requested. There may also be a fee involved; you can get this information from the librarian at the time you make your request.

Catalogs on computer or microfiche. An online catalog is a computerized catalog that gives you access to information about the library's holdings. Most systems are arranged so that you can request information by the author, the title, or the subject. In most libraries, card catalogs are now computerized.

A microfiche catalog is made by photographing information on microfiche. What appear to be tiny little negatives contain large amounts of information. You must use a special microfiche machine to read the information; usually the directions for using a microfiche machine are posted somewhere near the machine. You may also ask the librarian to help you.

Periodicals. A **periodical** is a publication that is issued at regular intervals, perhaps weekly, monthly, or several times a year. Magazines and journals are periodicals. All academic disciplines have their own scholarly journals. Not all libraries have all journals, but the larger libraries have many of them. The types of journals carried by the library may depend on the kind and size of the library and the kind of periodicals; for example, a law library will carry more journals devoted to that discipline. You can access periodicals through computers or bound volumes.

Various indexes. An index is a very quick and efficient way to find information on various sources. Some indexes are only for news articles, while others are for specific disciplines. Some well-known indexes you might use are listed below:

- *Reader's Guide to Periodical Literature*
- *News Bank*
- *New York Times Index*
- *Applied Science and Technology Index*
- *Social Sciences Index*
- *Humanities Index*

A librarian can direct you to an index and probably a listing of every index the library has to offer.

Abstracts. Abstracts, such as *Psychological Abstracts,* are summaries of journal articles. They are very helpful because you can read a short abstract instead of an entire article. The abstract contains enough information to determine the usefulness of the article for your paper.

Government publications. Different departments of the federal government, such as the Department of the Interior, publish facts on all subjects. The government publications are usually kept in a specific area of the library.

Specialized encyclopedias and dictionaries. In addition to regular encyclopedias and dictionaries, some are specific to one academic discipline. The following are only a few examples of the many specialized encyclopedias:

- *Encyclopedia of Religion and Ethics*
- *Encyclopedia of World Art*
- *Cyclopedia of World Authors*

The following are examples of the many specialized dictionaries:

- *Hammond Barnhart Dictionary of Science*
- *Dictionary of Mythology Folklore and Symbols*
- *Words of the Vietnam War*

 **CHECKLISTS**

After your paper is completed and your revisions have been made, use the following checklists to evaluate your paper before submitting it to the professor:

GRAMMAR AND MECHANICS CHECKLIST

1. Do subjects and verbs agree in number?
2. Do pronouns and antecedents agree in number?
3. Are pronouns used correctly?
4. Are adjectives and adverbs used correctly?
5. Were the correct forms of verbs used?
6. Are there any misplaced modifiers?
7. Were correct degrees of comparison used?
8. Have the first words in every sentence and all proper nouns been capitalized?
9. Are sufficient punctuation marks used and used correctly?
10. Are words spelled correctly?

COMPOSITION CHECKLIST

1. Are all sentences complete, with no sentence fragments or run-on sentences?
2. Are paragraph main ideas clear and supported by relevant details?
3. Does the overall organization center around an important idea or thesis?
4. Are paragraphs arranged so that there is an orderly flow of ideas from one section to another?
5. Are appropriate transition words and sentences used to connect ideas?

6. Have the various parts of the paper remained on the topic?

7. Does the conclusion appear logical?

8. If the paper is research, does it include an adequate number of references, and are they correctly documented?

9. Is there unnecessary repetition?

10. Is the written language more formal than everyday spoken language?

11. Is it clear which are the main ideas of the composition?

12. Is the paper interesting enough to cause the reader to want to know more?

VOCABULARY CHECKLIST

1. Are any words overused?

2. Are outdated expressions or clichés used?

3. Does the vocabulary reflect college-level writing?

4. Are words defined when appropriate?

5. If figures of speech are used, are they used appropriately?

6. Are literary allusions used correctly and accurately?

7. Have slang terms been avoided?

If you read the checklists and failed to understand some of the terms, you may need to improve your skills in grammar or composition. Writing instructors sometimes tell a student repeatedly to avoid using run-on sentences, only to find out later that the student had no concept of that term, *run-on sentence*. If you have a problem with any of the skills on the checklists, you should get advice from the university writing center about resources you could use to build skills. There are computer software programs to teach many of the skills on the checklists, and they may already be available in your university writing center or study skills lab. It would be time well spent to work through some of these programs.

SUMMARY

College students should anticipate numerous writing assignments across the curriculum. Depending on the academic discipline, there are many types of writing assignments, such as summaries, essays, narratives, laboratory reports, experimental studies, content journals, and research papers. The chapter presented guidelines for each type of writing assignment.

Students should also understand writing as both a process and a product. The writing process involves the stages of prewriting, writing a rough draft, revising, and sharing with others. Each stage is composed of different activities, and each stage is important to the finished product.

Colleges and universities offer valuable resources to help the college writer achieve success. There are learning labs and writing centers where students may go for individual assistance from both tutors and college instructors. In addition to these resources, computers enable students to write papers more efficiently because of the many tools simplifying the tasks of editing, rewriting, and rearranging material. Many software tutorial programs enable students who are deficient in grammar and composition skills to build skills that are needed for college work. The library is also rich in resources to help writers with research, including the resource of the research librarians. Even small college libraries can offer an unlimited supply of books through interlibrary loans. Students should be aware of the many resources available to them to aid in the writing process.

Cooperative Learning Activities

GROUP 1. Poll each member of the group concerning each person's idea of the "most difficult" writing assignment. Explain what makes each assignment difficult, and give suggestions from this chapter that will make all future assignments of this type less difficult.

GROUP 2. Make a list of all the writing you have done for your courses in the past week. Tell at least one challenging aspect of each writing activity.

GROUP 3. What are the writing demands for each of the following courses?

- English literature
- Mathematics
- Biology
- Art appreciation
- Psychology
- Composition
- Music

GROUP 4. List all of the resources you have used since you began attending college that have helped in completing writing assignments. Then compile a complete list of the resources available on *your* campus.

GROUP 5. Reread the grammar and mechanics checklist, the composition checklist, and the vocabulary checklist. Make notes of unfamiliar words and expressions as well as any items on the checklists that pose problems in your writing. Outline a plan for correcting all of your deficiencies so that you will become a better writer.

Reading Selection: *Essay*

Title: *For My Indian Daughter**
Author: L. P. Johnson

Activation of Prior Knowledge and Interest

1. What important advice did you receive from your father or some other relative?

   _____

   _____

   _____

   _____

2. What examples of racial prejudice have you witnessed recently?

   _____

   _____

   _____

   _____

3. Make a prediction about what the father will tell his daughter.

   _____

   _____

   _____

   _____

My little girl is singing herself to sleep upstairs, her voice mingling with the sounds of the birds outside in the old maple trees. She is two and I am nearly 50, and I am very taken with her. She came along late in my life, unexpected and unbidden, a startling gift.

Today at the beach my chubby-legged, brown-skinned daughter ran laughing into the water as fast as she could. My wife and I laughed watching her, until we heard behind us a low guttural curse and then an unpleasant voice raised in an imitation war whoop.

I turned to see a fat man in a bathing suit, white and soft as a grub, as he covered his mouth and prepared to make the Indian war cry again. He was middle-aged, younger than I, and had three little children lined up next to him, grinning foolishly. My wife suggested we leave the beach, and I agreed.

I knew the man was not unusual in his feelings against Indians. His beach behavior might have been socially unacceptable to more civilized whites, but his basic view of Indians is expressed daily in our small town, frequently on the editorial pages of the county newspaper, as white people speak out against Indian fishing rights and land rights, saying in essence, "Those Indians are taking our fish, our land." It doesn't matter to them that we were here first, that the U.S. Supreme Court has ruled in our favor. It matters to them that we have something they want, and they hate us for it. Backlash is the common explanation of the attacks on Indians, the bumper stickers that say, "Spear an Indian, Save a Fish," but I know better. The hatred of Indians goes back to the beginning when white people came to this country. For me it goes back to my childhood in Harbor Springs, Michigan.

Theft. Harbor Springs is now a summer resort for the very affluent, but a hundred years ago it was the Indian Village of my Ottawa ancestors. My grandmother, Anna Showanessy, and other Indians like her, had their land there taken by treaty, by fraud, by violence, by theft. They remembered how whites had burned down the village at Burt Lake in 1900 and pushed the Indians out. These were the stories in my family.

When I was a boy, my mother told me to walk down the alleys in Harbor Springs and not to wear my orange football sweater out of the house. This way I would not stand out, not be noticed, and not be a target.

I wore my orange sweater anyway and deliberately avoided the alleys. I was the biggest person I knew and wasn't really afraid. But I met my comeuppance when I enlisted in the U.S. Army. One night all the men in my barracks gathered together and, gang-fashion, pulled me into the shower and scrubbed me down with rough brushes used for floors, saying "We won't have any dirty Indian in our outfit." It is a point of irony that I was cleaner than any of them. Later in Korea I learned how to kill, how to bully, how to hate Koreans. I came out of the war tougher than ever and, strangely, white.

I went to college, got married, lived in La Porte, Indiana, worked as a surveyor, and raised three boys. I headed Boy Scout groups, never thinking it odd when the Scouts did imitation Indian dances, imitation Indian lore.

One day when I was 35 or thereabouts, I heard about an Indian powwow. My father used to attend them and so with great curiosity and a strange joy at discovering a part of my heritage, I decided the thing to do to get ready for this big event was to have my friend make me a spear in his forge. The steel was fine and blue and iridescent. The feathers on the shaft were bright and proud.

In a dusty state fairground in southern Indiana, I found white people dressed as Indians. I learned they were "hobbyists," that is, it was their hobby and leisure pastime to masquerade as Indians on weekends. I felt ridiculous with my spear, and I left.

It was years before I could tell anyone of the embarrassment of this weekend and see any humor in it. But in a way it was that weekend, for all its silliness, that was my awakening. I realized I didn't know who I was. I didn't have an Indian name. I didn't speak the Indian language. I didn't know the Indian customs. Dimly I remembered the Ottawa word for dog, but it was a baby word, *kahgee,* not the full word, *muhkahgee,* which I was later to learn. Even more hazily I remembered a naming ceremony (my own). I remember legs dancing around me, dust. Where had that been? Who had I been? "Suwaukquat," my mother told me when I asked, "where the tree begins to grow."

That was 1968, and I was not the only Indian in the country who was feeling the need to remember who he or she was. There were others. They had powwows, real ones, and eventually I found them. Together we researched our past, a search that for me culminated in the Longest Walk, a march on Washington in 1978. Maybe because I now know what it means to be Indian, it surprises me that others don't. Of course there aren't very many of us left. The chances of an average person knowing an average Indian in an average lifetime are pretty slim.

Circle. Still, I was amused one day when my small, four-year-old neighbor looked at me as I was hoeing in my garden and said, "You aren't a real Indian, are you?" Scotty is little, talkative, likable. Finally I said, "I'm a real Indian." He looked at me for a moment and then said, squinting into the sun, "Then where's your horse and feathers?" The child was simply a smaller, whiter version of my own ignorant self years before. We'd both seen too much TV, that's all. He was not to be blamed. And so, in a way, the moronic man on the beach today is blameless. We come full circle to realize other people are like ourselves, as discomfiting as that may be sometimes.

As I sit in my old chair on my porch, in a light that is fading so the leaves are barely distinguishable against the sky, I can picture my girl asleep upstairs. I would like to prepare her for what's to come, take her each step of the way saying, there's a place to avoid, here's what I know about this, but much of what's before her she must go through alone. She must pass through pain and joy and solitude and community to discover her own inner self that is unlike any other and come through that passage to the place where she sees all people are one, and in so seeing may live her life in a brighter future.

Critical Thinking Questions

1. After being in the U.S. Army and going to Korea, the author says, "I came out of the war tougher than ever and, strangely, white." Interpret this comment, based on the information given in the passage.

   _____

   _____

   _____

2. How does the author compare himself to the white man on the beach?

   _____

   _____

   _____

3. What does the author mean by saying that he had come "full circle"?

   _____

   _____

   _____

4. **Writing activity:** Write an essay about some form of discrimination you have experienced or witnessed.

REFERENCES

American Heritage Dictionary: Second College Edition. (1983). Boston: Houghton Mifflin.

Bromley, K. D., & McKeveny, L. (1986). Precis writing: Suggestions for instruction in summarizing. *Journal of Reading, 29,* 392–395.

Copi, I. M. (1986). *Introduction to Logic* (7th ed.). New York: Macmillan.

Harris, T. L., & Hodges, R. E. *A Dictionary of Reading and Related Terms.* Newark, DE: International Reading Association.

McCall, J. (1989). *How to Write Themes and Essays.* Upper Saddle River, NJ: Prentice-Hall.

Morris, C. G. (1996). *Psychology: An Introduction.* Upper Saddle River, NJ: Prentice-Hall, Inc.

Roe, B. D., Stoodt, B. D., & Burns, P. C. (1995). *Secondary School Reading Instruction: The Content Areas* (5th ed.). Boston: Houghton Mifflin.

Warriner, J. E., Ludwig, R. M., & Connolly, F. X. (1977). *Advanced Composition: A Book of Models for Writing.* New York: Harcourt Brace Jovanovich.

CREDITS

Davis, S. F., & Palladino, J. J. (1997). *Psychology* (2nd ed.). Upper Saddle River, NJ: Prentice-Hall, Inc.

Johnson, L. P. (1983). For my Indian daughter. *Newsweek, 102,* 8.

Test-Taking Skills

A major part of life for a college student is preparing for and taking tests. Although no one looks forward to tests, anyone can learn to use strategies that will make test performance a successful experience. This chapter begins with a brief discussion of test anxiety and then proceeds to specific guidelines for test preparation. There are suggestions for improvement on tests in general and then guidelines for each type of test that will be encountered in a college setting. Then there is a section on assessing performance after a test. This chapter is devoted to the idea that *anyone* can become a good test-taker.

ASSESSING THE REAL PROBLEM

Do you suffer from test anxiety? There is a simple way to determine whether the nervousness you feel is real test anxiety or merely a lack of preparation. In addition to the anxiety you feel before and during a test, you may also experience some physical discomfort, such as shaking or becoming nauseated. Your mind "goes blank." Ask yourself what happens when you leave the testing area after the test is over:

- Does all the information you had forgotten return to you shortly after the test?

- After the test is over, are you still unable to recall the information?

If you answered "yes" to the first question, it could be real test anxiety, and some relaxation techniques or counseling might be of some help. If, however, you answered "yes" to the second question, you simply were not prepared for the test. If you do not process academic material long enough or thoroughly enough to commit it to memory, you cannot expect to recall it on a test.

TEST PREPARATION

The best way to ensure a feeling of confidence on a test is adequate preparation; reading through a textbook chapter passively is never enough. Your extensive study should depend on your learning styles. However, there are some guidelines for preparation that are recommended for students in general, regardless of learning styles.

Ten Guidelines for Test Preparation

1. Try to find out in advance the type of test you will be having. When studying for an essay test, you will need to practice answering in paragraphs, and you will have to organize your thoughts in such a way that your main ideas will be evident and clear to the reader. If you know you will be answering dozens or hundreds of true-false or other objective items, you will need to learn many details instead of focusing on organized general topics. If the instructor does not announce the type of test, ask for this information. Even if the information is not forthcoming, you will know that instructor's format after the first test.

2. Always attend class the day before the test. This will be the time for any review or clues about the contents of the test. Many students decide to take this day off to study, but that is a mistake. If you are forced to miss this class because of illness or emergency, get another student to share the information with you.

3. Take advantage of any optional review sessions offered by the instructor. These sessions are usually before final exams and are not held during the regularly scheduled class time. Do attend, however, because it will be well worth your time.

4. If you are a social learner, organize study groups or work with a partner. Remember that the purpose of such groups is work, not socializing. Work with other students who are interested in their test performance and who really want to become better students.

5. Connect the class lectures with the textbook. After each lecture, review the lecture notes you made, and look over the textbook chapter to make connections and reinforce your learning. If you do this throughout the semester, you will not feel the need to "cram," or study all the material in one day.

6. Use prediction to get ready for a test. Make a habit of predicting what questions will be on the test. Then answer the questions. You will probably find that many of your predicted questions will actually be on the test.

7. Use distributed, or spaced, study. Plan on at least a week for major tests.

8. Organize your study notes in some form that works for you. Examples are note cards, mapping, outlining material, and recording notes.

9. Overlearn. When you think you know the test material, go a step further. Study a little longer or in a different way.

10. Study the different types of materials for a test different ways. Textbook chapters usually contain key vocabulary lists and chapter summaries; always reread those, as well as your underlining and any notes you made from the book. You should reread your lecture notes and mark in red the possible test questions. If you have access to any previous quizzes you have had over the same material, study those. Also look over any handouts the instructor has given and the readings on reserve in the library.

TAKING TESTS

Later in the chapter, you will learn specific suggestions for taking each type of test. However, there are several techniques you can use on any type of test that will increase your ability to do your best and get credit for all you know.

General Suggestions for Improvement

BEFORE THE TEST

1. *Practice with timed readings if you become anxious during timed tests.* You can find books of timed readings in study skills classes or in college learning labs. If these are not available, you can time yourself while doing homework or reading for pleasure.

2. *Make a habit of reading novels or other materials for fun to build concentration.* Reading has many rewards, and one is learning to concentrate for a sustained period of time. You are an active participant in the reading as you visualize the plot and characters and predict the action that will occur next.

3. *Practice good health habits.* Get a good night's sleep before a test because it is more difficult to recall information when you are tired or sleepy. Eat a good breakfast or lunch before the test. You should not be stuffed, but a reasonable amount of nourishing food can help you think clearly.

4. *Be on time at the test site with all of your materials.* Nothing can produce more test anxiety than rushing into a classroom late and then having to search frantically for pens and other materials. If possible, arrive early. Get your materials in order; then sit calmly for a few minutes or look over your notes.

5. *While waiting to begin the test, avoid conversations with classmates who are pessimistic or anxious.* There are always some students who engage in discussions about how difficult the instructor is, how impossible the test will be, and so on. If necessary, sit alone and take deep breaths, or think about a vacation spot you have enjoyed.

DURING THE TEST

1. *Preview the test before answering questions.* You need to know how long a test is, how many and what kinds of questions there are, and what point value is assigned to the different sections. When a test contains both objective and essay items, it is common for the essay items to count more points. You need to determine where to spend most of your time.

2. *Remember that on almost all classroom tests, there is no penalty for guessing.* Many students report feeling that they should leave questions blank if they are not sure of an answer. Some even leave true-false questions blank when there would have been a 50-50 chance of getting the correct answer by guessing. You will never get any credit for an unanswered question, whereas some instructors will give partial credit for an effort made or for partial answers.

3. If *you have test anxiety, answer some questions you are sure of first.* This strategy will have a calming effect and build confidence. Then you can proceed to the more difficult items, and you will probably perform better because of having a more positive attitude.

4. *When taking very long objective tests, check your place on the answer sheet every ten questions.* Some objective tests have one hundred or more questions, and skipping an item or simply getting on the wrong space on the answer sheet can cause you to miss the remaining questions on the test. You may discover your error at the end of the test, when there may be no time left to correct the mistakes.

5. *Read all questions carefully, and pay attention to all parts of the questions.* Don't overlook important words such as *not* or *the most important.* These words, and many others like them, can totally change the meaning of a question. Answer all parts of a question. Many students lose half of an item's points because they pay attention to only the first half of a question.

6. *Pace yourself on a test.* **Pacing** means to move along at a reasonable rate, not lingering too long on one question. Divide the number of test items into the number of minutes allotted for the test to make sure you do not leave any unfinished questions. Some of the most conscientious students labor over one question so long that they have no time left for part of the test.

7. *Allow time to proofread or check your answers at the end of the exam.* Obviously, if the test is composed of several hundred true-false or multiple-choice questions, there will not be time to actually proofread the entire test. You can, however, look over those items to be sure that none have been inadvertently skipped. When taking an essay test, allow enough time to proofread all answers.

 **MULTIPLE-CHOICE TESTS**

Many students prefer objective tests of any type because the answer appears on the test; they simply have to locate it. These tests do seem popular with instructors, and they are quick and easy to grade. However, on the college level, multiple-choice tests can be tricky. Many of the **distractors** (the answers that are not correct) may be similar, and many may seem to be correct. Sometimes choices include "none of the above" or "all of the above." Many college freshmen are not accustomed to multiple-choice questions that are not simple and literal. Therefore, some advice is needed to learn to perform to your maximum effectiveness on these commonly administered tests.

Eleven Suggestions for Taking Multiple-Choice Tests

1. Read the questions carefully, noting key words that can help you answer the questions. Many multiple-choice questions begin with phrases containing words that will change the meaning but that are often overlooked:

1. "The *first* explorer—"
2. "The *most* significant designer—"
3. "The *only* person who did *not*—"
4. "Which is the *only* statement that does *not* belong?"

Pay close attention to these key words.

2. Use the process of elimination. This strategy enables you to make educated guesses. You use your existing knowledge to eliminate the answers you know are incorrect. You may even be able to eliminate all of the choices except the correct one.

3. "Absolute" statements are usually distractors. **Absolute** words are those that leave no room for other choices. They are words such as *never, always, all,* and *none.* Common sense dictates that few things are absolute and that there are usually exceptions, as in the following:

1. Mentally healthy people
   a. never become upset.
   b. are always happy.
   c. are always successful on the job and in a relationship.
   d. are sometimes lonely.

The only choice not containing an absolute word is *d;* this question illustrates the reason absolute statements usually are not accurate.

4. Jokes and insults are usually distractors. College instructors often toss in distractors that they hope will add a little humor or that will simply break the monotony of making out so many test items. Unfortunately, the jokes are sometimes selected as the correct answer. Read the following question:

1. Most women who work outside the home do so because they
   a. need to earn a salary for economic reasons.
   b. get tired of soap operas and talk shows.
   c. want to meet men.
   d. need to fulfill the expectations of their parents.

Choices *b* and *c* are both in the category of jokes and/or insults. Those two choices should be eliminated, narrowing your options.

5. When one answer is more complete or inclusive, it is likely to be correct. You might have heard someone say that if one answer is the longest, it is usually the correct answer. This is not the same as the most complete or inclusive, and the longest answer may or may not be the correct choice. Which is the most inclusive answer in the following example?

1. People who work for public utility companies are usually
   a. from middle-class backgrounds.
   b. women.
   c. of European descent.
   d. from varied backgrounds.

Answer *d* is the most inclusive, and it is the correct answer.

6. Know what to do when answers contain confusing negatives. Some statements contain two or more negatives, such as the following sentence:

- "It is *not un*healthy to be *im*mature."

Obviously, this statement is confusing. The best way to process such statements is to eliminate the negatives, two at a time. In the example above, eliminate *not* and *un,* and you have the clarified statement of, "It is healthy to be immature." Now you can tell that this statement is a distractor.

7. "All of the above" is more likely to be the correct answer than is "none of the above." If you know that even one of the answers is incorrect, you also know that "all of the above" is not correct. On the other hand, if you know that one answer is correct, then you would eliminate "none of the above" as the answer. Read this example:

1. Which of the following topics would most likely be developed using the cause and effect pattern of writing?
   a. characteristics of a good academic counselor
   b. variables affecting job success
   c. three results of unemployment
   d. all of the above

Perhaps you know that *a* is not a topic that follows the cause and effect pattern of writing. If so, you could eliminate that choice as well as *d.*

8. When two answers are synonyms, eliminate both. Unless your test directions tell you otherwise, there can be only one answer. When two answers mean exactly the same, both can be eliminated:

1. According to your study skills handouts, the most important thing for college freshmen to learn is

   a. time management.

   b. metacognition.

   c. monitoring your own learning.

   d. organizational skills.

Choices *b* and *c* are synonyms and can be eliminated.

9. When two answers are similar in meaning, one is often the correct answer. Many test makers and instructors do include choices in which there are only slight variations in the answers. These are not the same as synonyms, so give each careful consideration.

1. Before reading an assigned chapter, you should do which of the following?

   a. a textbook preview

   b. a chapter preview

   c. a time management chart

   d. some deep-breathing exercises

The correct answer is *b,* but it is close in meaning to *a.*

10. If you have kept up with assignments fairly well, multiple-choice options that contain unfamiliar terms are usually distractors. College instructors are not likely to test students on terminology or other information that has not appeared in the lectures, the textbook, or the outside readings. The following example from a study skills test contains two terms unrelated to the course:

1. The term for your own awareness and understanding of your learning is

   a. echinoderms.

   b. metacognition.

   c. metatarsals.

   d. time management.

Options *a* and *c* would belong in science courses and would probably be out of place on a study skills test. They could both be eliminated.

11. Be careful when you are allowed to select two answers. These items will usually have options worded in the following ways:

a. metacognition

b. metatarsals

c. both *a* and *b*

d. neither *a* nor *b*

 **TRUE–FALSE TESTS**

True–False tests are popular with many students for the same reasons as multiple choice tests. Some of the same cautions are needed because, in haste, many students fail to read questions carefully, look at important words, and keep track of the time. True–false items can also be tricky.

Four Suggestions for Taking True–False Tests

1. For a statement to be true, all parts of the statement must be true. Students often relate that they marked a statement "true" because most of the statement was true or because the statement was more true than false. One detail can make the statement false:

- Four of our U.S. presidents were George Washington, Thomas Jefferson, Benjamin Franklin, and Woodrow Wilson.

Three of the men were presidents, but one was not, making the statement false.

2. Absolute words tend to make statements false. These same absolute words make multiple-choice answers the incorrect choices. Remember the power of these absolute words!

3. Words such as sometimes, usually, *and* often *tend to make statements true.* Read these examples:

- Secretaries are *sometimes* men.
- Secretaries are *usually* women.
- People *often* read for pleasure.

4. Be careful when statements contain confusing negatives. As with multiple-choice items, eliminate the negatives, two at a time.

MATCHING TESTS

College tests sometimes include a matching section, especially in survey or introductory courses taken by freshmen and sophomores. A matching test is composed of two columns of words or phrases that must be matched, based on some type of relationship. Some examples of items that could be matched follow:

- Terms and definitions
- Theorists and theories
- Explorers and countries
- Inventors and inventions
- Authors and literary works

There are several different types of matching tests, and each requires a different test-taking strategy. There are also different directions to follow in the various types of tests.

TYPES OF MATCHING TESTS

1. *Some tests contain the same number of items in both columns.* These are the least difficult. You are usually expected to use each answer once and only once. You should always answer the questions you know first and then eliminate the answers you have used by crossing them off in the answer column.

2. *Another type of matching test contains more answers than terms.* This type often is accompanied by the directions, "Some answers will not be used at all." This makes eliminating and guessing more difficult, but it is still a good idea to answer the items you are sure of first.

3. *A third type of matching test contains more question items than answers.* You often have the directions, "Some or many answers will be used more than once." Again, guessing will be of little use, but always answer the questions you know well so that you will get credit for those.

SHORT-ANSWER TESTS

Short-answer tests require the student to write a paragraph or two, or even to write a list. These tests will be differentiated from essay tests (discussed later in the chapter) by their answer length. It is common for college instructors to include a short-answer section in a test that may be largely objective (multiple-choice, true-false, matching, etc.). An example of a short-answer question is, "List and briefly explain the three stages of memory."

Five Guidelines for Taking Short-Answer Tests

1. Read the questions very carefully. Many students spend valuable test time answering questions that were not even asked. For example, if a question is, "List the stages in the development of humor in children," there is no need to define or discuss each stage. Listing is all that is required. On the other hand, many students answer only part of a question, losing valuable points.

2. Pay attention to the point distribution of the questions. Some short-answer questions on the same test will often count much more than the other questions. You should write more and spend more time on the questions with larger point values.

3. Think before you write. With all short-answer questions, decide what you want to write before beginning. This will save time, get your thoughts in order, and give a sense of organization to your answer. This is especially important with questions having higher point values and requiring more writing.

4. Put forth your best effort on composition and spelling. Although the instructor may value your content over writing form, all college instructors expect high school graduates to know the basics in terms of complete sentences, grammar, and spelling.

5. Use clues on the test when in doubt. For example, you may feel that you do not know how much to write on some questions. If the instructor leaves space for the answers, the amount of space is a clue to how much to write. Sometimes you will be given directions about continuing on another sheet; you would know that this answer will be longer. Even the wording of the questions can be a clue. If a question states that you should compare two forms of poetry, you know that you are expected to tell something about each form, telling how they are alike and perhaps how they are different.

 **PROBLEM-SOLVING TESTS**

Students generally expect to solve problems on math, chemistry, or statistics tests. However, these are not the only subjects that involve problem solving, especially with the current emphasis on higher-level thinking and reasoning skills. Following are some examples of test items from the social sciences in which problem solving is required:

1. Many inner cities are experiencing an increase in violent crime among juveniles. Referring to facts and concepts learned in the course about pre-

vention of crime, describe a plan for an after-school program for at-risk teenagers.

2. Devise a plan of action to encourage a city of 500,000 people to (a) conserve water, (b) recycle plastic, and (c) use 25% less gasoline. Be able to explain to the community the benefits of each.

3. After having completed a unit on phobias, tell how you would encourage an agoraphobic woman to leave her house for the first time in ten years.

Four Suggestions for Taking Problem-Solving Tests

1. Be sure of what is expected on each question. Be careful to answer all parts of the question instead of offering only a partial solution. If in doubt, ask the instructor for clarification.

2. On mathematics tests, find out if points will be assigned for correct answers only or if partial credit will be given for proper procedures. Many instructors now give partial credit for using the correct steps or operations. This type of test might relieve anxiety because you will not lose all the points if you make a careless error.

3. Know ahead of time if you are expected to memorize formulas. If the formulas will be provided for you, you can save valuable time by not memorizing this information. Instead, you can use your preparation time studying concepts and working practice problems.

4. Take all calculators and other materials allowed to the testing situation. Know in advance if you can bring calculators, dictionaries, charts, or any other material. This will be announced in class if it is allowed.

ESSAY TESTS

Many students dread essay tests more than any other type of test because these examinations require more actual physical work and also because they require complete recall. No clues are given, and there are no choices.

Eleven Suggestions for Taking Essay Tests

1. Plan your time before writing your answers, and pace yourself. This could make the difference between passing and failing because you must, at least, finish a major portion of the test in order to pass.

2. Leave some blank space if you feel that you would like to write more if there is time. Some questions may not require as much of your time, so there will be time left for you to add more information to earlier questions.

3. Outline your ideas before you begin to write. This strategy will prevent the omission of some important points.

4. Write organized answers, and resist rambling. Instructors do not like to have to search for your main ideas. Sometimes in their enthusiasm and desire to write all the facts or concepts they know, students jump from one idea to another. Number your main points if necessary, and include essential details under each point.

5. Stick to the question asked. You may feel that you want to include additional information, but it probably will not be graded, and you will be wasting time. Also *avoid giving your opinion* unless specifically asked. Most instructors will not give credit for answering questions that are not asked.

6. If you do not know a complete answer, write a partial answer that includes what you do know. Remember that if an essay question counts fifty points, you may earn from zero to fifty. It is not an all-or-nothing proposition; get as much credit as you possibly can.

7. Write legibly. Instructors become very frustrated when they cannot read an answer or when it is a great effort to do so. Some may even give up and assign no points at all.

8. Use correct composition, grammar, and spelling. Even if you have been told by the instructor that content counts 100 percent, all instructors prefer a composition that is college-level writing. People may actually perceive the content to be better if the essay reads like a composition of an educated person.

9. If essay exams make you nervous, first answer a question you know well. This strategy will calm you and give you confidence to continue with the remaining questions.

10. Leave time at the end of the test to proofread your answers. You should use this time to check for content as well as composition errors.

11. Understand the directions by paying close attention to the cue words. Become familiar with the words used in essay tests, and answer in the correct manner. (Figure 12.1 contains commonly used direction words, the definitions of each, and an example of a test item using the word.)

Figure 12.1   *Direction words used on essay tests.*

Direction Word	Definition	Example of Essay Question
Analyze	Break into parts and explain.	Analyze the background of a typical repeat offender.
Apply	Show how a principle works in a real situation.	Apply the concept of consumerism to the automobile industry.
Choose	Favor one over another.	Choose the most outstanding poem of John Keats and tell why you chose it.
Comment	Discuss briefly.	Comment on Freud's theory of the *id.*
Compare	Tell how two or more things are alike.	Compare communism and fascism.
Contrast	Tell how two or more things are different.	Contrast a neurosis and a psychosis.
Criticize	Give your judgment with evidence.	Criticize the poem, "Ode to a Grecian Urn."
Define	Give the meaning or definition.	Define "megacognition."
Describe	Give the features or characteristics.	Describe family life in the 1700s.
Diagram	Draw and label.	Diagram the bones of the head.
Differentiate	Same as "contrast."	Differentiate between life in Germany and France in the present time.
Discuss	Tell everything you can about a subject.	Discuss the French economy.
Distinguish	Same as "contrast."	Distinguish between Judaism and Christianity.
Enumerate	Make a list.	Enumerate six positive skills for job interviews.
Evaluate	Discuss positive and negative points, and draw a conclusion.	Evaluate capital punishment.
Explain	Discuss a topic, telling the specifics as fully as possible.	Explain the reasons for the Depression.
Give an example	Write an example from the textbook or from personal experience.	Give an example of a social problem that could lead to alienation.
Identify	Give the distinguishing characteristics.	Identify the tenets of Buddhism.
Illustrate	Draw a picture and label.	Illustrate the parts of a cell.
Interpret	Tell the meaning in everyday terms.	Interpret the symbolism in "Rime of the Ancient Mariner."

(continued)

Figure 12.1 *Continued.*

Direction Word	Definition	Example of Essay Question
Justify	Defend and present reasons for your beliefs.	Justify government subsidies for day care.
List	Enumerate and number items.	List the first ten U.S. presidents in order.
Outline	Make a well-organized list.	Outline the strategies for taking essay tests.
Prove	Establish the truth with evidence.	Prove the need for government intervention in an issue of your choice.
Relate	Discuss the connection between two things.	Relate time spent doing homework to school achievement.
Review	Briefly cover the main points.	Review Supreme Court decisions from 1950–1975.
State	Write the main points.	State the reasons for the French Revolution.
Summarize	Give only the main points in a concise manner.	Summarize the early childhood developmental stages.
Trace	Discuss in a logical sequence.	Trace the events leading to U.S. involvement in World War II.

OPEN-BOOK TESTS

Students who are inexperienced in taking open-book tests may expect them to be so easy that they make little or no preparation. At the college level, this is a serious mistake. Most open-book tests are not composed of simple, literal questions, but even the answers to literal questions would be difficult to locate without having read and studied the material beforehand. The majority of open-book tests assess your higher-level thinking skills, expecting you to apply, organize, or evaluate the factual material. Many of the open-book tests are actually essays. You should plan to answer the questions as you would any other essay question.

TAKE-HOME TESTS

Many students also feel that a take-home test will be very easy, and they make the mistake of not taking the test seriously enough. Some students fail to answer some of the questions. This is a mistake because, with planning, you should be able to earn a good grade on a take-home test. You are allowed to locate information from any source or to work with another student. There is no excuse for blanks.

At the time the test is distributed, read the directions and clarify anything about which you are in doubt. You may need to ask about the instructor's expectations concerning length, number of sources, or format to be used. Some take-home tests are somewhat difficult because much research is expected. Set goals for what you want to finish each day that you are allowed to work on the test.

ASSESSING PERFORMANCE AFTER TAKING A TEST

What do you do after you have taken a test and it is returned to you by the instructor? Do you look at your grade and then put the test away? Do you check to see if the instructor has subtracted the correct number of points? You need to do more than that if you expect your test performance to improve in the future. Here are some suggestions.

Look at the types of errors you made on the test. You may have done well on the objective questions but not the essay questions. If so, try to discover the reason for this. Look back over the guidelines for each type of test to determine the source of your problem. Perhaps you did well on the questions covering certain chapters but not others. This would be a reflection of your inadequate preparation; next time you should strive to study all of the material better.

Try to determine whether you interpreted the questions correctly. Because of haste or anxiety, you may have misunderstood the questions even though you might have known the material. If this was a problem, you can work on this before the next test.

See if you skipped any questions or parts of questions. This is a very common error, which could be corrected by proofreading and by reading more carefully.

If you did not perform as well as you should have and cannot determine the reason, have a conference with the instructor. Another person may observe problems with your test taking that you may overlook. The instructor will be pleased that you want to improve your test performance.

If you have the opportunity to locate a fellow classmate who did well on the test, have a conference with him or her. This student may offer insight or may agree to study with you. Don't be embarrassed about your grade because most students have problems with tests sooner or later.

Remember that anyone *can become an effective test-taker.* You simply have to work at this skill the way you would work at becoming better at a sport. Practice and preparation will help you reach your goal.

SUMMARY

Preparing for and taking tests are skills that any determined student can master. Strategies were presented for (1) test preparation, (2) test taking, and (3) assessment of performance after a test. Strategies presented should be employed on each and every test.

General guidelines for improving performance on all tests were presented first. Then the chapter discussed strategies to employ when taking the different types of tests, from objective to essay. The various objective tests were explained with specific suggestions for approaching each. There was an emphasis on cue words used in essay tests as well as suggestions for writing complete essay answers. There were additional suggestions for taking open-book and take-home tests.

There are many different types of tests, each with unique strategies. All of these tests will be a part of college courses at one time or another. While students may never look forward to tests, they can enter a testing situation without anxiety and can learn to perform to their maximum potential.

EXERCISE 12.1 MULTIPLE-CHOICE

Directions: Look back and review the guidelines for taking multiple-choice tests; then select the best answer for each of the following items.

_____ 1. A weekly to-do list
     a. will eliminate the need to study.
     b. should work in conjunction with your semester plan.
     c. will interfere with your academic goals.
     d. will inhibit your ability to achieve your academic objectives.

_____ 2. Distributed learning is an effective study strategy because
     a. your mind never wanders.
     b. organizational processing and review can occur several times.
     c. you will remember all of the facts you study.
     d. it will eliminate external distractions.

_____ 3. People of all ages are attending college these days because

    a. old people are trying to relieve boredom.

    b. society is more accepting of varied lifestyles and ambitions.

    c. professors are tired of young people who are not motivated.

    d. college has become easier.

_____ 4. An important step in solving a problem is

    a. defining the problem.

    b. analyzing the problem.

    c. formulating possible solutions.

    d. all of the above.

_____ 5. A hypothesis is

    a. an educated guess.

    b. a memory technique to remember strings of information.

    c. the author's opinion of other authors.

    d. none of the above.

_____ 6. Successful college students

    a. never worry about the future.

    b. usually have a clearly identified goal.

    c. always participate in extracurricular activities.

    d. never have a full-time job.

_____ 7. The most important thing to remember when taking an essay test is to

    a. learn the terminology of the course.

    b. know the definitions of all the important vocabulary words.

    c. pace yourself.

    d. write as much as you can on another question if you do not know the question that was asked.

_____ 8. An informed opinion is the opinion of

    a. a famous person.

    b. an expert on the subject.

    c. the encyclopedia.

    d. the dictionary.

_____ 9. Persuasive writing is often found in

     a. advertisements.

     b. editorials.

     c. both *a* and *b*.

     d. neither *a* nor *b*.

_____10. Which of the following is an example of a stereotype?

     a. the absent-minded professor

     b. the mother-in-law

     c. the teenager

     d. all of the above

EXERCISE 12.2 TRUE–FALSE

Directions: In order for a true–false statement to be true, all parts of the statement must be true; one small detail can make it false. In the following statements, cross out the part of the statement that makes it false.

Example: Some foods with a very high fat content are chocolate, milk, radishes, and cooking oil.

1. Some famous explorers were Christopher Columbus, Ferdinand Magellan, and Benjamin Franklin.

2. Subjects in the social sciences department include geology, sociology, psychology, and anthropology.

3. Subjects in the natural sciences department include biology, chemistry, botany, and communications.

4. Some of the most widely spoken languages in the world are English, Creole, Chinese, and Spanish.

5. Astrology is the scientific study of how the planets and the signs under which people are born affect people's lives.

6. Study skills books recommend much review, distributed study, and Cornell note taking, but they do not recommend taking a learning styles inventory since all students need to review, study, and take good notes.

7. Disney World, located in Miami, Florida, is the favorite vacation spot for people visiting America from other countries.

8. Montana had the distinction of being the largest state in the United States until Alaska was admitted to the Union.

9. New England states include Vermont, New Hampshire, and Pennsylvania.

10. In the bluegrass state of Kentucky, the capital, Frankfort, is also the largest city.

11. Criminologists study societal problems caused by violent crimes like assault, rape, embezzlement, and murder.

12. A famous honeymoon spot is Niagara Falls, located on the U.S.-Mexican border.

EXERCISE 12.3 TRUE–FALSE

Directions: Absolute words generally make statements false. On the other hand, words that are not absolute, such as *some, a few, usually,* and *often,* are usually found in true statements. Look for absolute words in the following statements, and then mark each statement T (True) or F (False).

_____ 1. College students, though resentful of many policies, never complain to the college dean.

_____ 2. Throughout history, women have usually held less powerful positions than men.

_____ 3. People who are emotionally well adjusted always feel optimistic about the future.

_____ 4. None of the countries of the world has had a woman as leader.

_____ 5. It is generally acknowledged by psychologists and psychiatrists that most people feel despondent at times.

_____ 6. Some people have never been physically sick in their entire lives.

_____ 7. No one has more than ten fingers.

_____ 8. All secretaries and nurses are women.

_____ 9. People often spend more than anticipated on vacations.

_____10. Many people leave their country of origin.

_____11. Several famous rulers have been dictators.

_____12. All U.S. presidents have been married at the time they were elected to the presidency.

EXERCISE 12.4 TRUE–FALSE

Directions: Statements can be very confusing if they contain multiple negatives. To clarify the statement, eliminate the negatives, two at a time. In the following statements, cross out the unnecessary negatives; then mark each statement T (True) or F (False).

Example: An ~~un~~expected dinner guest is ~~not~~ unusual.

_____ 1. It is not impolite to be unkind to the host or hostess at a dinner party.

_____ 2. Students who are unable to read are not illiterate.

_____ 3. It is not uncommon for twelve-year-olds to attend college.

_____ 4. A child who does not go to the doctor's office unwillingly is unusual.

_____ 5. Contraband items are those that are not illegal.

_____ 6. The evidence heard in court cases is not ever irrefutable.

_____ 7. It is not illegal for two people over the age of 21 to be unmarried.

_____ 8. Some dogs are not unable to become guides for the blind.

_____ 9. It would not be unintentional to trip and fall on the icy sidewalk.

_____ 10. An uninvited guest is not unexpected.

EXERCISE 12.5 MATCHING ESSAY TERMS

Directions: All of the following are terms used in the directions of essay tests. On this matching test, there are an equal number of items in each column. Each answer will be used once and only once.

_____ 1. analyze   a. give the features or characteristics

_____ 2. compare   b. discuss in a logical sequence

_____ 3. describe   c. establish the truth with evidence

_____ 4. enumerate   d. break into parts and explain

_____ 5. evaluate   e. defend and present reasons for your beliefs

_____ 6. identify   f. make a list

_____ 7. illustrate   g. tell how two or more things are alike

_____ 8. interpret   h. give only the main points in a concise manner

_____ 9. justify   i. give the distinguishing characteristics

_____10. prove   j. discuss positive and negative points, and draw a
                              conclusion

_____11. summarize   k. draw a picture and label

_____12. trace   l. tell the meaning in everyday terms

Cooperative Learning Activities

GROUP 1. Students often allow other activities to take the place of adequate test preparation. Have your group list as many excuses for not studying as you have ever used. After your group has compiled the list, give a solution in the form of a strategy to get back on track. In other words, tell how you would remove each excuse from the list in order to be a better student in the future.

GROUP 2. Fred prefers to take objective tests. He performs well on multiple-choice, true-false, or matching tests. However, he has never passed an essay test in his high school or college career. He says that he studies just as long for the essay tests as he does for the objective tests on which he performs well. First, brainstorm among your group members, and state possible reasons for Fred's unusual testing history. Then formulate a plan of action that will enable Fred to perform as well on essay tests as he does on objective tests.

GROUP 3. Have a volunteer from the group bring in an old test on which he or she did not perform as well as desired. Let the members of the group examine the test and the pattern of errors to determine the cause of the problem. The group members may ask questions about study habits, test anxiety, past testing history, or anything else that might enable them to determine the cause of the unsatisfactory grade. Present the analysis and a future plan of action to the student who brought the test.

GROUP 4. The group should brainstorm about tests in the various subjects they are currently taking or have taken in the past. Formulate a list of specific study strategies for the following academic disciplines: (1) history, (2) mathematics, (3) science, and (4) English literature. As you make your lists of strategies, think about the skills that are necessary for each course and how the courses are different from each other.

GROUP 5. Each member of the group should think of one teacher in the past or present who gives "hard" tests. Discuss the teachers and the tests, and determine what caused each student to consider these particular tests more difficult than other tests he or she has taken. What strategies could have been used to better prepare for these tests?

Reading Selection: *Biography*

Title: Excerpt from *Gather Together in My Name**
Author: Maya Angelou

Activation of Prior Knowledge and Interest

1. Oprah Winfrey names the author, Maya Angelou, as her *mentor.* What do you think Angelou did for her in the role of mentor?

   _____

   _____

   _____

2. Describe an incident of great disappointment for you, and tell how you overcame the disappointment.

   _____

   _____

   _____

3. Name one possible significance of the title of the book.

   _____

   _____

   _____

---

*From GATHER TOGETHER IN MY NAME by Maya Angelou. Copyright © 1974 by Maya Angelou. Reprinted by permission of Random House, Inc.

I was mortified. A silly white woman who probably counted on her toes looked me in the face and said I had not passed. The examination had been constructed by morons for idiots. Of course I breezed through without thinking much about it.

Rearrange these letters: A C T - A R T - A S T

Okay. CAT. RAT. SAT. Now what?

She stood behind her make-up and coiffed hair and manicured nails and dresser-drawers of scented angora sweaters and years of white ignorance and said that I had not passed.

"The telephone company spends thousands of dollars training operators. We simply cannot risk employing anyone who made the marks you made. I'm sorry."

She was sorry? I was stunned. In a stupor I considered that maybe my outsized intellectual conceit had led me to take the test for granted. And maybe I deserved this high-handed witch's remarks.

"May I take it again?" That was painful to ask.

"No, I'm sorry." If she said she was sorry one more time, I was going to take her by her sorry shoulders and shake a job out of her.

"There is an opening, though"—she might have sensed my unspoken threat—"for a bus girl in the cafeteria."

"What does a bus girl do?" I wasn't sure I could do it.

"The boy in the kitchen will tell you."

After I filled out forms and was found uninfected by a doctor, I reported to the cafeteria. There the boy, who was a grandfather, informed me, "Collect the dishes, wipe the tables, make sure the salt and pepper shakers are clean, and here's your uniform."

The coarse white dress and apron had been starched with concrete and was too long. I stood at the side of the room, the dress hem scratching my calves, waiting for the tables to clear.

Many of the trainee operators had been my classmates. Now they stood over laden tables waiting for me or one of the other dumb bus girls to remove the used dishes so that they could set down their trays.

I lasted at the job a week, and so hated the salary that I spent it all the afternoon I quit.

Critical Thinking Questions

1. Why do you think Maya Angelou lasted only one week at this job? Support your answer with evidence from the passage.

_____

_____

_____

2. Why does she refer to herself and others as the "dumb bus girls"?

_____

_____

_____

3. What did you learn about the woman who administered the test? Do you know someone like her?

_____

_____

_____

REFERENCES

Boyd, R. T. C. (1988). *Improving Your Test-Taking Skills*. Washington, DC: Institute for Research.

Flippo, R. F. (1988). *Testwise: Strategies for Success in Taking Tests*. Belmont, CA: David S. Lake.

CREDIT

Angelou, M. (1974). *Gather Together in My Name*. New York: Random House.

Glossary

absolute word a word that leaves no room for other choices, such as the words *never* and *always*

abstract a brief summary of a much longer work, such as a journal article

acronym a word formed from initials of other words, such as *MADD* for *Mothers Against Drunk Driving*

acrostic the use of the first letters of the words to be remembered being used as the first letters in other words, as in *Every good boy does fine* to remember the musical notes *EGBDF*

affix a word part that is attached to the root, or main part, of the word

alternate goal a goal or objective that a person would consider secondary to the original or top-priority goal

analogy a comparison of two or more things, people, or situations

analyze to break into parts and explain

annotation marking a textbook for study, including underlining and marginal notes

appendix a supplement in a book that contains additional information which may pertain to a specific academic discipline

apply show how a principle works in a real situation

assumption a statement or an idea that is taken for granted

authority an accepted source of information

bar graph a graph illustration having either vertical or horizontal bars to represent amounts

bias a type of viewpoint that leaves out or alters facts in order to support a certain side of an issue

card stacking presenting only one side of an issue, giving only the facts that support the favored argument

cause the person, thing, or event responsible for something

chunking the mental act of putting information into meaningful units to aid recall

circle graph a circle that is divided in the manner of a pie to show the size of the parts and the relationship between the parts

circular reasoning a restatement of the original assertion, such as "School prayer should remain illegal because children should not pray at school."

cluster reading looking at several words in one fixation

colloquial expression a word or phrase that is used only in certain areas of the country

comparison the describing of how two or more things are alike

comprehension connecting new information to known information

context clues the use of surrounding words in a sentence or in nearby sentences to discover the meaning of an unknown word

contrast the describing of how two or more things are different

Cornell notes a notetaking system developed by Walter Pauk at Cornell University

cramming learning or attempting to learn large amounts of information at one time, often shortly before a test

critical thinking a purposeful and deliberate evaluation of all evidence on all sides of an issue in order to form a judgment about the value of information, arguments, or opinions

criticize a direction word often used on essay tests and meaning to give your judgment with evidence

deductive a process in which a conclusion or most important point is given first, and the supporting facts follow

diagram a drawing or other graphic illustration to show a process or to demonstrate how something works or is arranged

distractor an incorrect choice in the list of responses following a multiple choice item on a test

distributed study study in smaller amounts of time spread over several study sessions

effect the result of an action or event

encoding putting information into some form which can be placed into memory

enumerate to make a list; a term often used on essay tests

essay a relatively brief literary composition, usually in prose, giving the author's views on a particular topic

etymology the study of the origins of words

evaluate to discuss positive and negative points and then draw a conclusion

EVOKER a study method that is often used for studying literature and contains the steps: explore, vocabulary, oral reading, key ideas, evaluate, and recapitulation

expressive vocabulary a person's spoken vocabulary, or the words actually used in spoken communication

external distraction an interruption or hindrance which is outside the student, being something in the environment

extrinsic motivation rewards outside the learner, such as grades, money, and recognition

eye span the amount of print that the eyes can physically see during a fixation

fact a statement that is true or verifiable

fixation the stop the eyes make on a word when reading

flexibility the use of different reading rates for different materials

general embracing the whole, not local or partial

generalization the drawing of a conclusion based on an experience

general vocabulary those words in a language that can be shared by everyone and are not a part of a particular academic discipline

glossary a mini-dictionary in a textbook that gives the definitions that apply to the particular course for which the textbook was written

graphics drawings or other types of illustrations

hypothesis a tentative assumption that accounts for a fact or set of facts and that can be tested by further investigation

index an alphabetized list of all of the subjects covered in a book

inductive a process in which the supporting points are given first, in a logical manner, and the conclusion is given last

intent to remember a conscious effort to recall information

internal distraction an interruption or hindrance that is within the person, not contingent on the surroundings

interpret tell the meaning in everyday terms

intrinsic motivation satisfaction derived from an activity itself, needing no external rewards

keyword method a multi-stage process of word learning that involves translating an unknown word into a familiar, sound-alike counterpart, such as *country band* for the word *contraband*

learning style the way a person learns most effectively

left-to-right progression the eye movement from left to right, as when reading in English

legend a caption that explains how certain symbols, drawings, or abbreviations are to be used on a map or other graphic display

linear (line) graph a graph that shows points representing the frequency of relations or connections among data by using lines, dots, or dashes to connect points

loci a method of remembering items by visualizing them in specific locations

locus of control the way in which people evaluate situations, or whether they feel they themselves or outside influences are in control

long-term goal a goal that may take an extended period of time to achieve

long-term memory the mental receptacle for all of a person's accumulated knowledge, where information can remain indefinitely

main idea the most important point an author is trying to make about a topic

mass study study for several hours at a sitting

mnemonics specific memory techniques

motivation a desire to do something

narrative a form of writing in which a fictional or nonfictional story is told, in either prose or poetry

opinion someone's judgment or belief

organizational pattern the writing form by which a paragraph or series of paragraphs are developed

overgeneralization a conclusion that has been reached with inadequate and incomplete evidence

paraphrase to retell in one's own words instead of by repeating verbatim

periodical a publication which is issued at regular intervals, perhaps weekly, monthly, or several times a year

pictograph a graphic illustration which uses pictures to represent amounts

pie graph See *circle graph*

precis a type of summary that is written from the point of view of the author, not the person writing the precis

prediction anticipating what is to come next in a narrative or in expository writing

prefix an affix that is added to the beginning of a word

previewing an examination of a chapter or a textbook to get a general idea of features and/or main ideas

prior knowledge the accumulated knowledge a learner takes to a new task

process approach an approach to writing that has the stages of prewriting, writing a draft, revision, and publishing or sharing

receptive vocabulary those words a person understands when reading or hearing them

ROWAC a study method that stresses writing in the steps: read, organize, write, active reading, and correct predictions

saccade the jerky movement, or jump, made by the eyes when reading

scanning a type of reading in which the reader searches for a particular word or phrase while skipping over the remainder of the material

selective attention screening out some information entering a sensory organ, while attending to other information

semantic mapping a system of placing material into meaningful categories

sensory memory a brief lingering of sensory information after the stimulus has been removed

short-term goal a goal that is made for the immediate future

short-term memory working memory that has the capacity to hold information for only about twenty seconds unless some active strategies are employed to retain the information

skimming reading very fast by paying attention to some parts of a selection and skipping other parts in order to get only the main ideas of a selection

source the publication in which a selection is located; the origin of information

specialized vocabulary those words belonging to a specific discipline instead of being in general use

specific peculiar to a certain larger element

SQRQCQ a study method for mathematics which contains the steps: survey, question, read, question, compute, and question

SQ3R a study method which has the steps: survey, question, read, recite, and review

stacked line graph a line graph which has several lines, instead of only one, to represent the frequency of relations or connections among data

stereotype a fixed idea about a group of people, an idea which gives to everyone in the group the same or similar characteristics

subvocalizing hearing each word in the mind while reading

suffix an affix that is added to the end of a word

summary a brief statement that contains the most important points of a longer selection

surveying See *previewing*

table a systematic listing of data in rows and columns

theme an underlying message, purpose, or lesson which is contained in a literary work

topic a word or phrase that is the subject of a paragraph or a series of paragraphs

trace a term often used on essay tests, meaning to discuss in a logical sequence

Venn diagram a graphic representation often used in a comparison and contrast situation

vocalizing moving the lips while reading

word by word reading the practice of making a stop, or fixation, on each word while reading

Index